C.S. PACAT   JOHANNA THE MAD   JOANA LAFUENTE

™

VOLUME THREE

BOOm!
BOX™

BOOm! BOX™

FENCE Volume Three, August 2019. Published by BOOM! Box, a division of Boom Entertainment, Inc. Fence is ™ & © 2019 C.S. Pacat. Originally published in single magazine form as FENCE No. 9-12. ™ & © 2018 C.S. Pacat. All rights reserved. BOOM! Box™ and the BOOM! Box logo are trademarks of Boom Entertainment, Inc., registered in various countries and categories. All characters, events, and institutions depicted herein are fictional. Any similarity between any of the names, characters, persons, events, and/or institutions in this publication to actual names, characters, and persons, whether living or dead, events, and/or institutions is unintended and purely coincidental. BOOM! Studios does not read or accept unsolicited submissions of ideas, stories, or artwork.

For information regarding the CPSIA on this printed material, call: (203) 595-3636 and provide reference #RICH - 825783.

BOOM! Studios, 5670 Wilshire Boulevard, Suite 400, Los Angeles, CA 90036-5679. Printed in USA. First Printing.

ISBN: 978-1-68415-334-3 eISBN: 978-1-64144-187-2

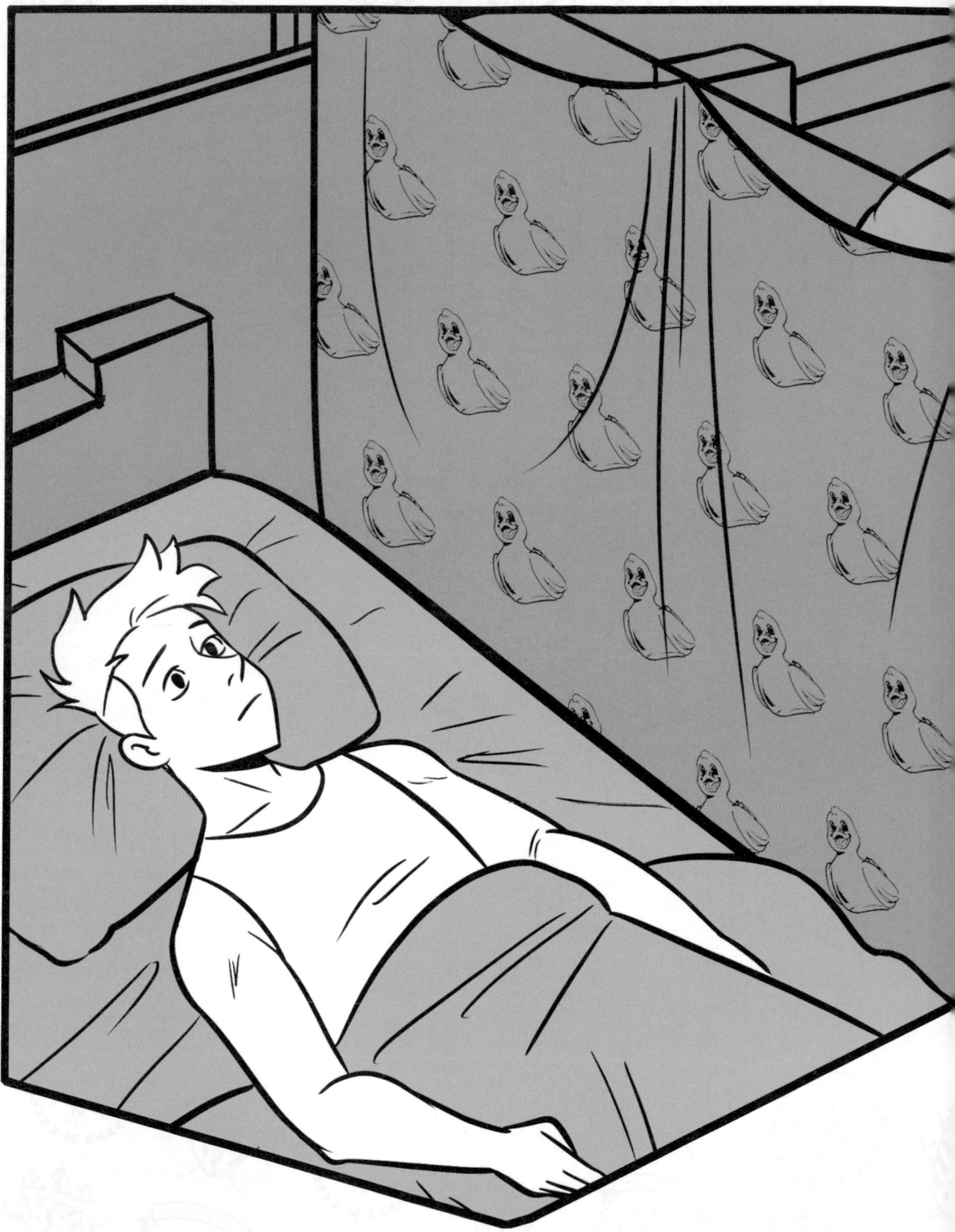

WRITTEN BY
C.S. Pacat

ILLUSTRATED BY
Johanna the Mad

COLORS BY
Joana LaFuente

LETTERS BY
Jim Campbell

TECHNICAL CONSULTANT
Pieter Leeuwenburgh

SCHOOL LOGO DESIGNS
Fawn Lau

COVER BY
Johanna the Mad

SERIES DESIGNER
Marie Krupina

COLLECTION DESIGNER
Kara Leopard

ASSISTANT EDITOR
Sophie Philips-Roberts

EDITORS
Shannon Watters & Dafna Pleban

CREATED BY
C.S. Pacat & Johanna the Mad

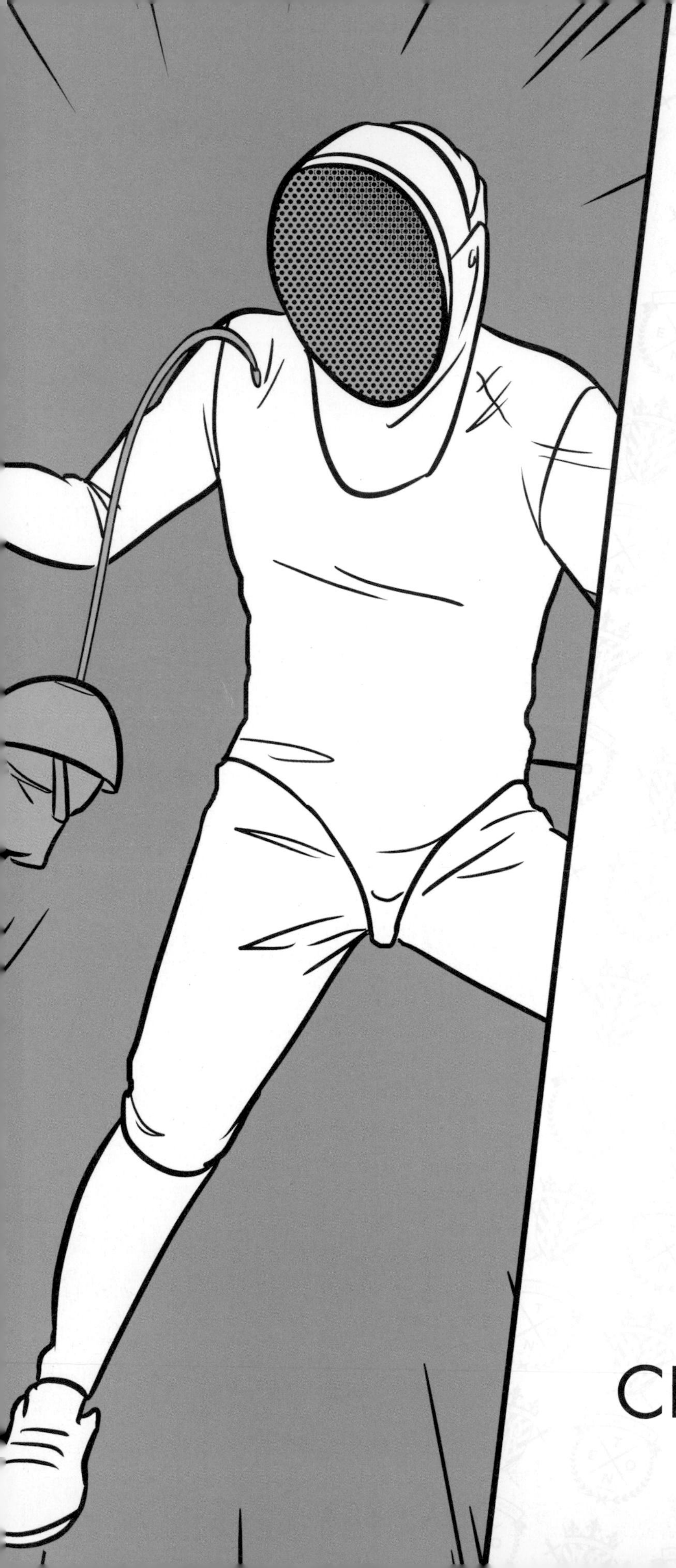

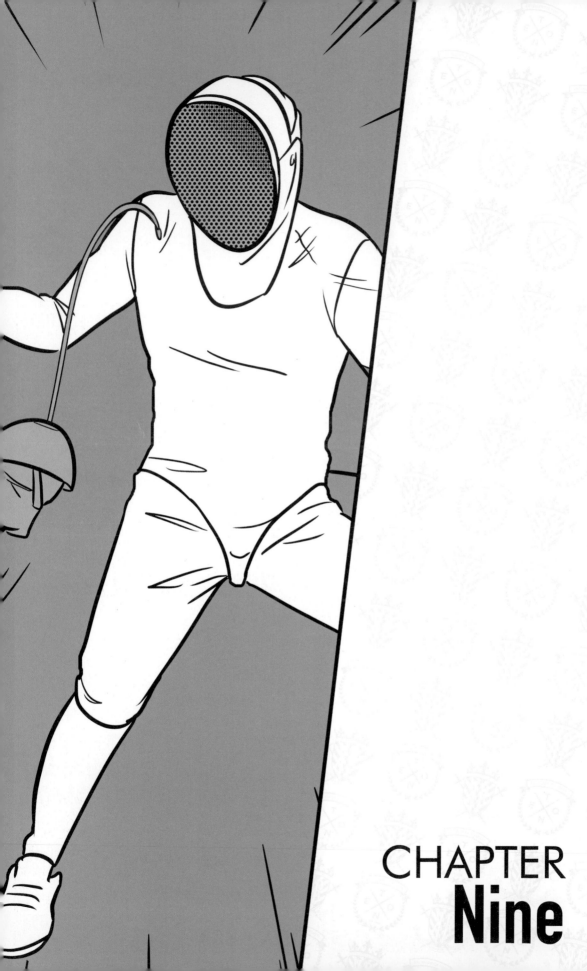

CHAPTER
Nine

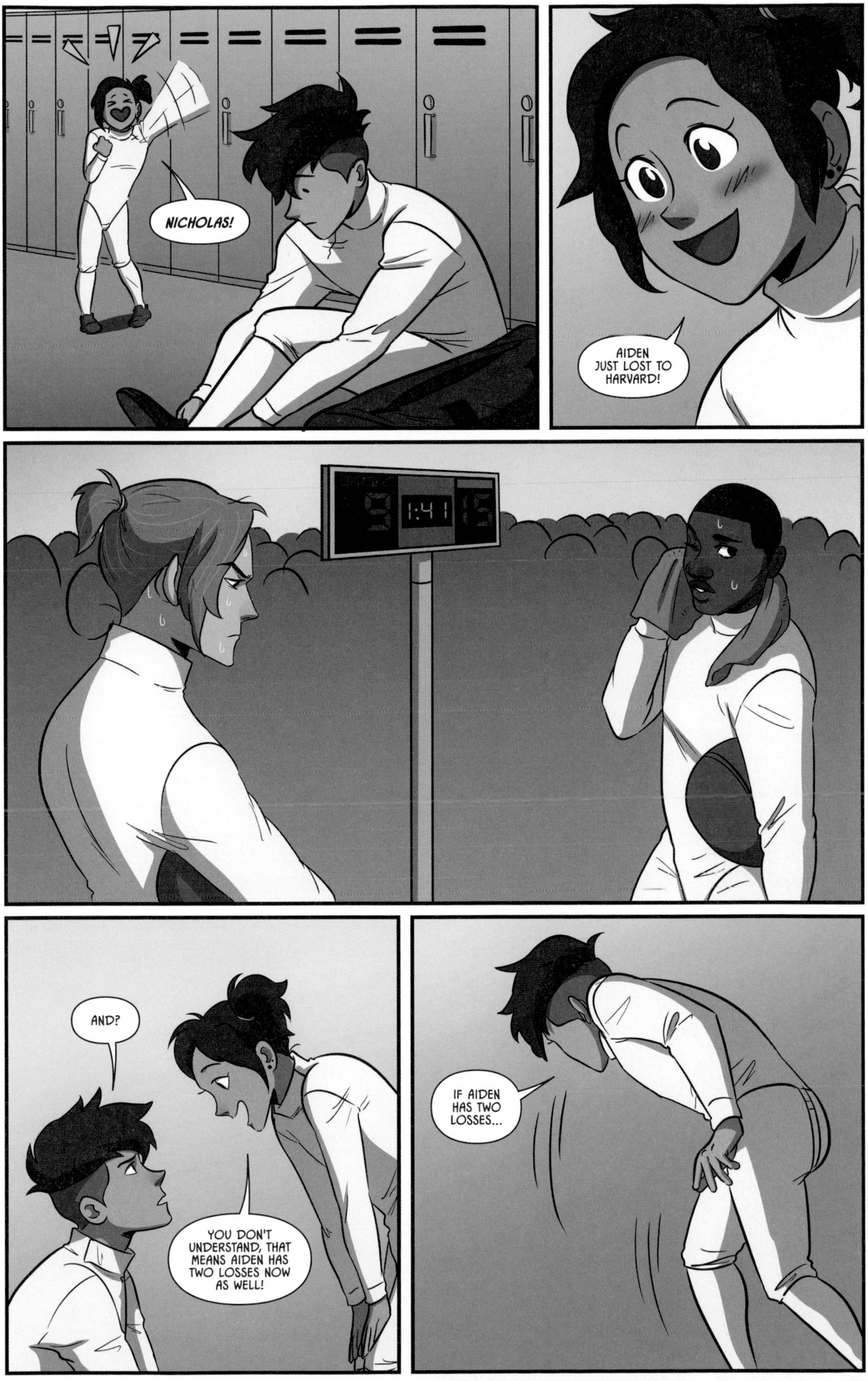
NICHOLAS!
AIDEN JUST LOST TO HARVARD!
AND?
YOU DON'T UNDERSTAND, THAT MEANS AIDEN HAS TWO LOSSES NOW AS WELL!
IF AIDEN HAS TWO LOSSES...

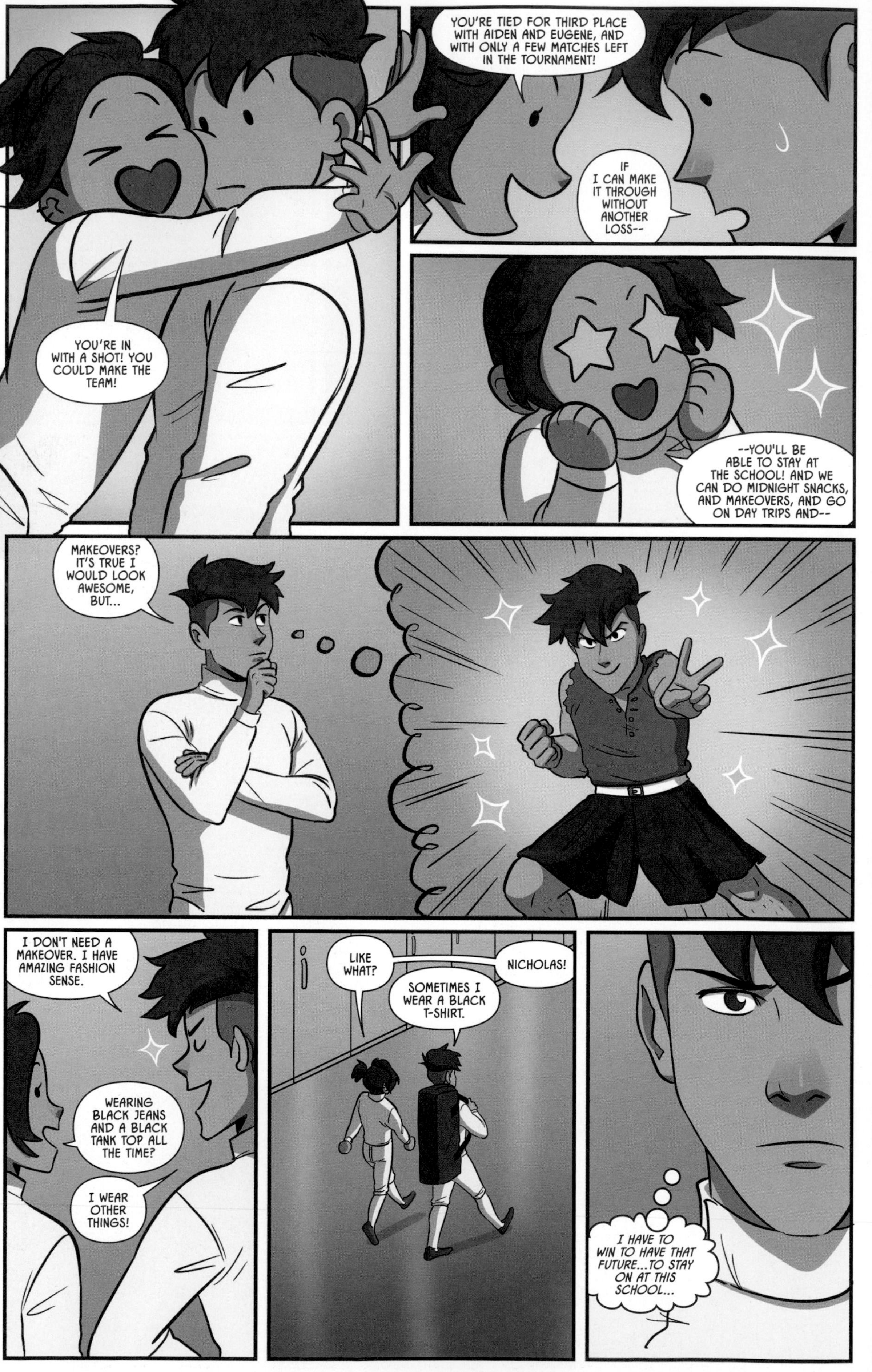

YOU'RE IN WITH A SHOT! YOU COULD MAKE THE TEAM!
YOU'RE TIED FOR THIRD PLACE WITH AIDEN AND EUGENE, AND WITH ONLY A FEW MATCHES LEFT IN THE TOURNAMENT!
IF I CAN MAKE IT THROUGH WITHOUT ANOTHER LOSS--
--YOU'LL BE ABLE TO STAY AT THE SCHOOL! AND WE CAN DO MIDNIGHT SNACKS, AND MAKEOVERS, AND GO ON DAY TRIPS AND--
MAKEOVERS? IT'S TRUE I WOULD LOOK AWESOME, BUT...
I DON'T NEED A MAKEOVER. I HAVE AMAZING FASHION SENSE.
WEARING BLACK JEANS AND A BLACK TANK TOP ALL THE TIME?
I WEAR OTHER THINGS!
LIKE WHAT?
SOMETIMES I WEAR A BLACK T-SHIRT.
NICHOLAS!
I HAVE TO WIN TO HAVE THAT FUTURE...TO STAY ON AT THIS SCHOOL...

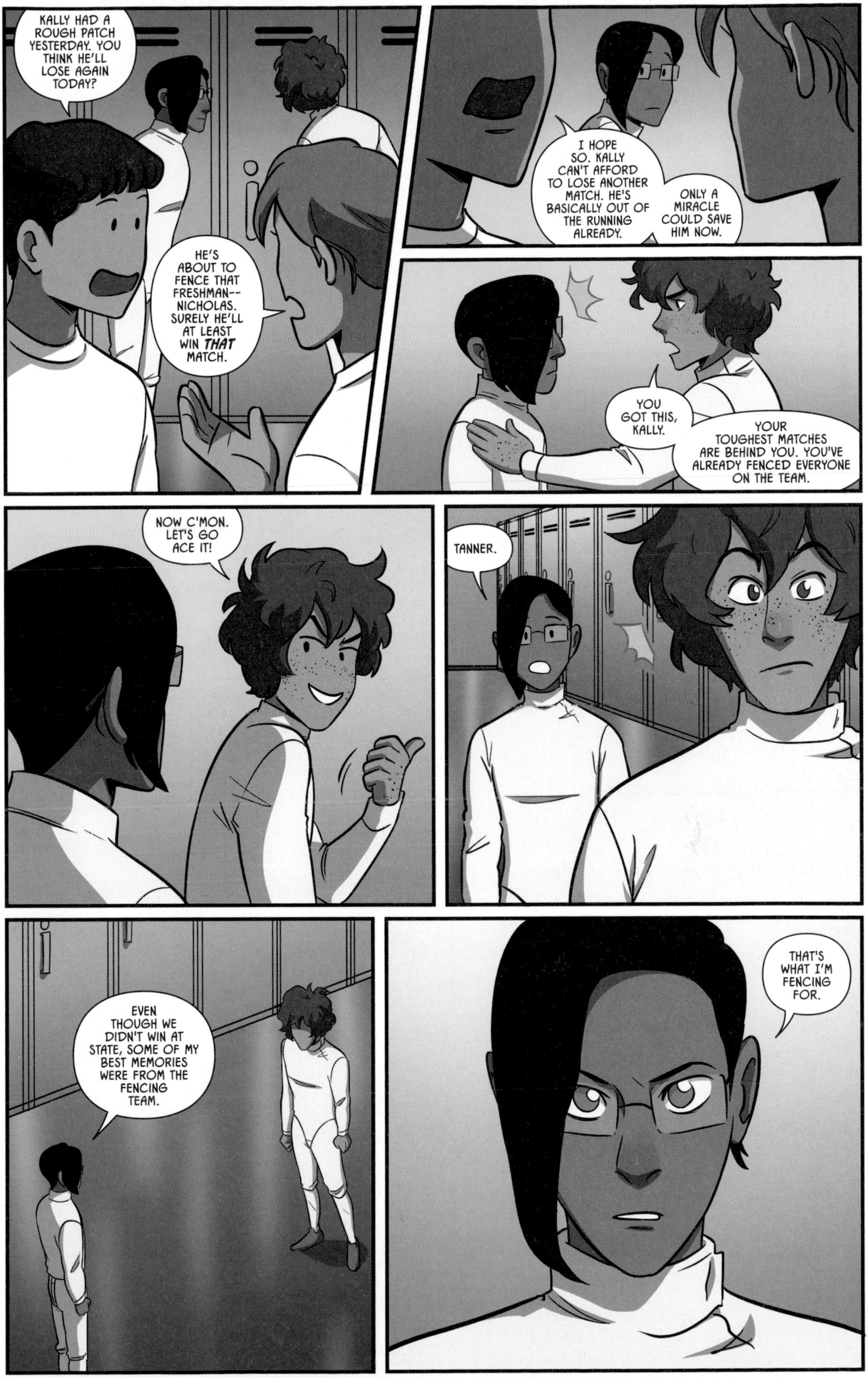
KALLY HAD A ROUGH PATCH YESTERDAY. YOU THINK HE'LL LOSE AGAIN TODAY?
HE'S ABOUT TO FENCE THAT FRESHMAN-- NICHOLAS. SURELY HE'LL AT LEAST WIN *THAT* MATCH.
I HOPE SO. KALLY CAN'T AFFORD TO LOSE ANOTHER MATCH. HE'S BASICALLY OUT OF THE RUNNING ALREADY.
ONLY A MIRACLE COULD SAVE HIM NOW.
YOU GOT THIS, KALLY.
YOUR TOUGHEST MATCHES ARE BEHIND YOU. YOU'VE ALREADY FENCED EVERYONE ON THE TEAM.
NOW C'MON. LET'S GO ACE IT!
TANNER.
EVEN THOUGH WE DIDN'T WIN AT STATE, SOME OF MY BEST MEMORIES WERE FROM THE FENCING TEAM.
THAT'S WHAT I'M FENCING FOR.

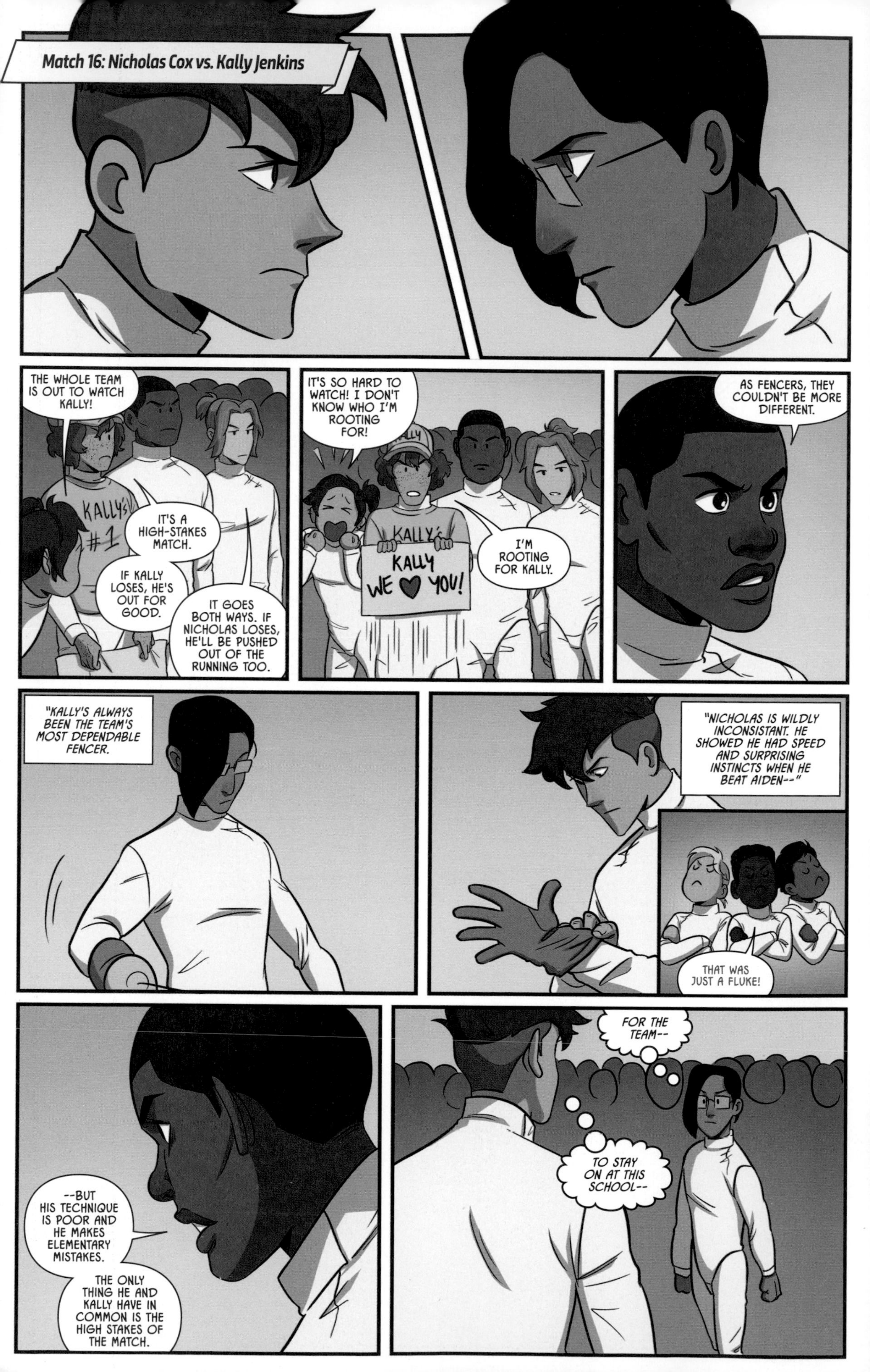
Match 16: Nicholas Cox vs. Kally Jenkins
THE WHOLE TEAM IS OUT TO WATCH KALLY!
KALLY'S #1
IT'S A HIGH-STAKES MATCH.
IF KALLY LOSES, HE'S OUT FOR GOOD.
IT GOES BOTH WAYS. IF NICHOLAS LOSES, HE'LL BE PUSHED OUT OF THE RUNNING TOO.
IT'S SO HARD TO WATCH! I DON'T KNOW WHO I'M ROOTING FOR!
KALLY
KALLY'S
KALLY WE ♥ YOU!
I'M ROOTING FOR KALLY.
AS FENCERS, THEY COULDN'T BE MORE DIFFERENT.
"KALLY'S ALWAYS BEEN THE TEAM'S MOST DEPENDABLE FENCER.
"NICHOLAS IS WILDLY INCONSISTANT. HE SHOWED HE HAD SPEED AND SURPRISING INSTINCTS WHEN HE BEAT AIDEN--"
THAT WAS JUST A FLUKE!
--BUT HIS TECHNIQUE IS POOR AND HE MAKES ELEMENTARY MISTAKES.
THE ONLY THING HE AND KALLY HAVE IN COMMON IS THE HIGH STAKES OF THE MATCH.
FOR THE TEAM--
TO STAY ON AT THIS SCHOOL--

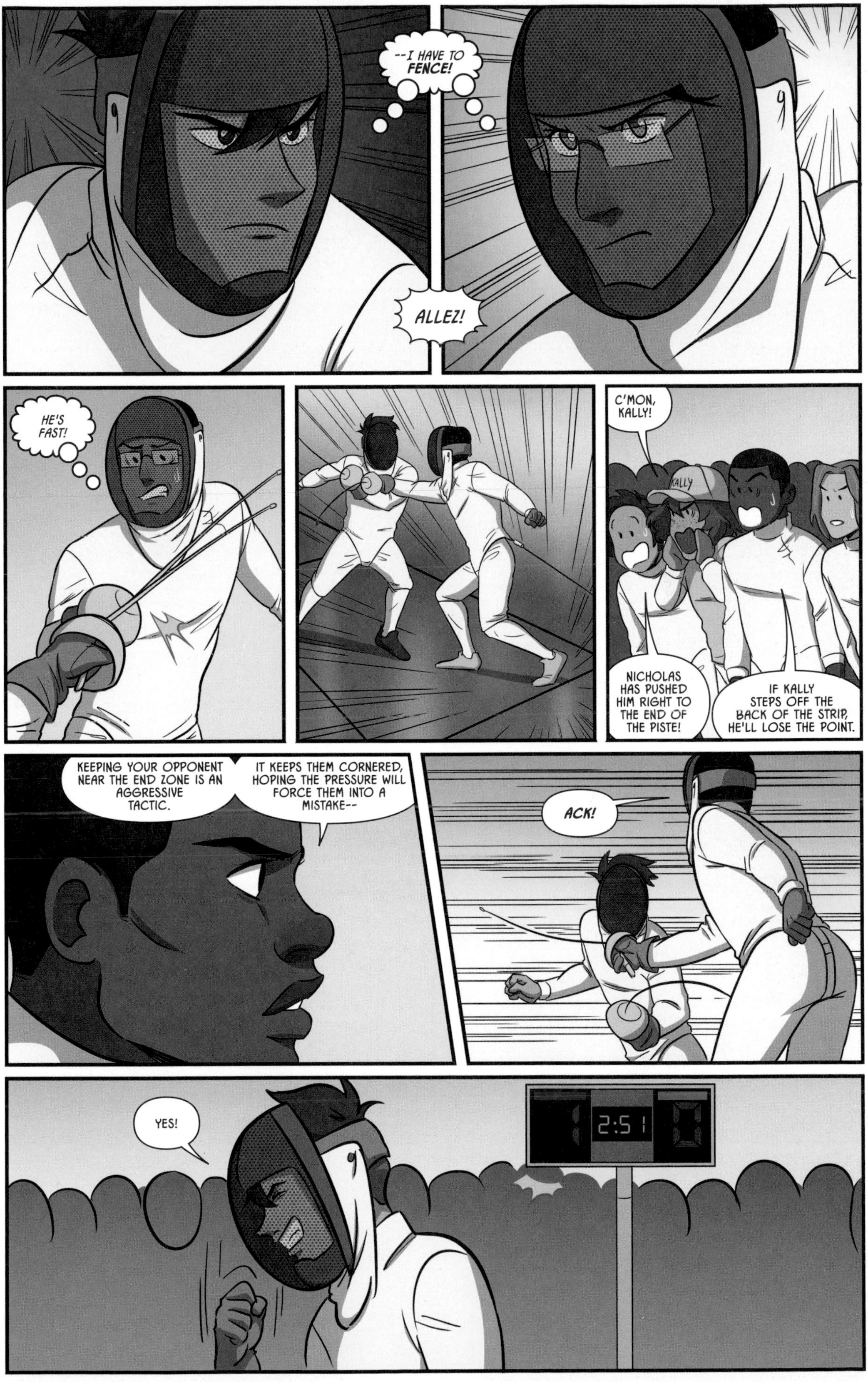
--I HAVE TO FENCE!
ALLEZ!
HE'S FAST!
C'MON, KALLY!
KALLY
NICHOLAS HAS PUSHED HIM RIGHT TO THE END OF THE PISTE!
IF KALLY STEPS OFF THE BACK OF THE STRIP, HE'LL LOSE THE POINT.
KEEPING YOUR OPPONENT NEAR THE END ZONE IS AN AGGRESSIVE TACTIC.
IT KEEPS THEM CORNERED, HOPING THE PRESSURE WILL FORCE THEM INTO A MISTAKE--
ACK!
YES!
2:51

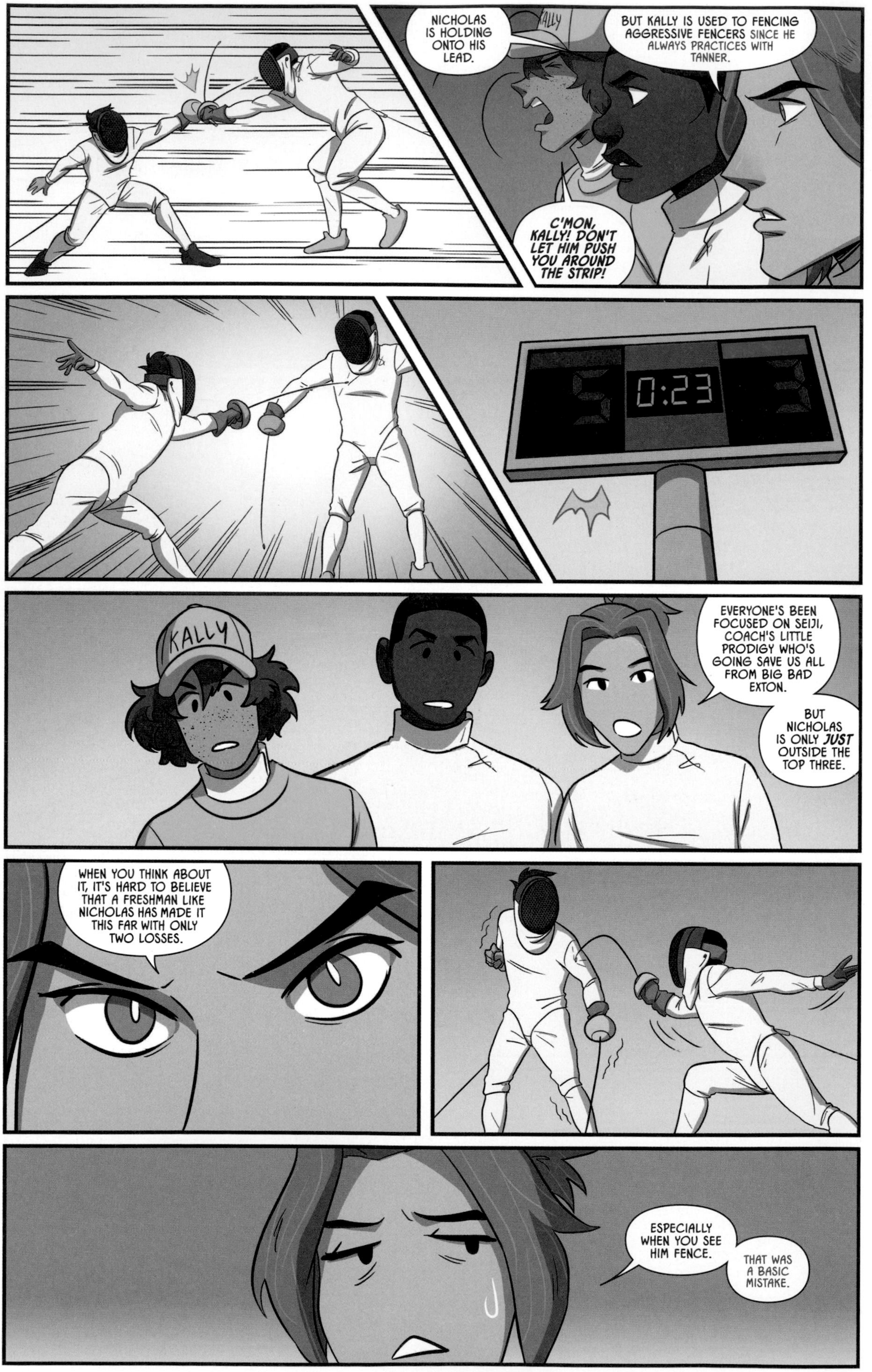
NICHOLAS IS HOLDING ONTO HIS LEAD.
BUT KALLY IS USED TO FENCING AGGRESSIVE FENCERS SINCE HE ALWAYS PRACTICES WITH TANNER.
KALLY
C'MON, KALLY! DON'T LET HIM PUSH YOU AROUND THE STRIP!
0:23
KALLY
EVERYONE'S BEEN FOCUSED ON SEIJI, COACH'S LITTLE PRODIGY WHO'S GOING SAVE US ALL FROM BIG BAD EXTON.
BUT NICHOLAS IS ONLY JUST OUTSIDE THE TOP THREE.
WHEN YOU THINK ABOUT IT, IT'S HARD TO BELIEVE THAT A FRESHMAN LIKE NICHOLAS HAS MADE IT THIS FAR WITH ONLY TWO LOSSES.
ESPECIALLY WHEN YOU SEE HIM FENCE.
THAT WAS A BASIC MISTAKE.

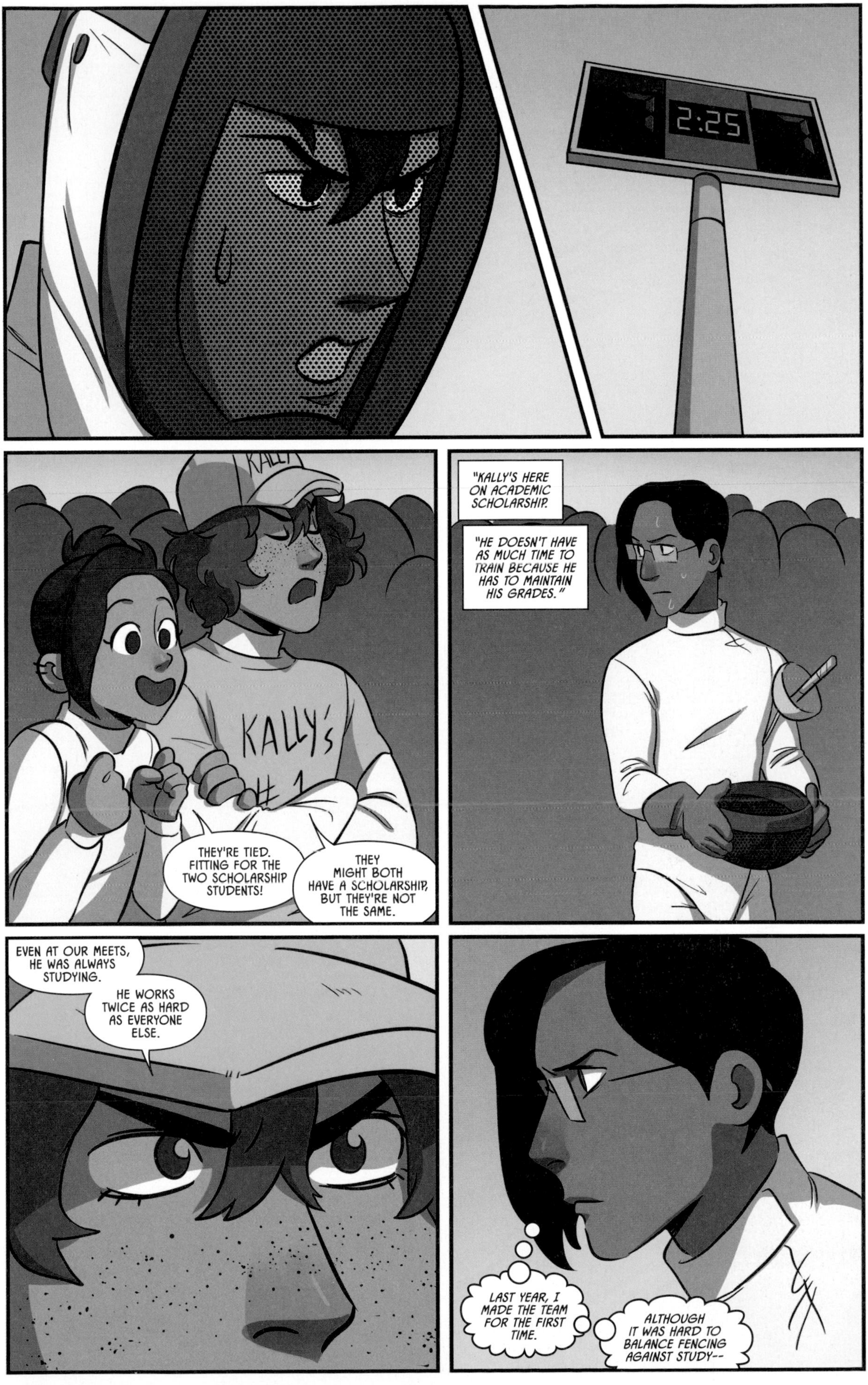
2:25
KALLY
KALLY'S #1
THEY'RE TIED. FITTING FOR THE TWO SCHOLARSHIP STUDENTS!
THEY MIGHT BOTH HAVE A SCHOLARSHIP, BUT THEY'RE NOT THE SAME.
"KALLY'S HERE ON ACADEMIC SCHOLARSHIP.
"HE DOESN'T HAVE AS MUCH TIME TO TRAIN BECAUSE HE HAS TO MAINTAIN HIS GRADES."
EVEN AT OUR MEETS, HE WAS ALWAYS STUDYING.
HE WORKS TWICE AS HARD AS EVERYONE ELSE.
LAST YEAR, I MADE THE TEAM FOR THE FIRST TIME.
ALTHOUGH IT WAS HARD TO BALANCE FENCING AGAINST STUDY--

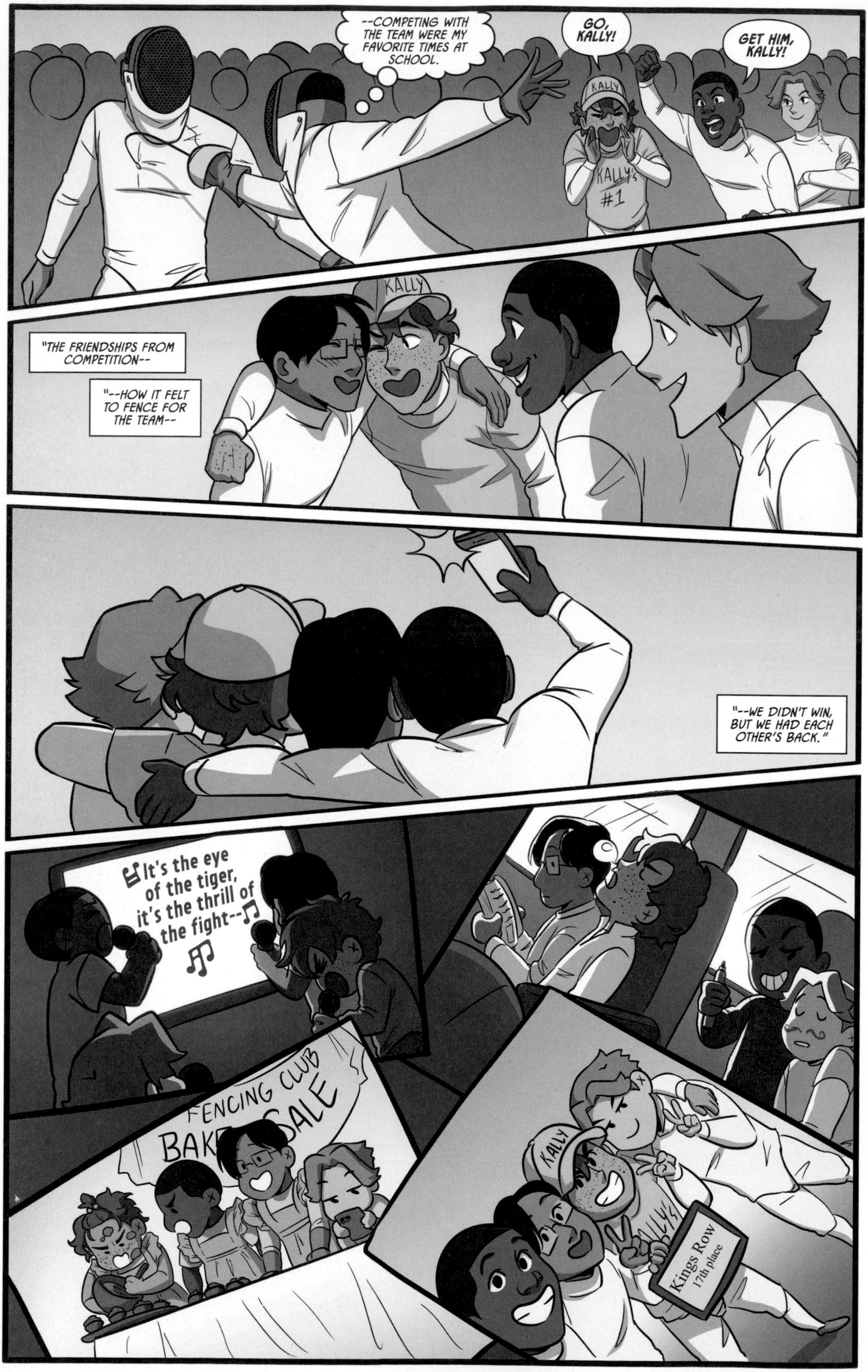
--COMPETING WITH THE TEAM WERE MY FAVORITE TIMES AT SCHOOL.
GO, KALLY!
GET HIM, KALLY!
KALLY
KALLY'S #1
"THE FRIENDSHIPS FROM COMPETITION--
"--HOW IT FELT TO FENCE FOR THE TEAM--
"--WE DIDN'T WIN, BUT WE HAD EACH OTHER'S BACK."
It's the eye of the tiger, it's the thrill of the fight--
FENCING CLUB BAKE SALE
KALLY
Kings Row 17th place

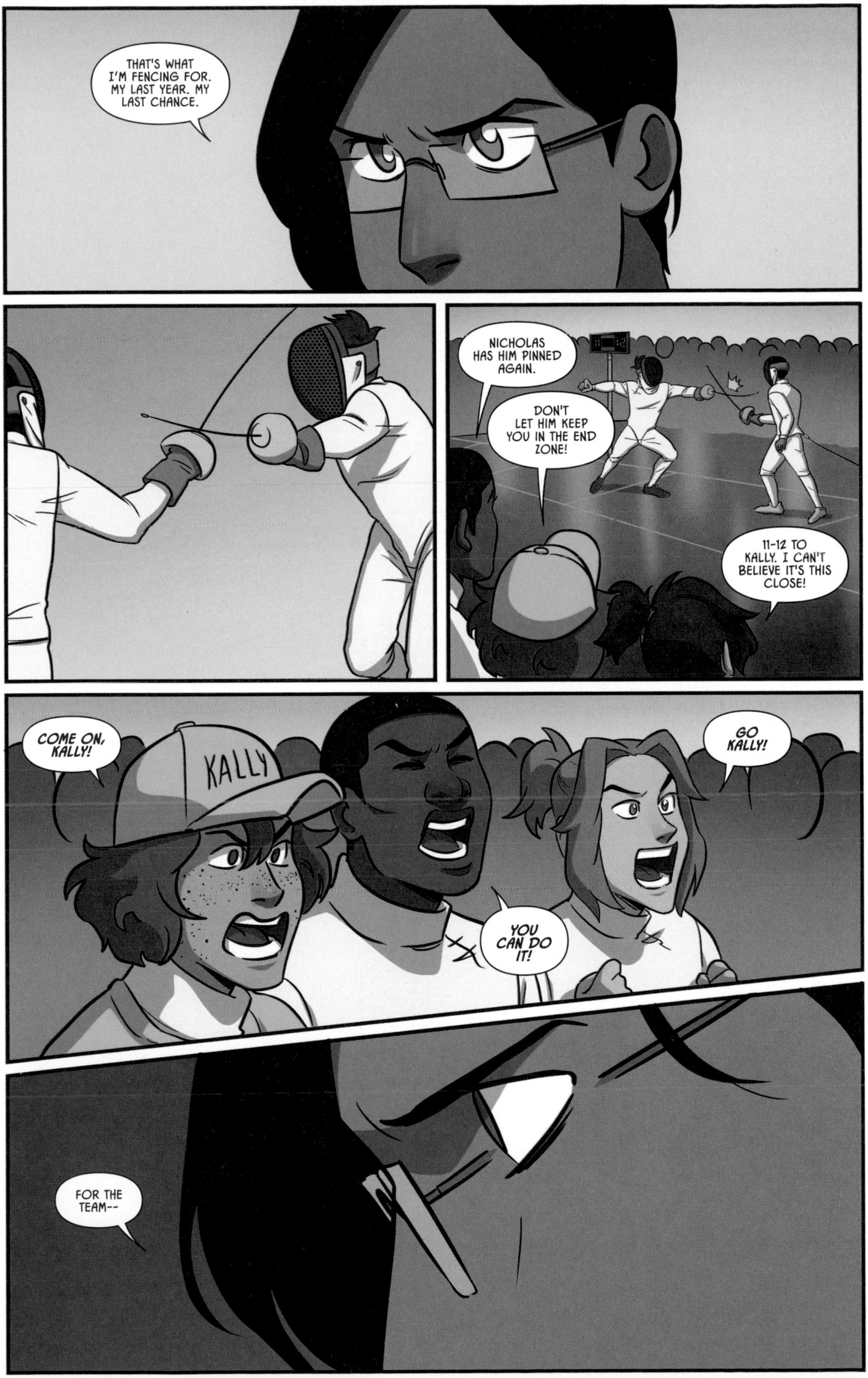
THAT'S WHAT I'M FENCING FOR. MY LAST YEAR. MY LAST CHANCE.
NICHOLAS HAS HIM PINNED AGAIN.
DON'T LET HIM KEEP YOU IN THE END ZONE!
11-12 TO KALLY. I CAN'T BELIEVE IT'S THIS CLOSE!
COME ON, KALLY!
KALLY
GO KALLY!
YOU CAN DO IT!
FOR THE TEAM--

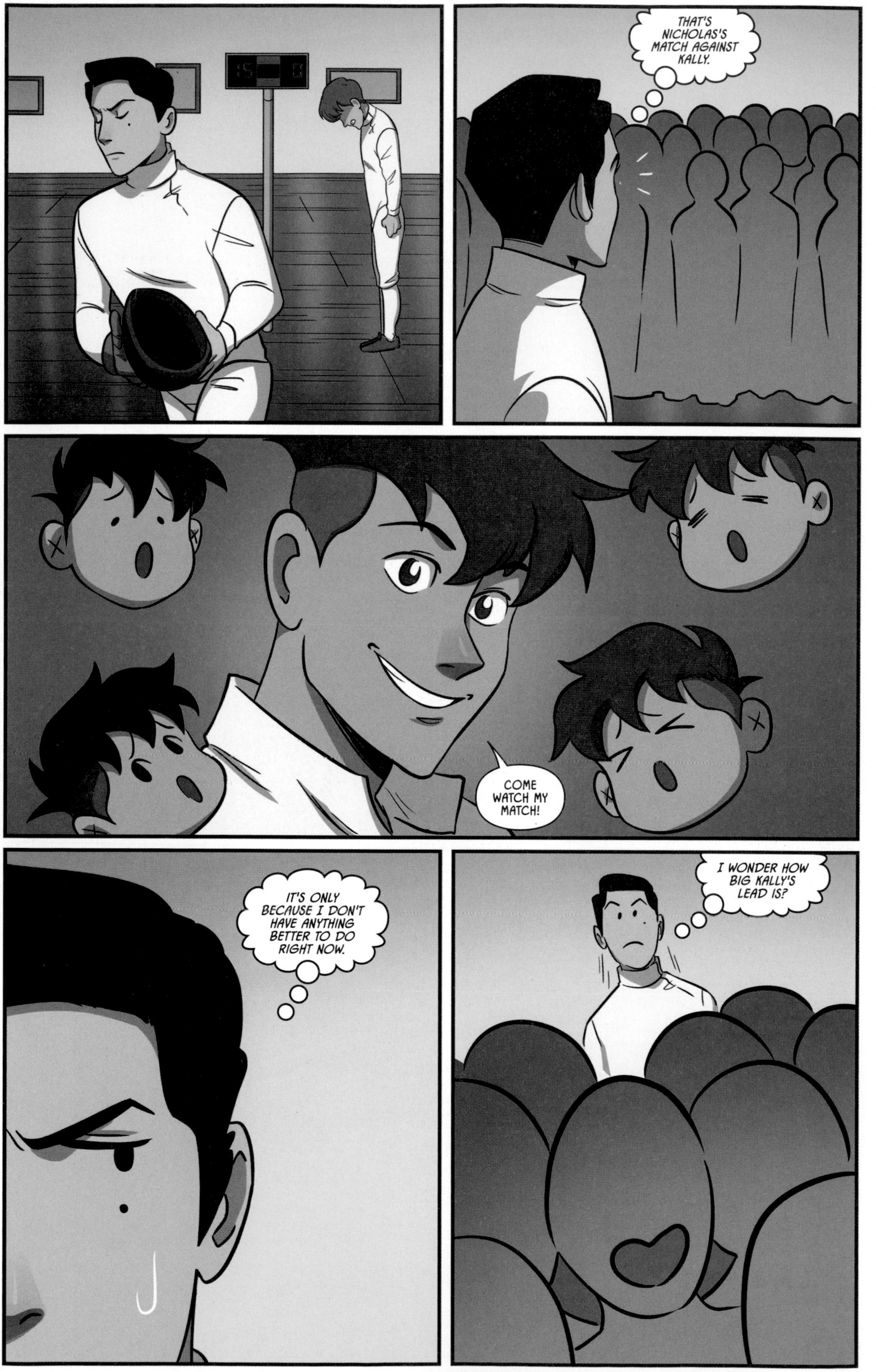
15 0
THAT'S NICHOLAS'S MATCH AGAINST KALLY.
COME WATCH MY MATCH!
IT'S ONLY BECAUSE I DON'T HAVE ANYTHING BETTER TO DO RIGHT NOW.
I WONDER HOW BIG KALLY'S LEAD IS?

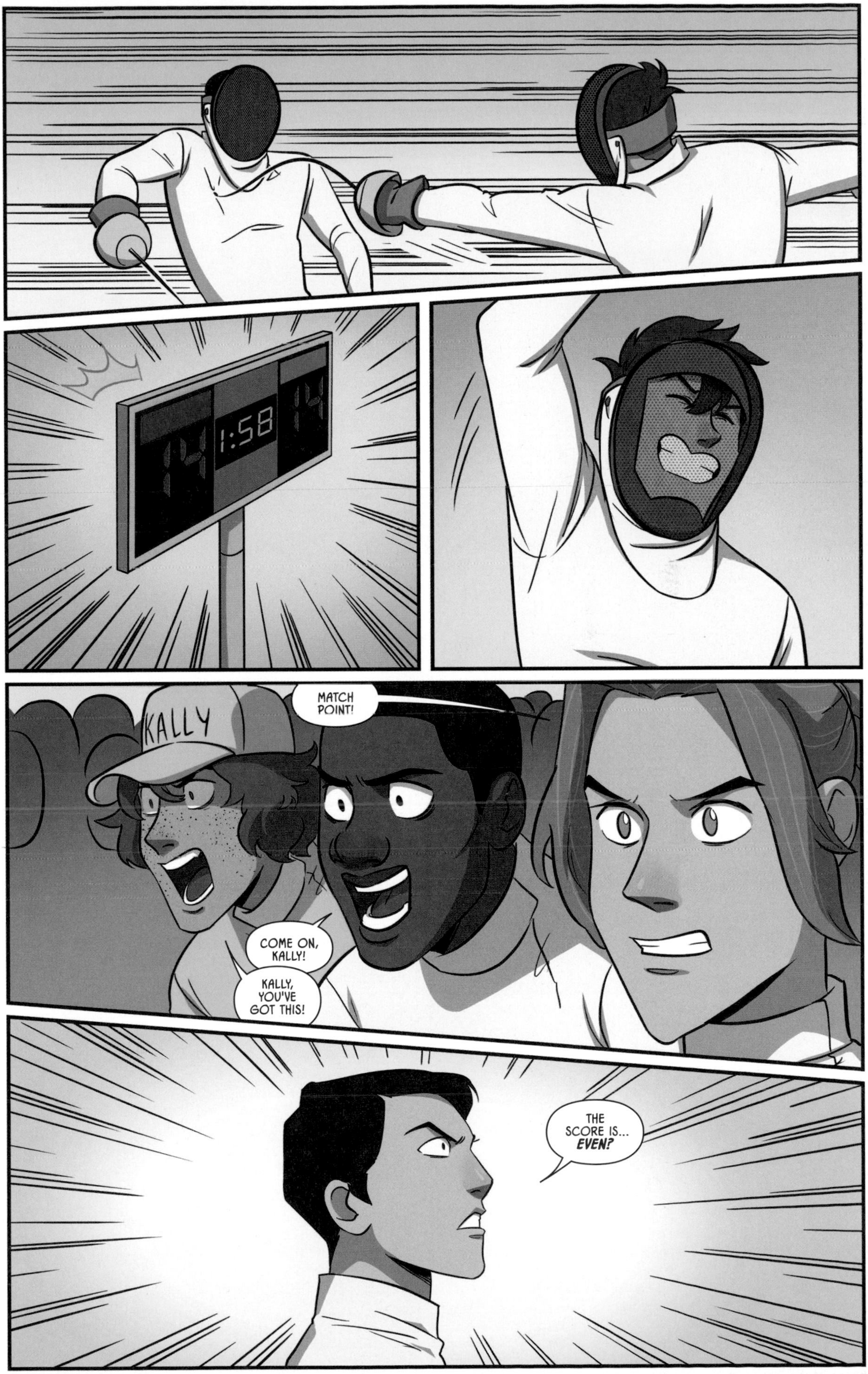
14
1:58
14
KALLY
MATCH POINT!
COME ON, KALLY!
KALLY, YOU'VE GOT THIS!
THE SCORE IS... *EVEN?*

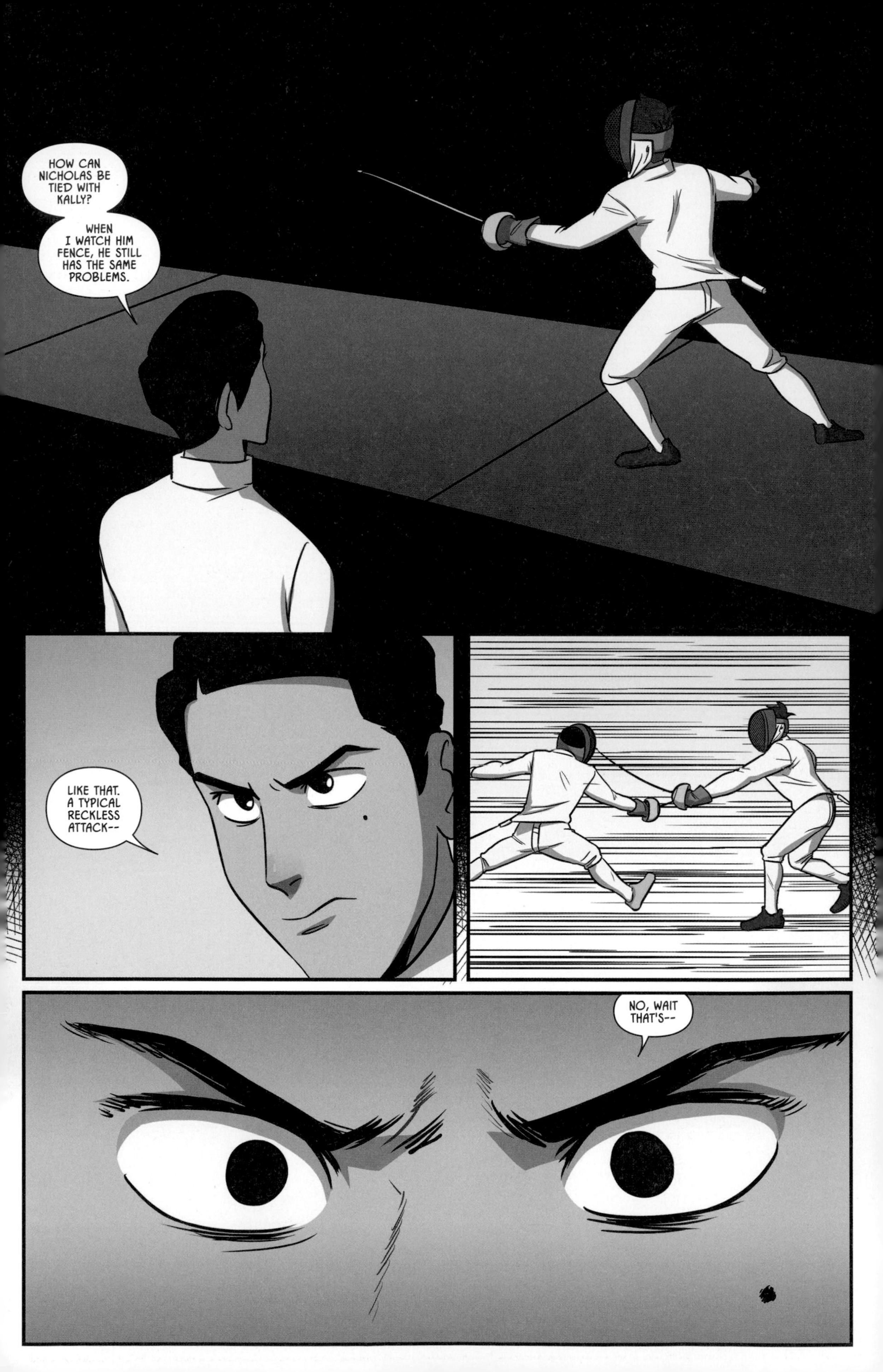
HOW CAN NICHOLAS BE TIED WITH KALLY?
WHEN I WATCH HIM FENCE, HE STILL HAS THE SAME PROBLEMS.
LIKE THAT. A TYPICAL RECKLESS ATTACK--
NO, WAIT THAT'S--

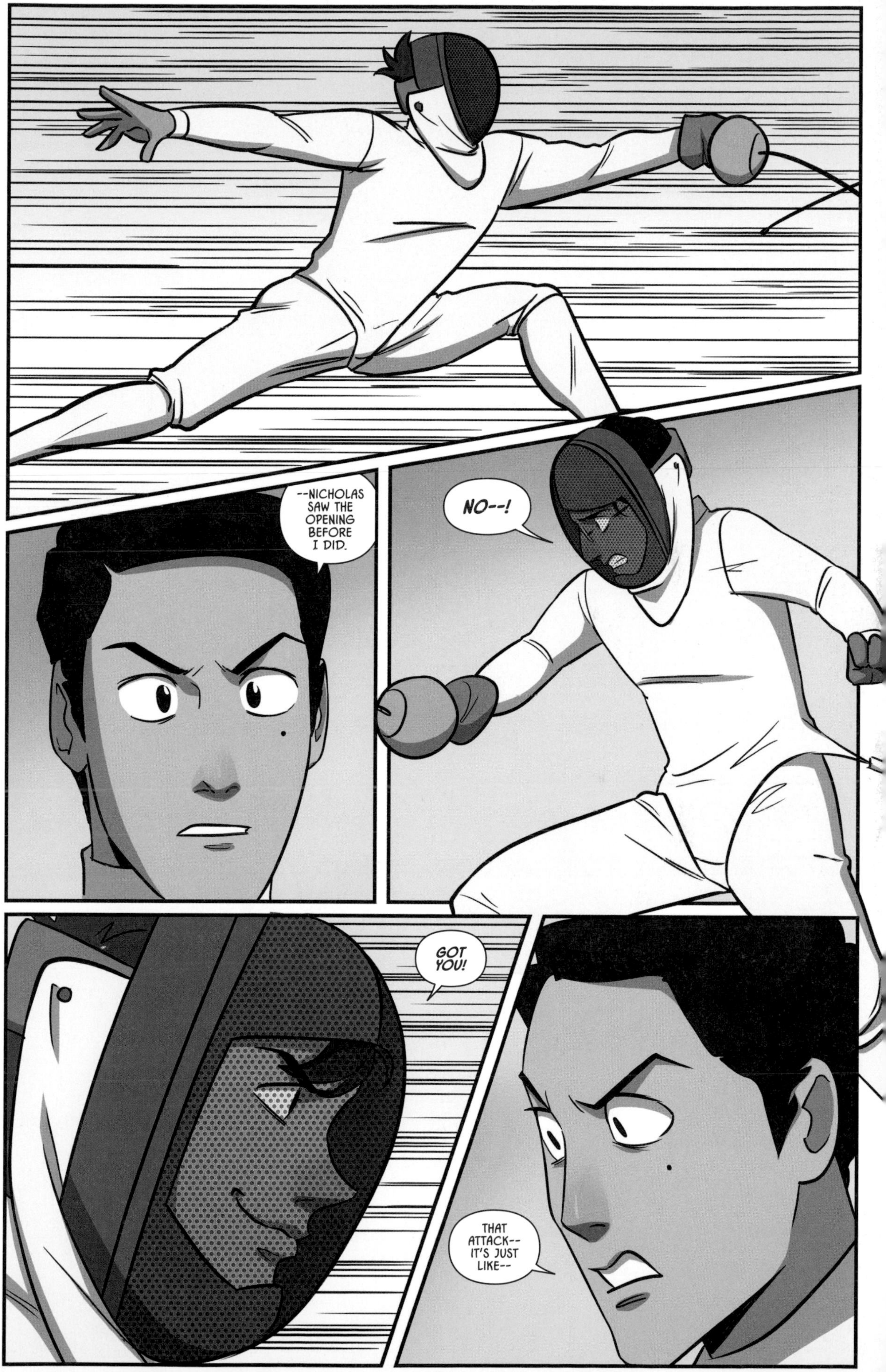
--NICHOLAS SAW THE OPENING BEFORE I DID.
NO--!
GOT YOU!
THAT ATTACK-- IT'S JUST LIKE--

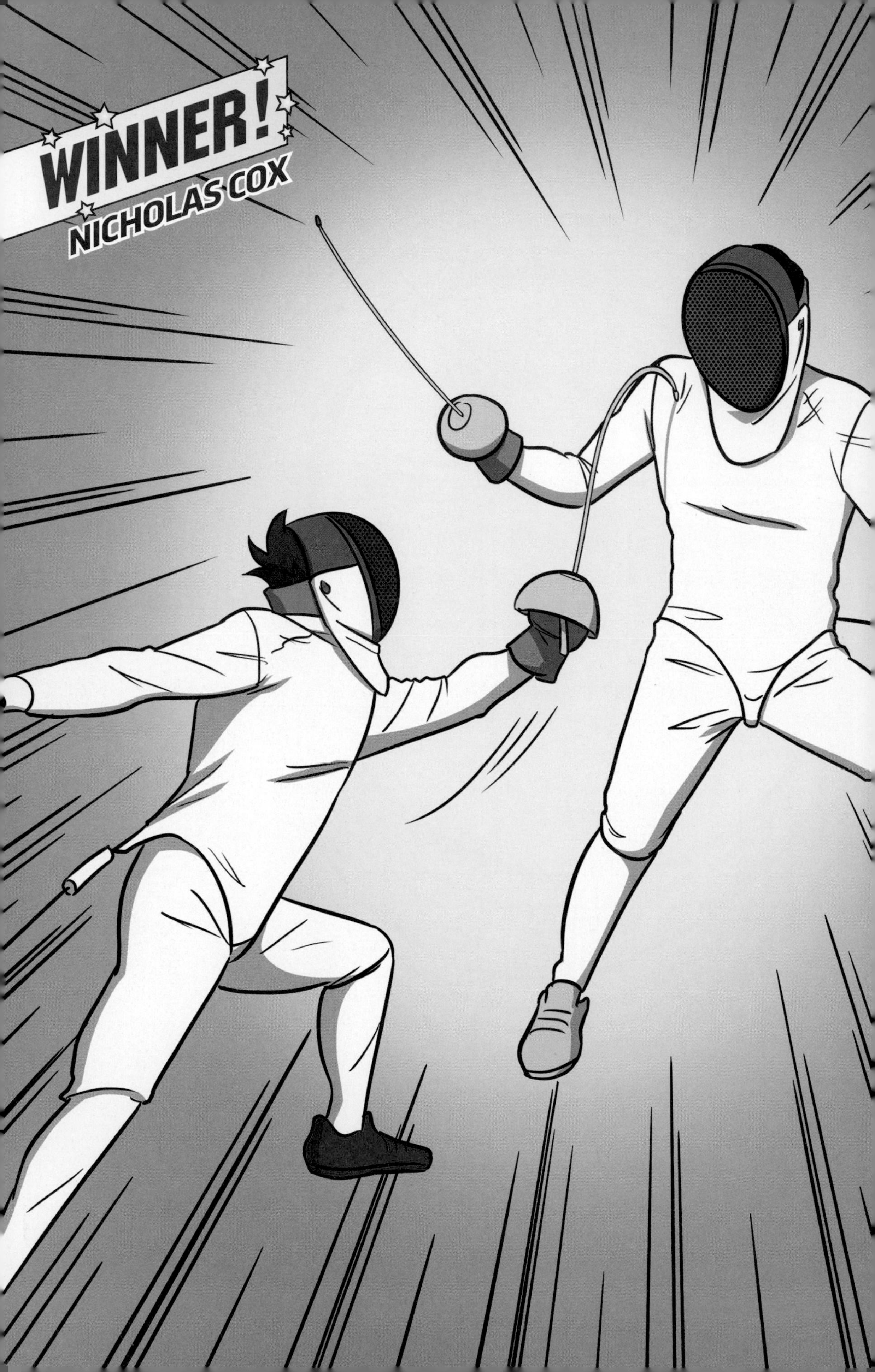
WINNER!
NICHOLAS COX

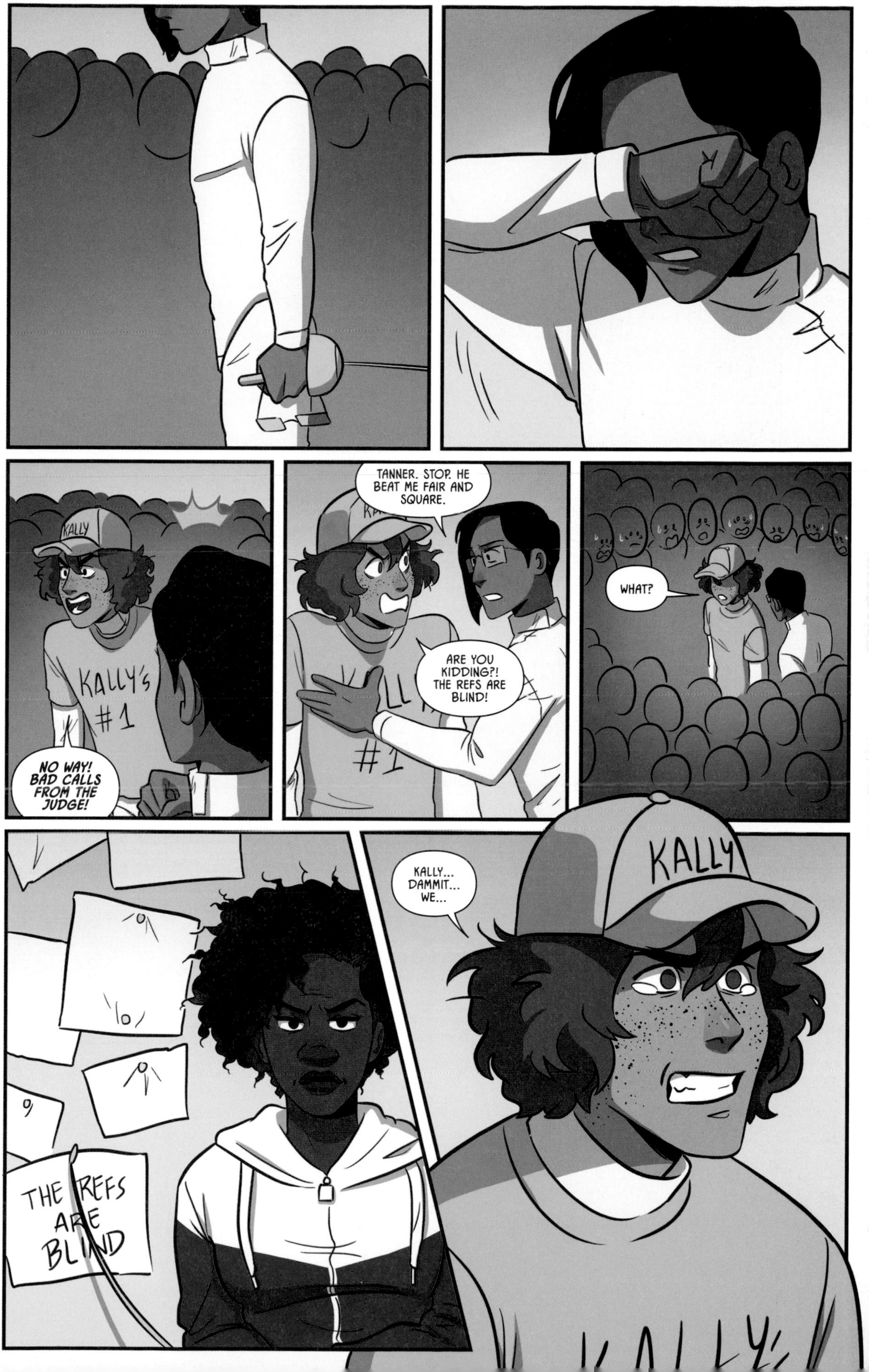
NO WAY! BAD CALLS FROM THE JUDGE!
KALLY
KALLY'S #1
TANNER. STOP. HE BEAT ME FAIR AND SQUARE.
ARE YOU KIDDING?! THE REFS ARE BLIND!
WHAT?
THE REFS ARE BLIND
KALLY... DAMMIT... WE...
KALLY

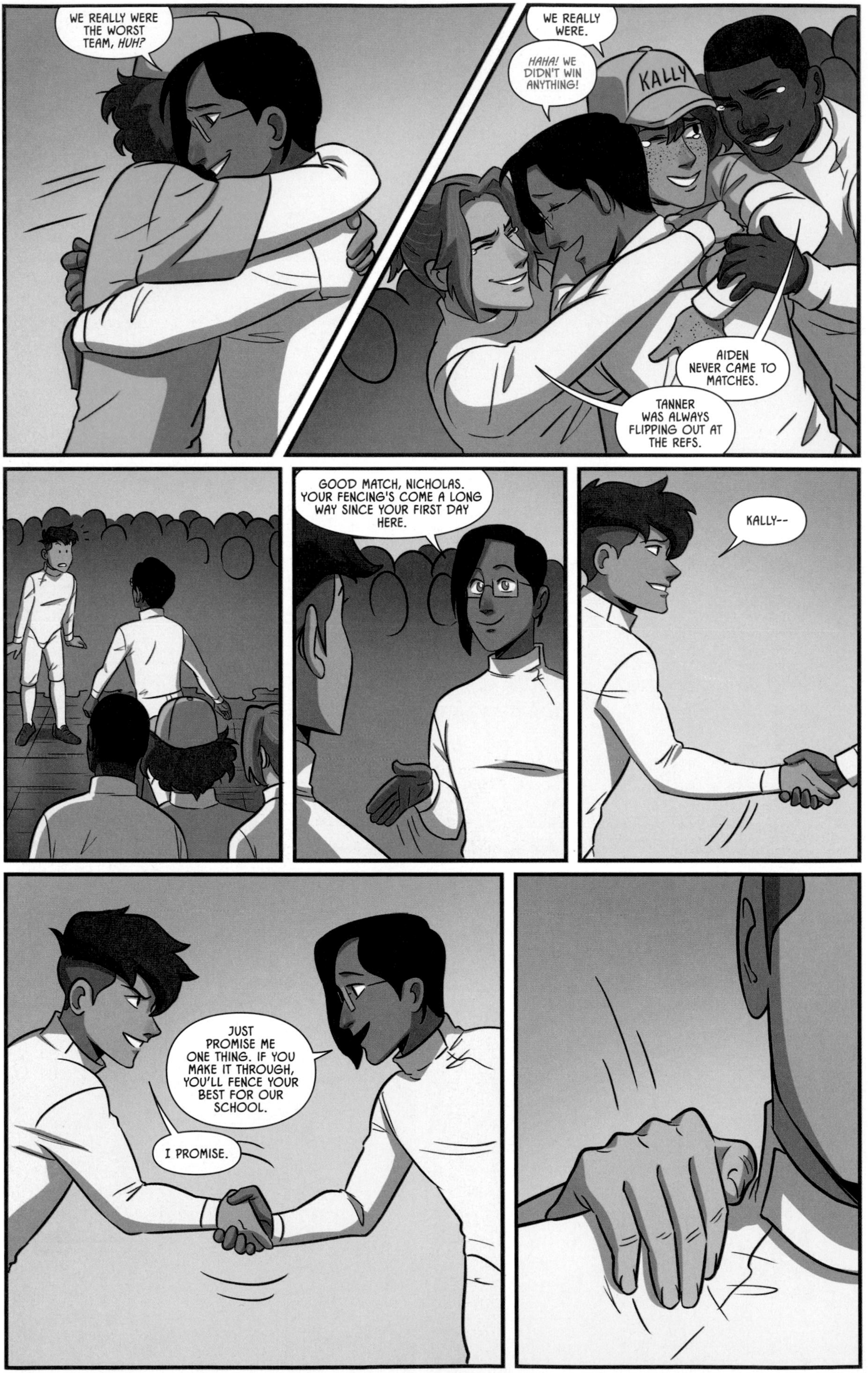
WE REALLY WERE THE WORST TEAM, *HUH?*
WE REALLY WERE.
HAHA! WE DIDN'T WIN ANYTHING!
AIDEN NEVER CAME TO MATCHES.
TANNER WAS ALWAYS FLIPPING OUT AT THE REFS.
GOOD MATCH, NICHOLAS. YOUR FENCING'S COME A LONG WAY SINCE YOUR FIRST DAY HERE.
KALLY--
JUST PROMISE ME ONE THING. IF YOU MAKE IT THROUGH, YOU'LL FENCE YOUR BEST FOR OUR SCHOOL.
I PROMISE.

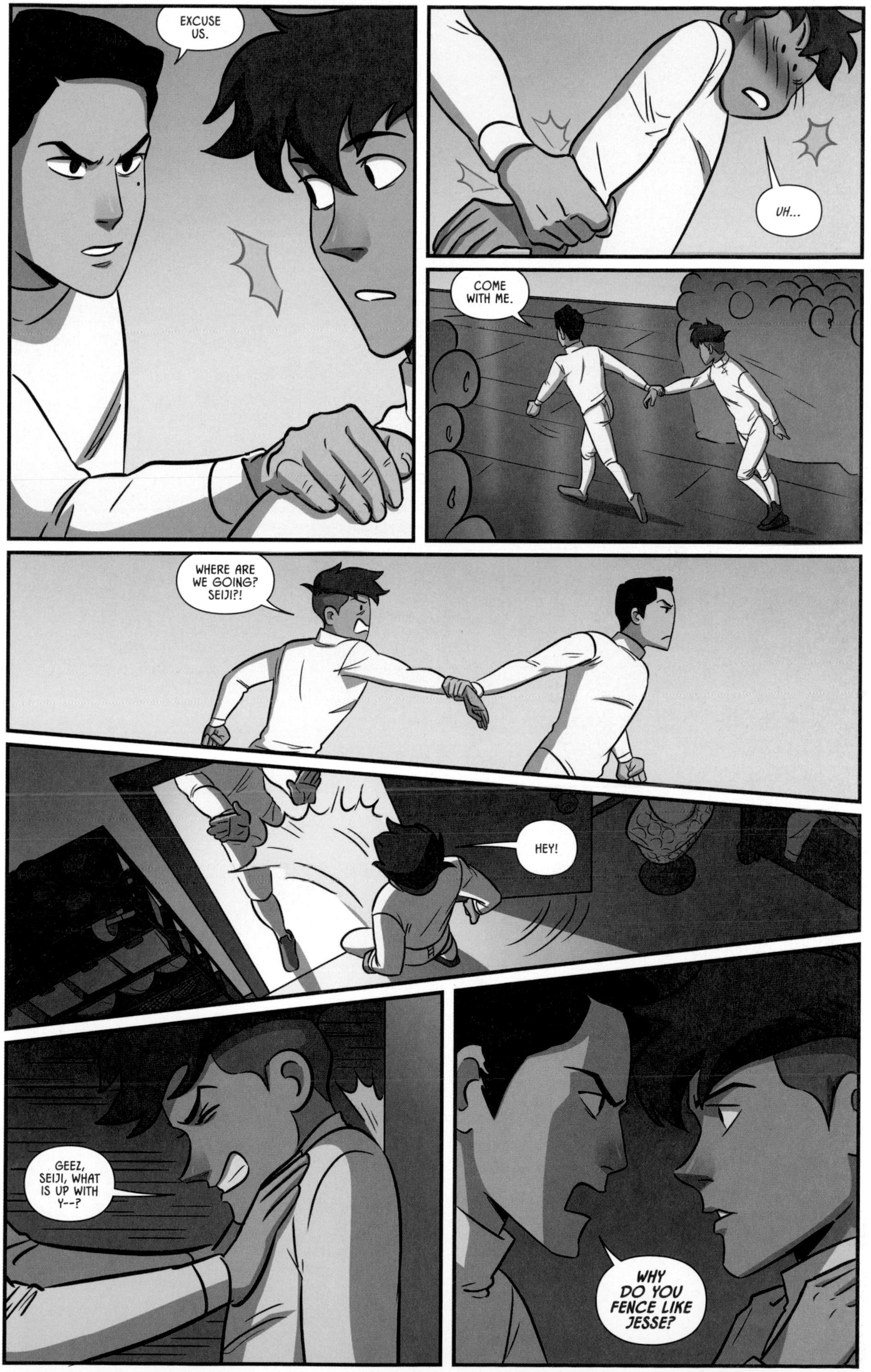
EXCUSE US.
UH...
COME WITH ME.
WHERE ARE WE GOING? SEIJI?!
HEY!
GEEZ, SEIJI, WHAT IS UP WITH Y--?
WHY DO YOU FENCE LIKE JESSE?

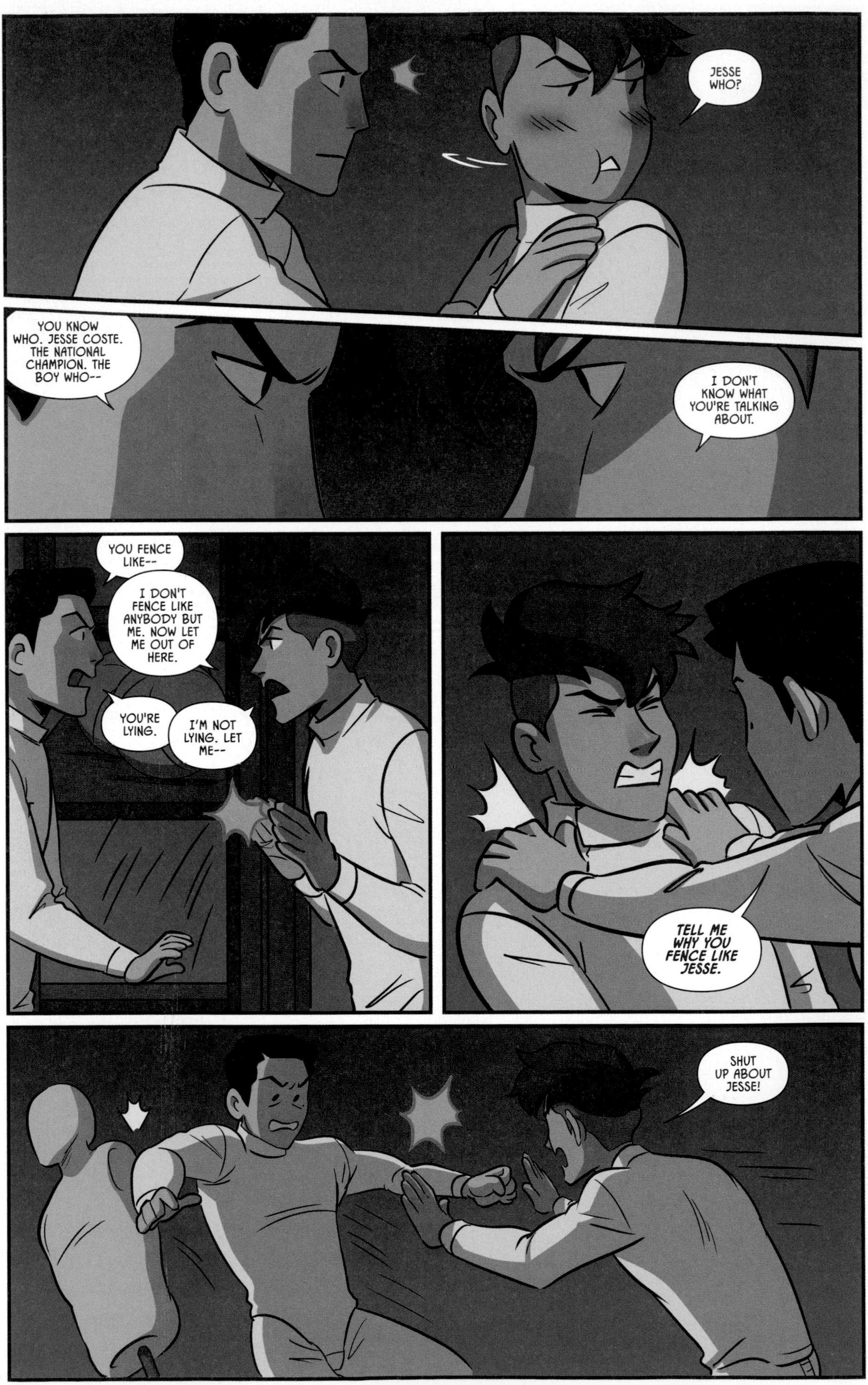
JESSE WHO?
YOU KNOW WHO. JESSE COSTE. THE NATIONAL CHAMPION. THE BOY WHO--
I DON'T KNOW WHAT YOU'RE TALKING ABOUT.
YOU FENCE LIKE--
I DON'T FENCE LIKE ANYBODY BUT ME. NOW LET ME OUT OF HERE.
YOU'RE LYING.
I'M NOT LYING. LET ME--
TELL ME WHY YOU FENCE LIKE JESSE.
SHUT UP ABOUT JESSE!

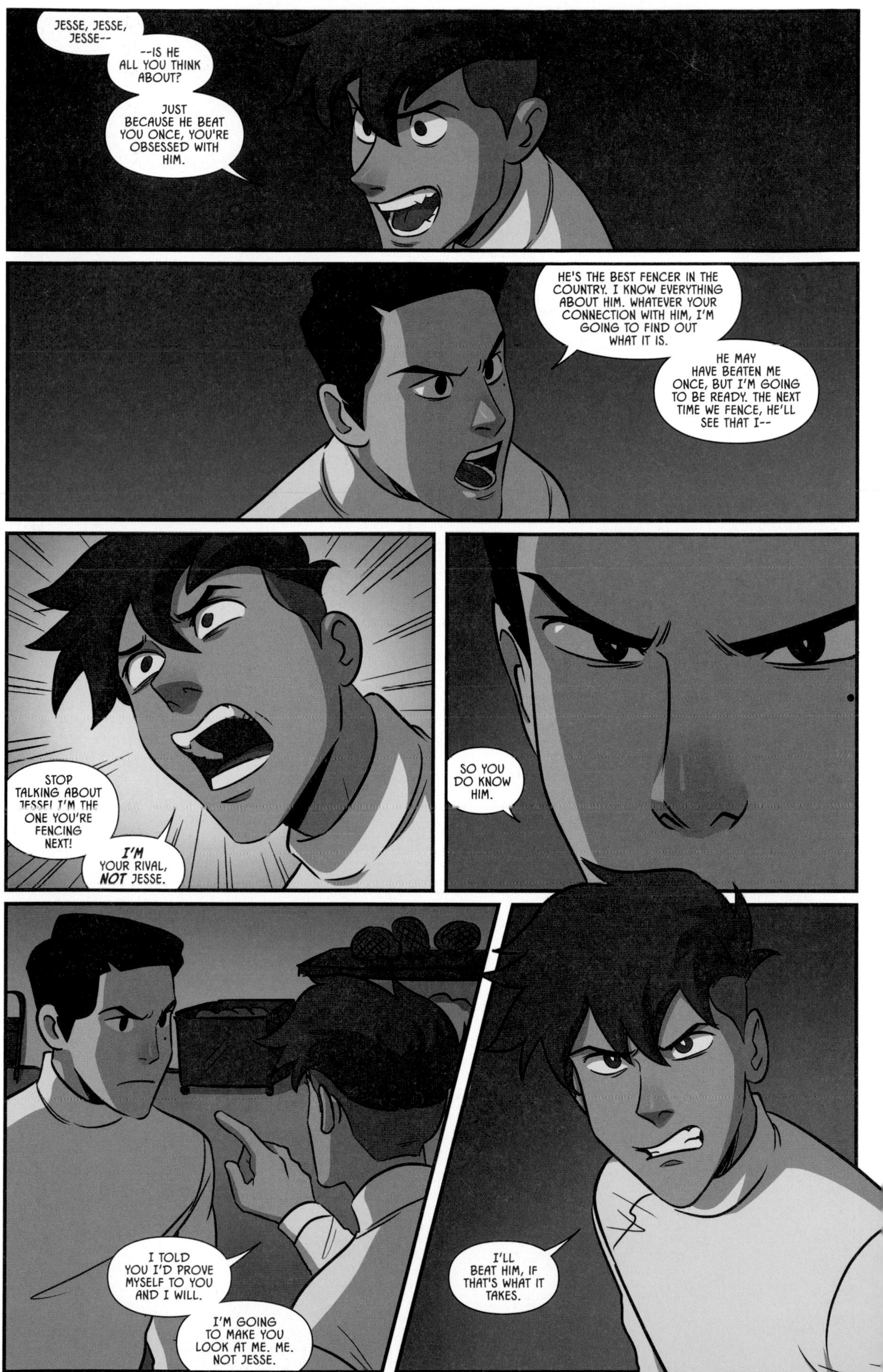
JESSE, JESSE, JESSE--
--IS HE ALL YOU THINK ABOUT?
JUST BECAUSE HE BEAT YOU ONCE, YOU'RE OBSESSED WITH HIM.
HE'S THE BEST FENCER IN THE COUNTRY. I KNOW EVERYTHING ABOUT HIM. WHATEVER YOUR CONNECTION WITH HIM, I'M GOING TO FIND OUT WHAT IT IS.
HE MAY HAVE BEATEN ME ONCE, BUT I'M GOING TO BE READY. THE NEXT TIME WE FENCE, HE'LL SEE THAT I--
STOP TALKING ABOUT JESSE! I'M THE ONE YOU'RE FENCING NEXT!
I'M YOUR RIVAL, NOT JESSE.
SO YOU DO KNOW HIM.
I TOLD YOU I'D PROVE MYSELF TO YOU AND I WILL.
I'M GOING TO MAKE YOU LOOK AT ME. ME. NOT JESSE.
I'LL BEAT HIM, IF THAT'S WHAT IT TAKES.

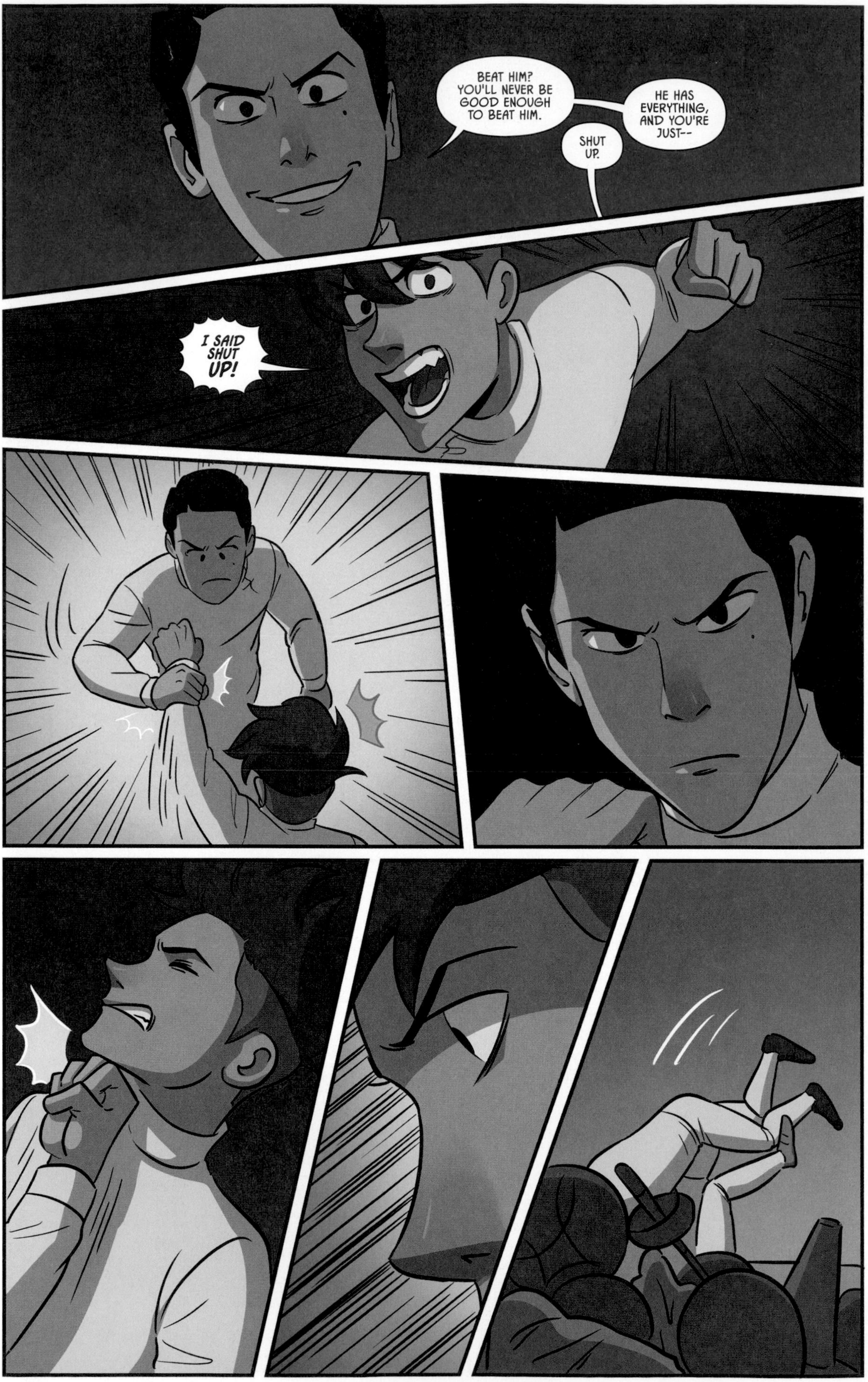
BEAT HIM? YOU'LL NEVER BE GOOD ENOUGH TO BEAT HIM.
HE HAS EVERYTHING, AND YOU'RE JUST--
SHUT UP.
I SAID SHUT UP!

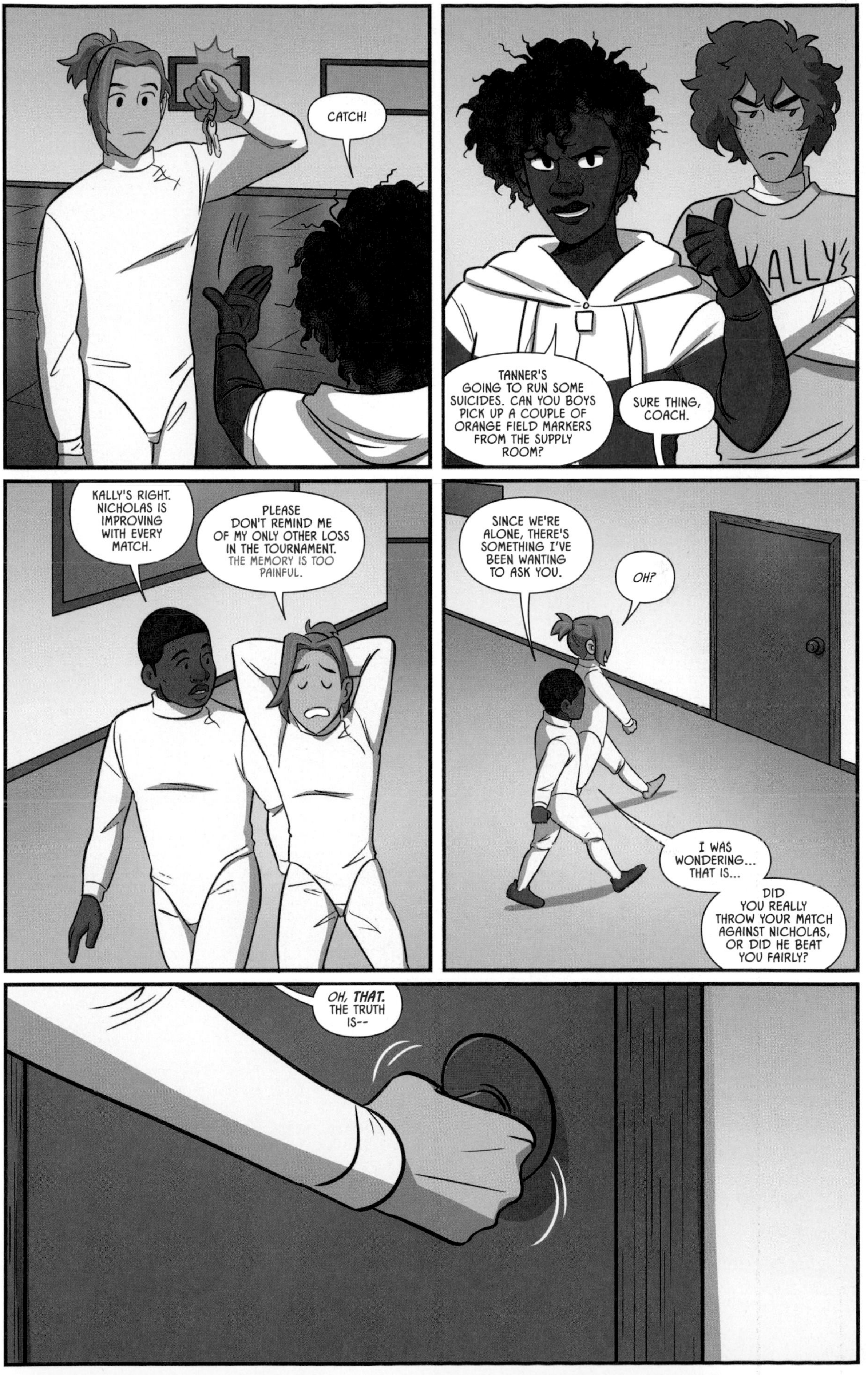
CATCH!
TANNER'S GOING TO RUN SOME SUICIDES. CAN YOU BOYS PICK UP A COUPLE OF ORANGE FIELD MARKERS FROM THE SUPPLY ROOM?
SURE THING, COACH.
KALLY'S
KALLY'S RIGHT. NICHOLAS IS IMPROVING WITH EVERY MATCH.
PLEASE DON'T REMIND ME OF MY ONLY OTHER LOSS IN THE TOURNAMENT. THE MEMORY IS TOO PAINFUL.
SINCE WE'RE ALONE, THERE'S SOMETHING I'VE BEEN WANTING TO ASK YOU.
OH?
I WAS WONDERING... THAT IS...
DID YOU REALLY THROW YOUR MATCH AGAINST NICHOLAS, OR DID HE BEAT YOU FAIRLY?
OH, THAT. THE TRUTH IS--

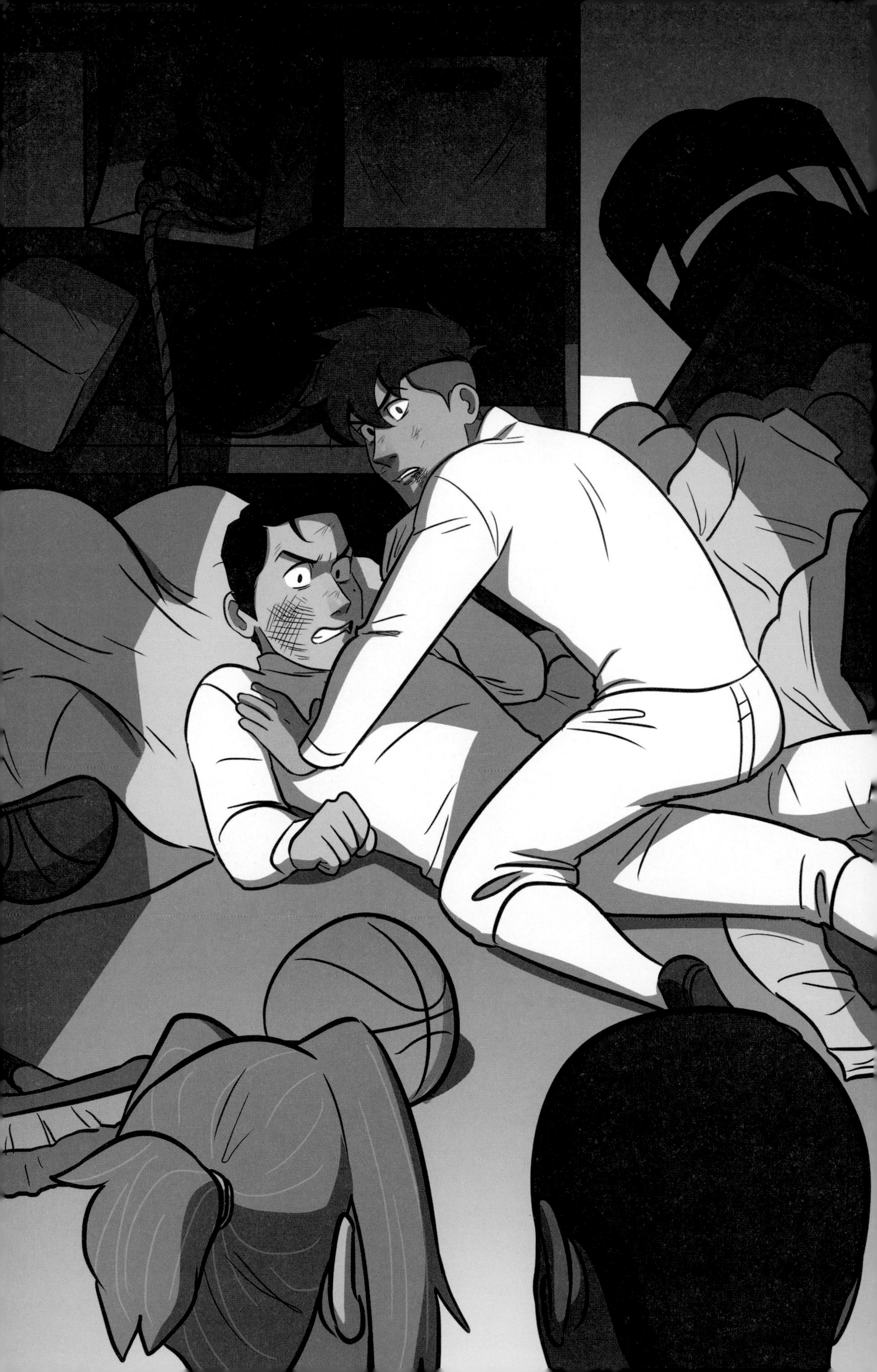

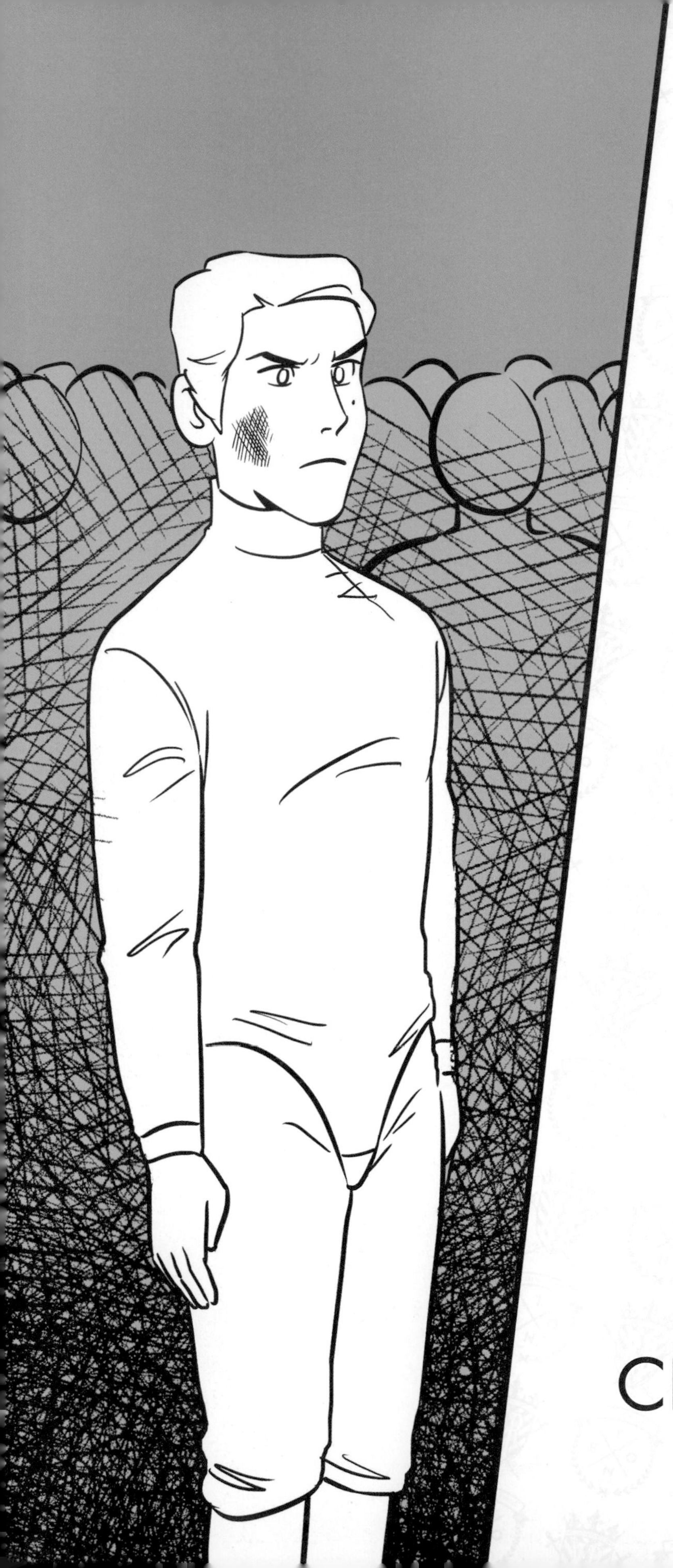

CHAPTER Ten

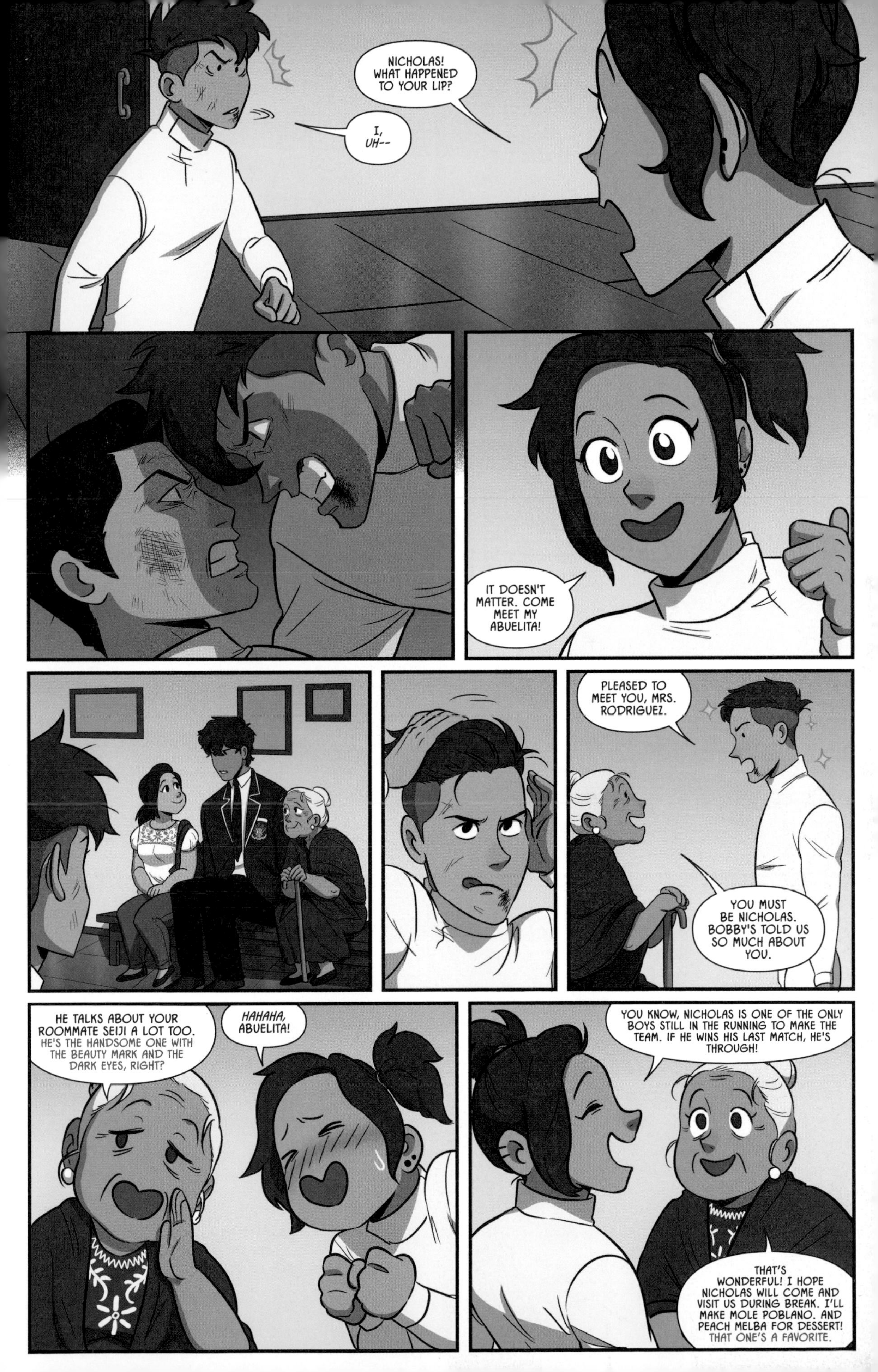
NICHOLAS! WHAT HAPPENED TO YOUR LIP?
I, UH--
IT DOESN'T MATTER. COME MEET MY ABUELITA!
PLEASED TO MEET YOU, MRS. RODRIGUEZ.
YOU MUST BE NICHOLAS. BOBBY'S TOLD US SO MUCH ABOUT YOU.
HE TALKS ABOUT YOUR ROOMMATE SEIJI A LOT TOO. HE'S THE HANDSOME ONE WITH THE BEAUTY MARK AND THE DARK EYES, RIGHT?
HAHAHA, ABUELITA!
YOU KNOW, NICHOLAS IS ONE OF THE ONLY BOYS STILL IN THE RUNNING TO MAKE THE TEAM. IF HE WINS HIS LAST MATCH, HE'S THROUGH!
THAT'S WONDERFUL! I HOPE NICHOLAS WILL COME AND VISIT US DURING BREAK. I'LL MAKE MOLE POBLANO. AND PEACH MELBA FOR DESSERT! THAT ONE'S A FAVORITE.

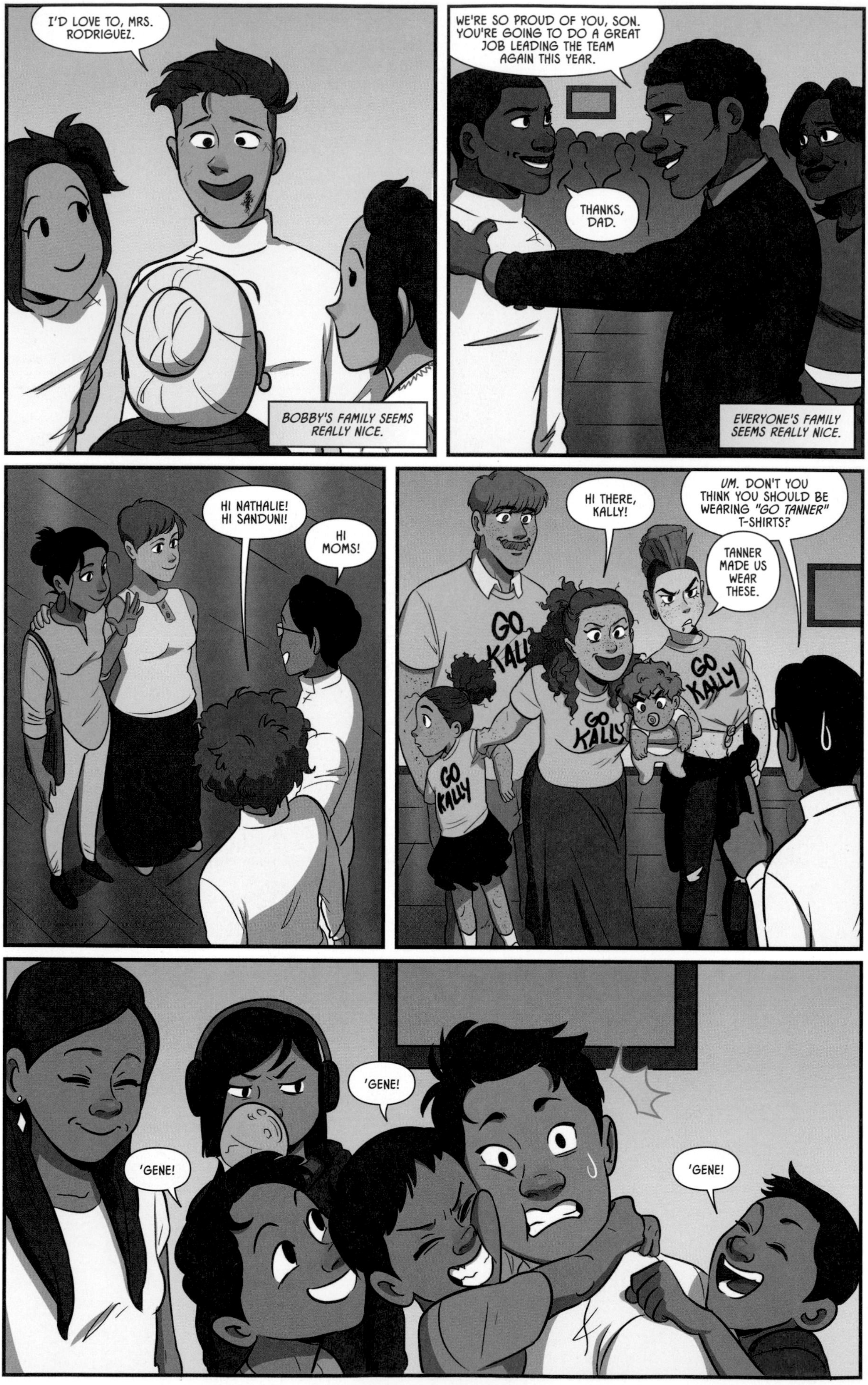
I'D LOVE TO, MRS. RODRIGUEZ.
BOBBY'S FAMILY SEEMS REALLY NICE.
WE'RE SO PROUD OF YOU, SON. YOU'RE GOING TO DO A GREAT JOB LEADING THE TEAM AGAIN THIS YEAR.
THANKS, DAD.
EVERYONE'S FAMILY SEEMS REALLY NICE.
HI NATHALIE! HI SANDUNI!
HI MOMS!
HI THERE, KALLY!
UM. DON'T YOU THINK YOU SHOULD BE WEARING "GO TANNER" T-SHIRTS?
TANNER MADE US WEAR THESE.
GO KALLY
GO KALLY
GO KALLY
GO KALLY
'GENE!
'GENE!
'GENE!

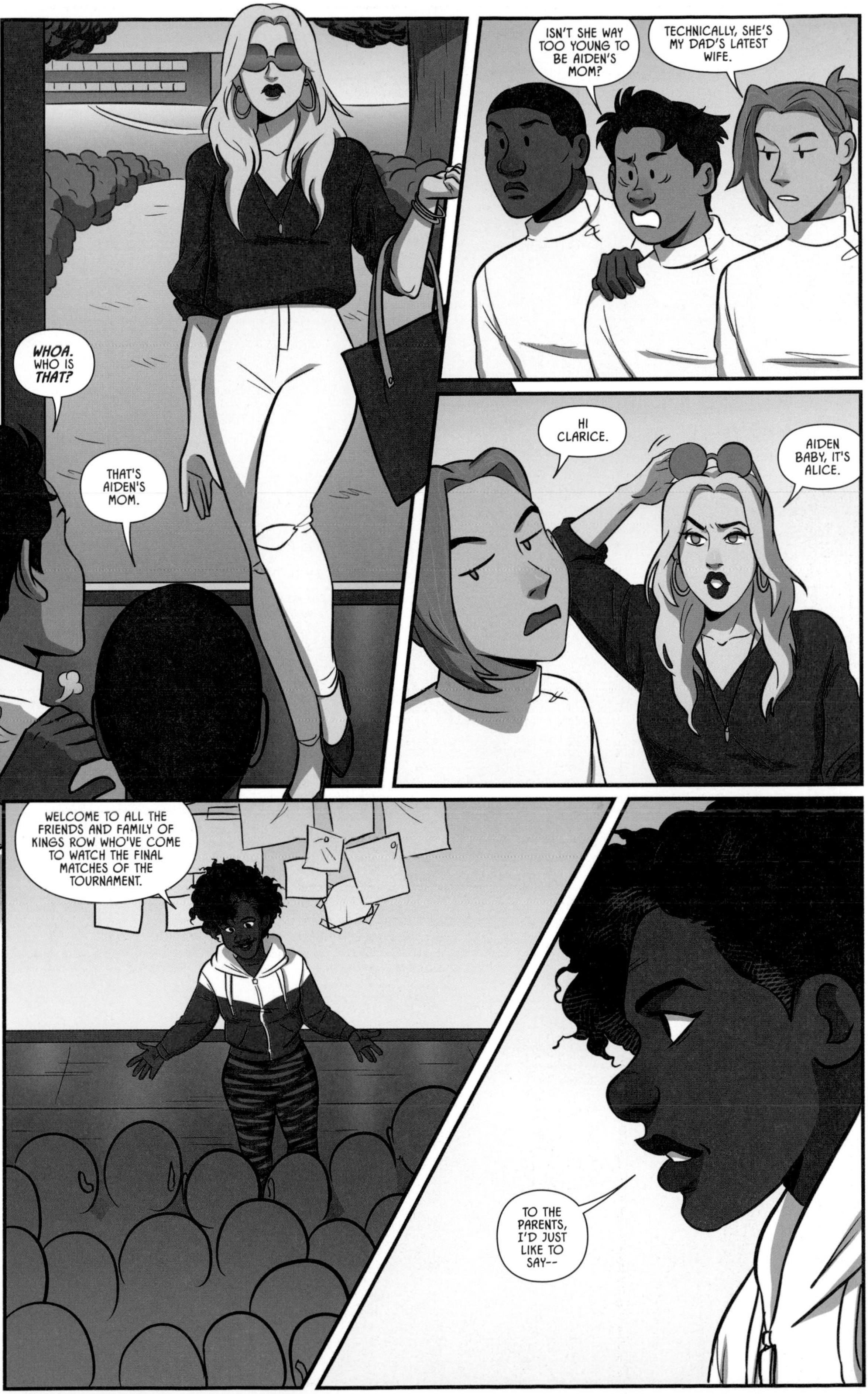

WHOA. WHO IS THAT?
THAT'S AIDEN'S MOM.
ISN'T SHE WAY TOO YOUNG TO BE AIDEN'S MOM?
TECHNICALLY, SHE'S MY DAD'S LATEST WIFE.
HI CLARICE.
AIDEN BABY, IT'S ALICE.
WELCOME TO ALL THE FRIENDS AND FAMILY OF KINGS ROW WHO'VE COME TO WATCH THE FINAL MATCHES OF THE TOURNAMENT.
TO THE PARENTS, I'D JUST LIKE TO SAY--

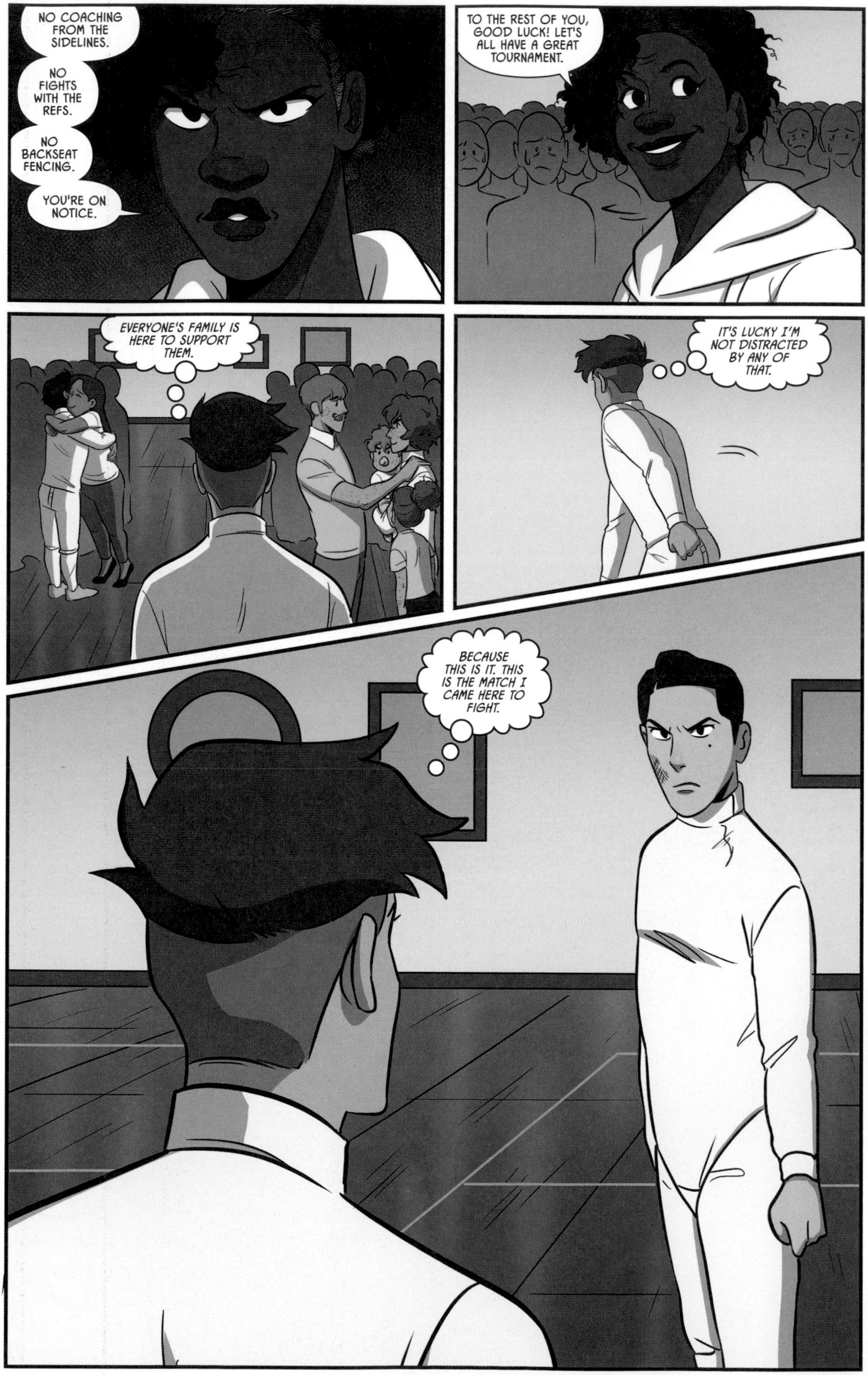
NO COACHING FROM THE SIDELINES.
NO FIGHTS WITH THE REFS.
NO BACKSEAT FENCING.
YOU'RE ON NOTICE.
TO THE REST OF YOU, GOOD LUCK! LET'S ALL HAVE A GREAT TOURNAMENT.
EVERYONE'S FAMILY IS HERE TO SUPPORT THEM.
IT'S LUCKY I'M NOT DISTRACTED BY ANY OF THAT.
BECAUSE THIS IS IT. THIS IS THE MATCH I CAME HERE TO FIGHT.

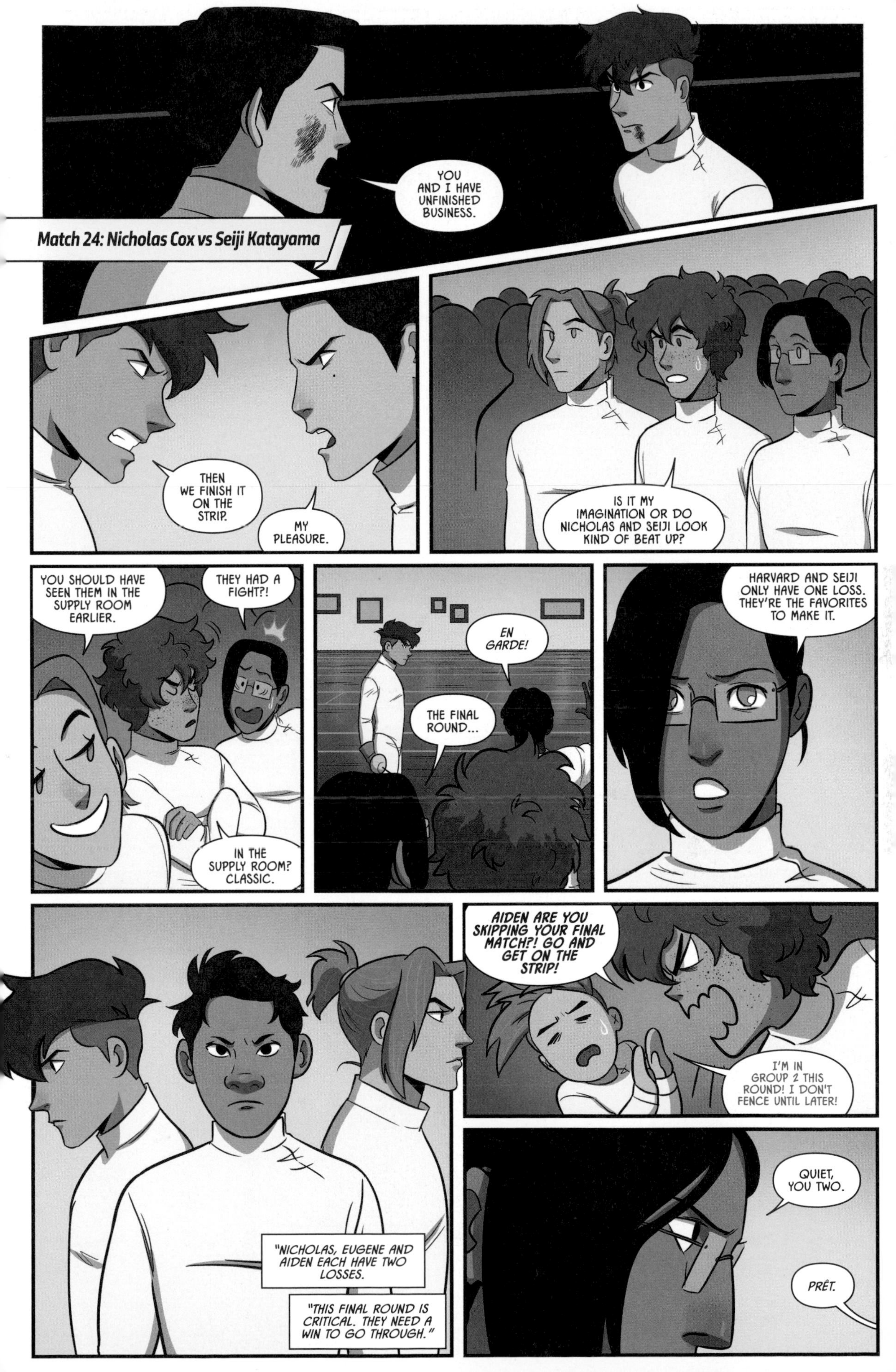
YOU AND I HAVE UNFINISHED BUSINESS.
Match 24: Nicholas Cox vs Seiji Katayama
THEN WE FINISH IT ON THE STRIP.
MY PLEASURE.
IS IT MY IMAGINATION OR DO NICHOLAS AND SEIJI LOOK KIND OF BEAT UP?
YOU SHOULD HAVE SEEN THEM IN THE SUPPLY ROOM EARLIER.
THEY HAD A FIGHT?!
IN THE SUPPLY ROOM? CLASSIC.
EN GARDE!
THE FINAL ROUND...
HARVARD AND SEIJI ONLY HAVE ONE LOSS. THEY'RE THE FAVORITES TO MAKE IT.
"NICHOLAS, EUGENE AND AIDEN EACH HAVE TWO LOSSES.
"THIS FINAL ROUND IS CRITICAL. THEY NEED A WIN TO GO THROUGH."
AIDEN ARE YOU SKIPPING YOUR FINAL MATCH?! GO AND GET ON THE STRIP!
I'M IN GROUP 2 THIS ROUND! I DON'T FENCE UNTIL LATER!
QUIET, YOU TWO.
PRÊT.

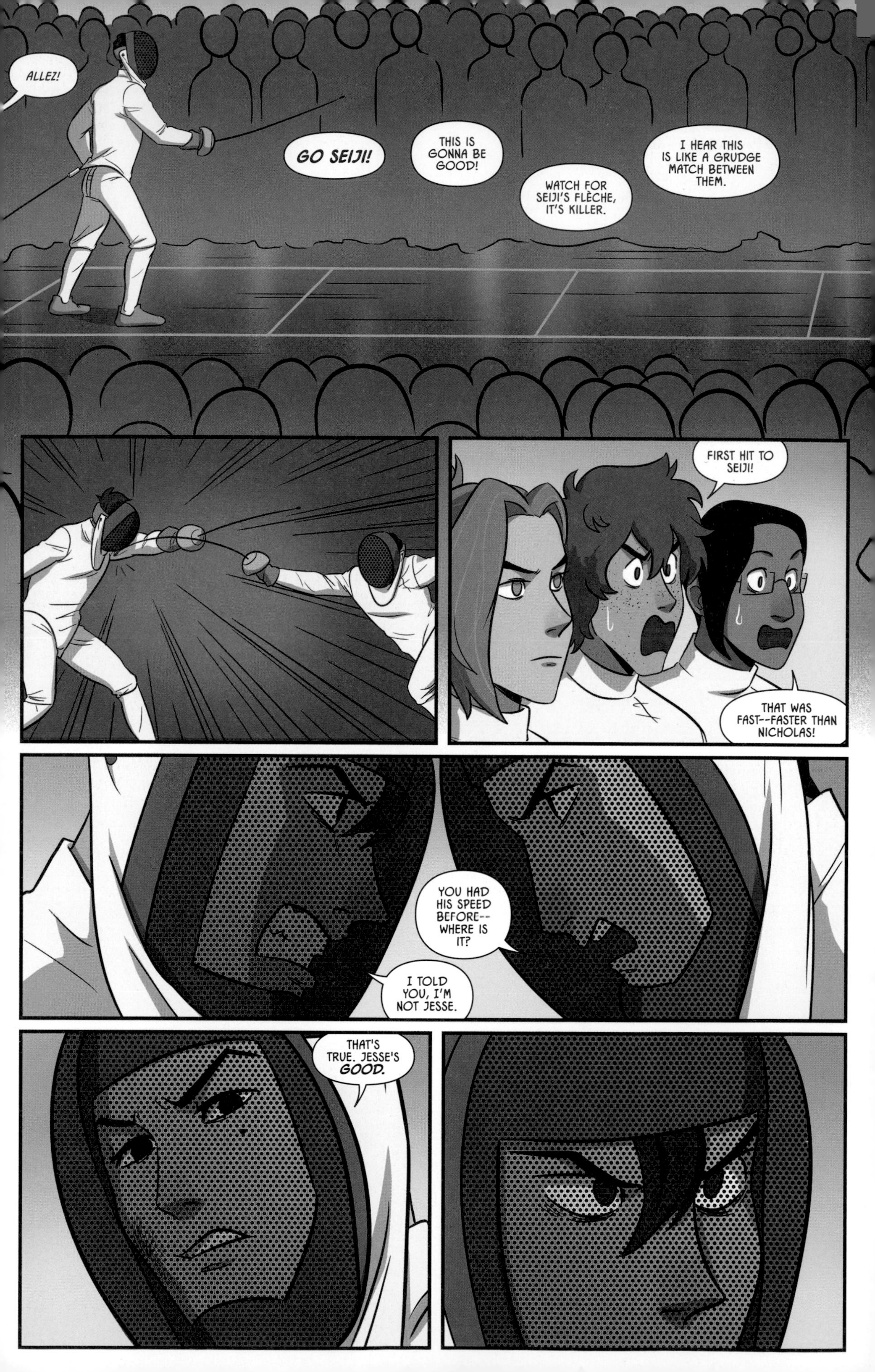
ALLEZ!
GO SEIJI!
THIS IS GONNA BE GOOD!
WATCH FOR SEIJI'S FLÈCHE, IT'S KILLER.
I HEAR THIS IS LIKE A GRUDGE MATCH BETWEEN THEM.
FIRST HIT TO SEIJI!
THAT WAS FAST--FASTER THAN NICHOLAS!
YOU HAD HIS SPEED BEFORE--WHERE IS IT?
I TOLD YOU, I'M NOT JESSE.
THAT'S TRUE. JESSE'S GOOD.

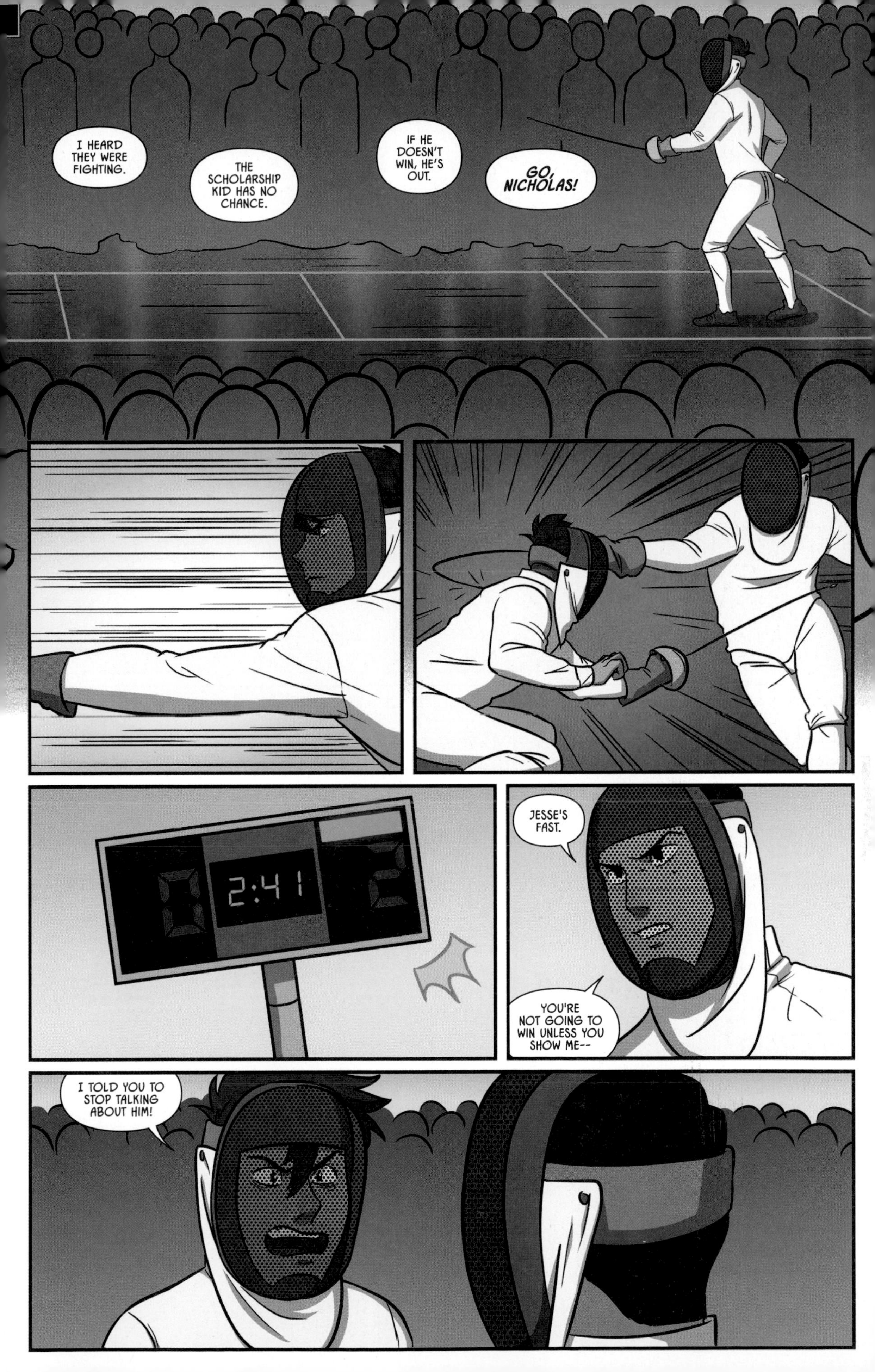

I HEARD THEY WERE FIGHTING.
THE SCHOLARSHIP KID HAS NO CHANCE.
IF HE DOESN'T WIN, HE'S OUT.
GO, NICHOLAS!
2:41
JESSE'S FAST.
YOU'RE NOT GOING TO WIN UNLESS YOU SHOW ME--
I TOLD YOU TO STOP TALKING ABOUT HIM!

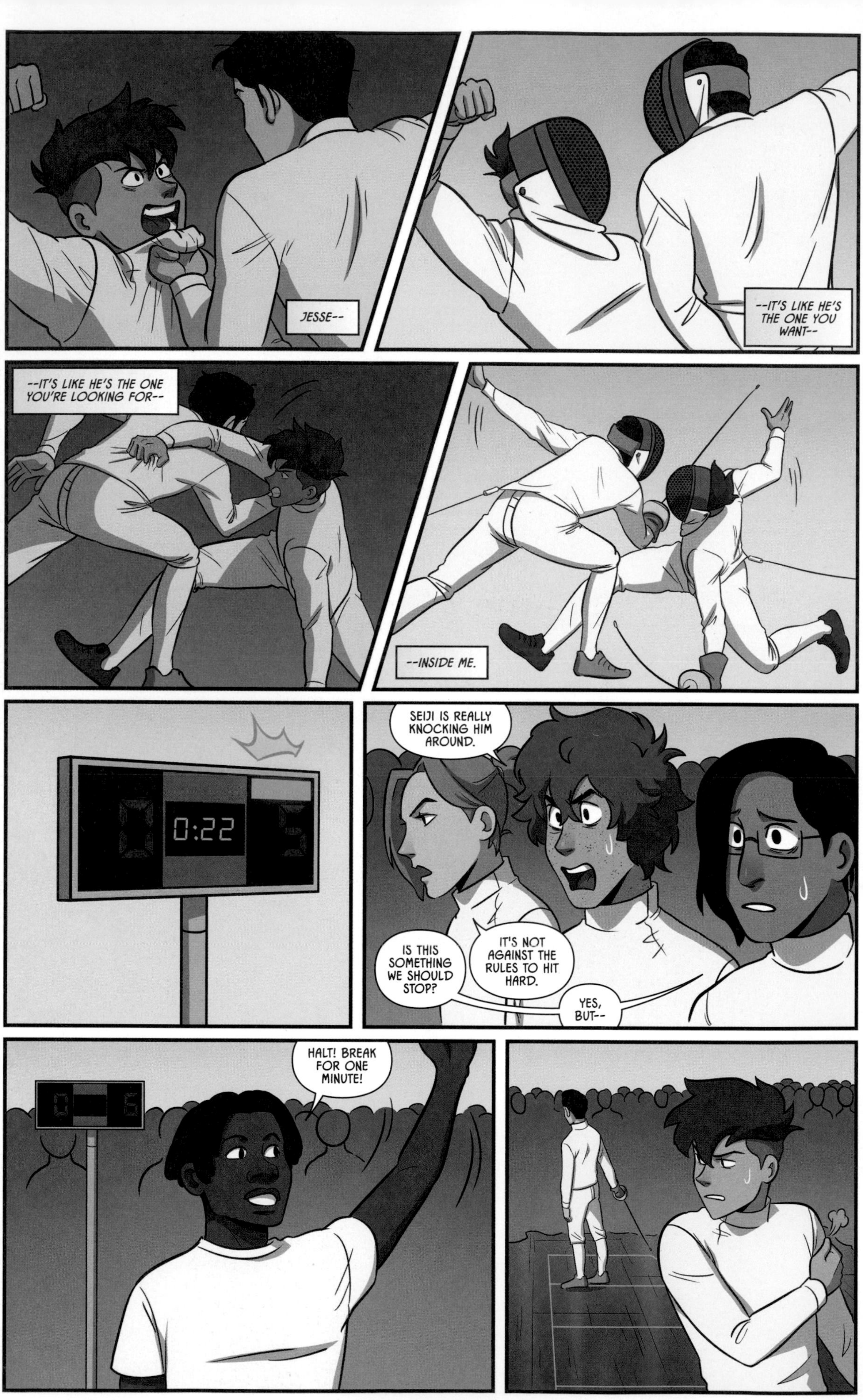

JESSE--
--IT'S LIKE HE'S THE ONE YOU WANT--
--IT'S LIKE HE'S THE ONE YOU'RE LOOKING FOR--
--INSIDE ME.
0:22
SEIJI IS REALLY KNOCKING HIM AROUND.
IS THIS SOMETHING WE SHOULD STOP?
IT'S NOT AGAINST THE RULES TO HIT HARD.
YES, BUT--
HALT! BREAK FOR ONE MINUTE!

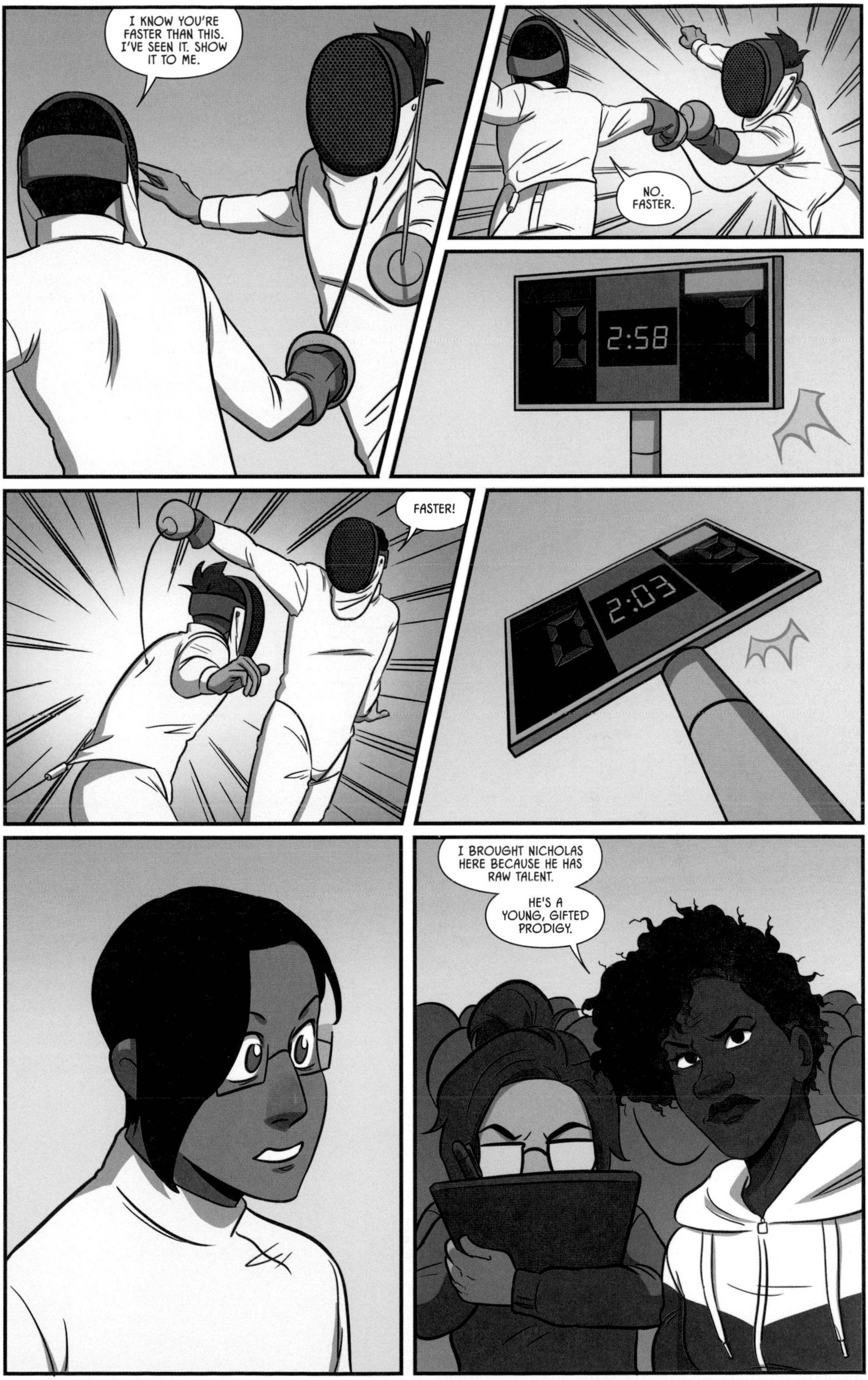
I KNOW YOU'RE FASTER THAN THIS. I'VE SEEN IT. SHOW IT TO ME.
NO. FASTER.
2:58
FASTER!
2:03
I BROUGHT NICHOLAS HERE BECAUSE HE HAS RAW TALENT.
HE'S A YOUNG, GIFTED PRODIGY.

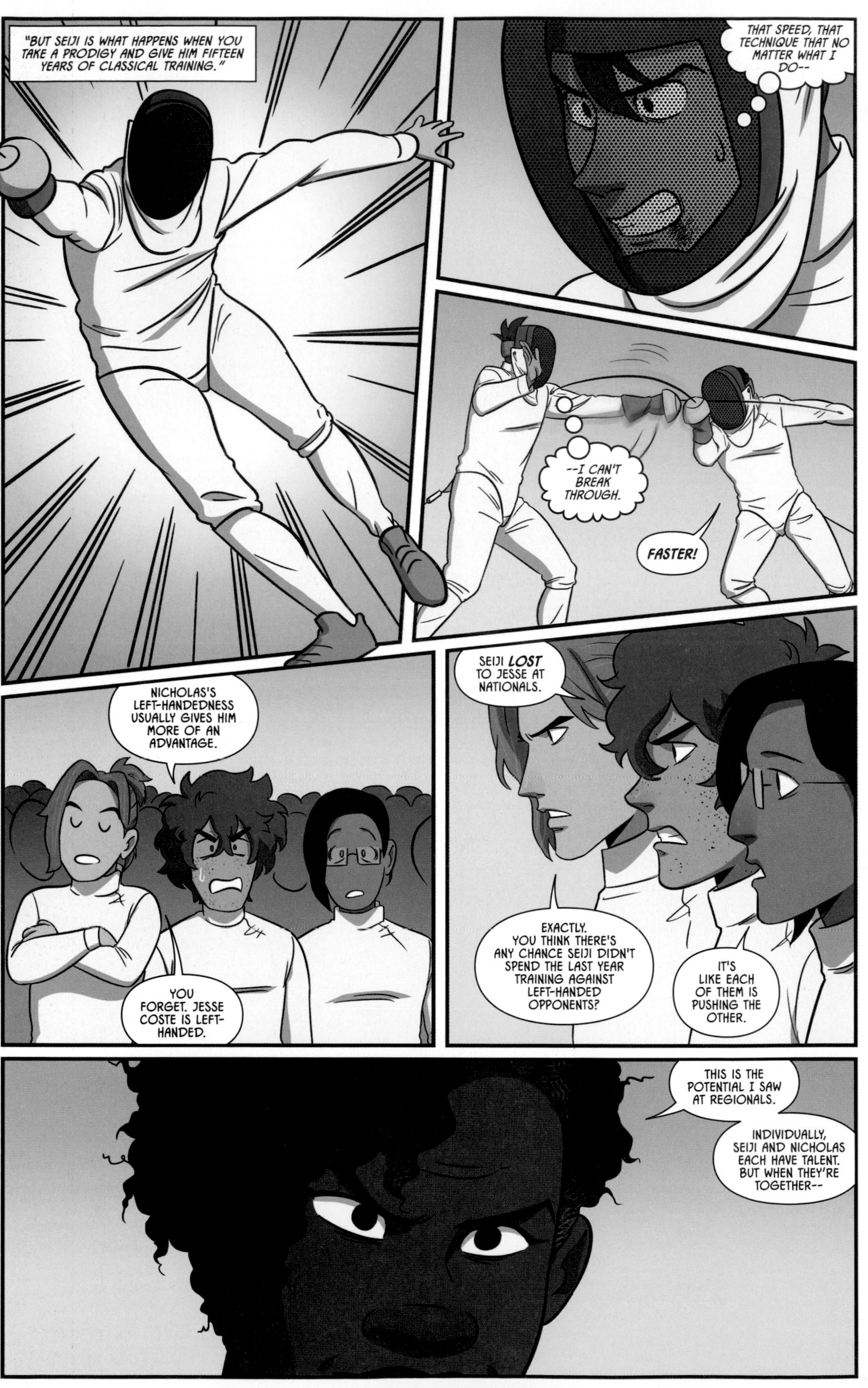
"BUT SEIJI IS WHAT HAPPENS WHEN YOU TAKE A PRODIGY AND GIVE HIM FIFTEEN YEARS OF CLASSICAL TRAINING."
THAT SPEED, THAT TECHNIQUE THAT NO MATTER WHAT I DO--
--I CAN'T BREAK THROUGH.
FASTER!
NICHOLAS'S LEFT-HANDEDNESS USUALLY GIVES HIM MORE OF AN ADVANTAGE.
YOU FORGET. JESSE COSTE IS LEFT-HANDED.
SEIJI LOST TO JESSE AT NATIONALS.
EXACTLY. YOU THINK THERE'S ANY CHANCE SEIJI DIDN'T SPEND THE LAST YEAR TRAINING AGAINST LEFT-HANDED OPPONENTS?
IT'S LIKE EACH OF THEM IS PUSHING THE OTHER.
THIS IS THE POTENTIAL I SAW AT REGIONALS.
INDIVIDUALLY, SEIJI AND NICHOLAS EACH HAVE TALENT. BUT WHEN THEY'RE TOGETHER--

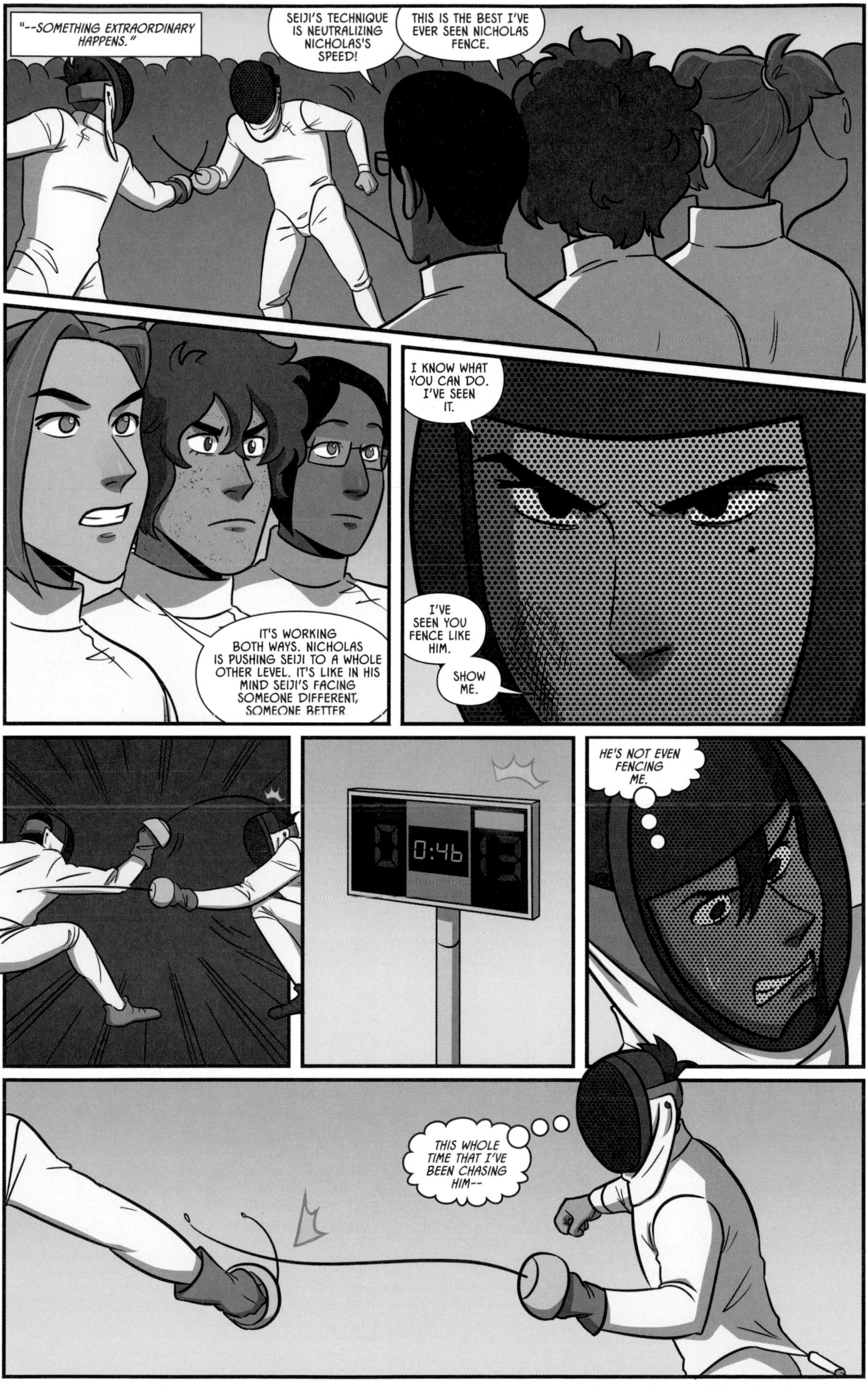
"--SOMETHING EXTRAORDINARY HAPPENS."
SEIJI'S TECHNIQUE IS NEUTRALIZING NICHOLAS'S SPEED!
THIS IS THE BEST I'VE EVER SEEN NICHOLAS FENCE.
IT'S WORKING BOTH WAYS. NICHOLAS IS PUSHING SEIJI TO A WHOLE OTHER LEVEL. IT'S LIKE IN HIS MIND SEIJI'S FACING SOMEONE DIFFERENT, SOMEONE BETTER.
I KNOW WHAT YOU CAN DO. I'VE SEEN IT.
I'VE SEEN YOU FENCE LIKE HIM.
SHOW ME.
0:46
HE'S NOT EVEN FENCING ME.
THIS WHOLE TIME THAT I'VE BEEN CHASING HIM--

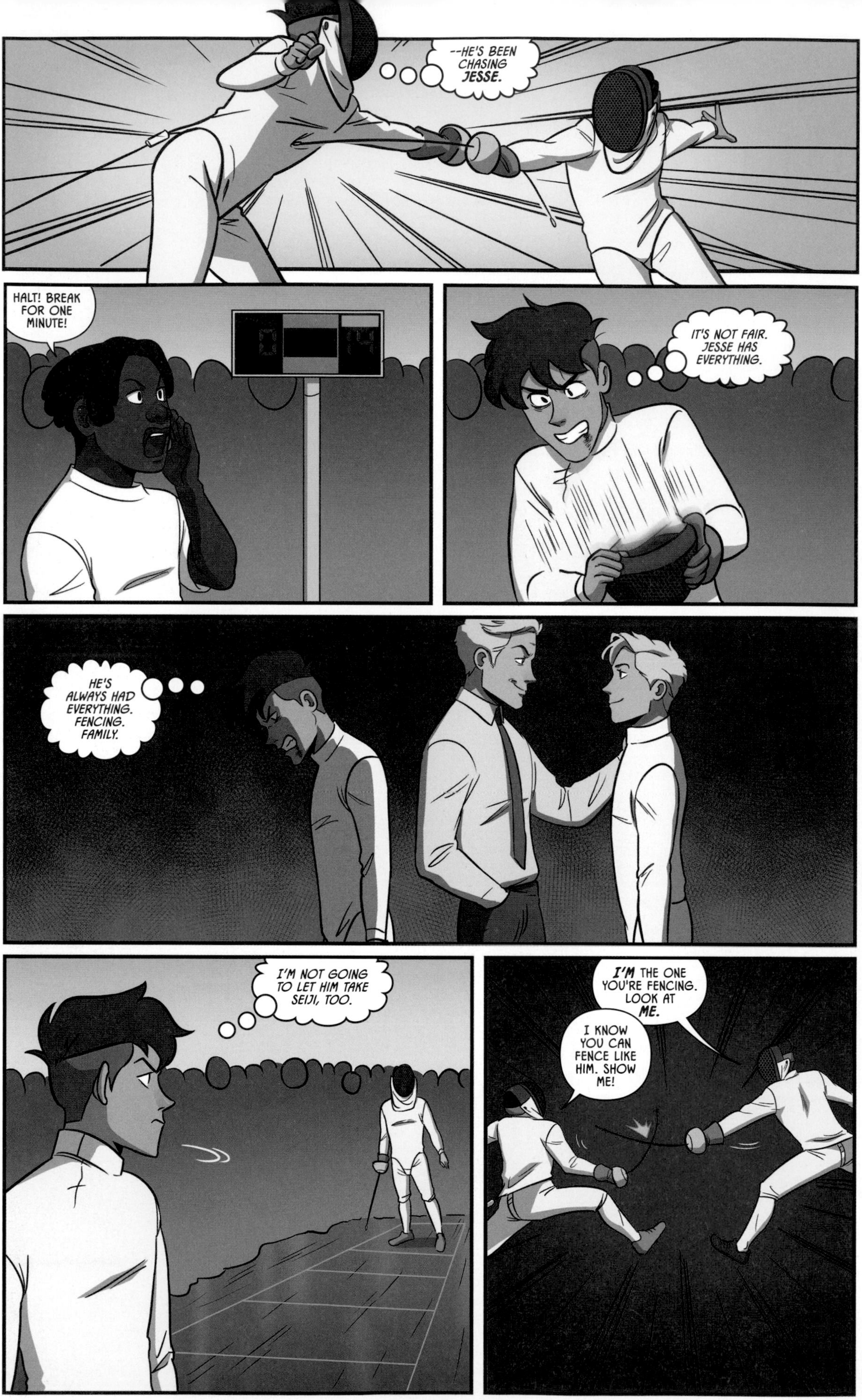
--HE'S BEEN CHASING JESSE.
HALT! BREAK FOR ONE MINUTE!
IT'S NOT FAIR. JESSE HAS EVERYTHING.
HE'S ALWAYS HAD EVERYTHING. FENCING. FAMILY.
I'M NOT GOING TO LET HIM TAKE SEIJI, TOO.
I'M THE ONE YOU'RE FENCING. LOOK AT ME.
I KNOW YOU CAN FENCE LIKE HIM. SHOW ME!

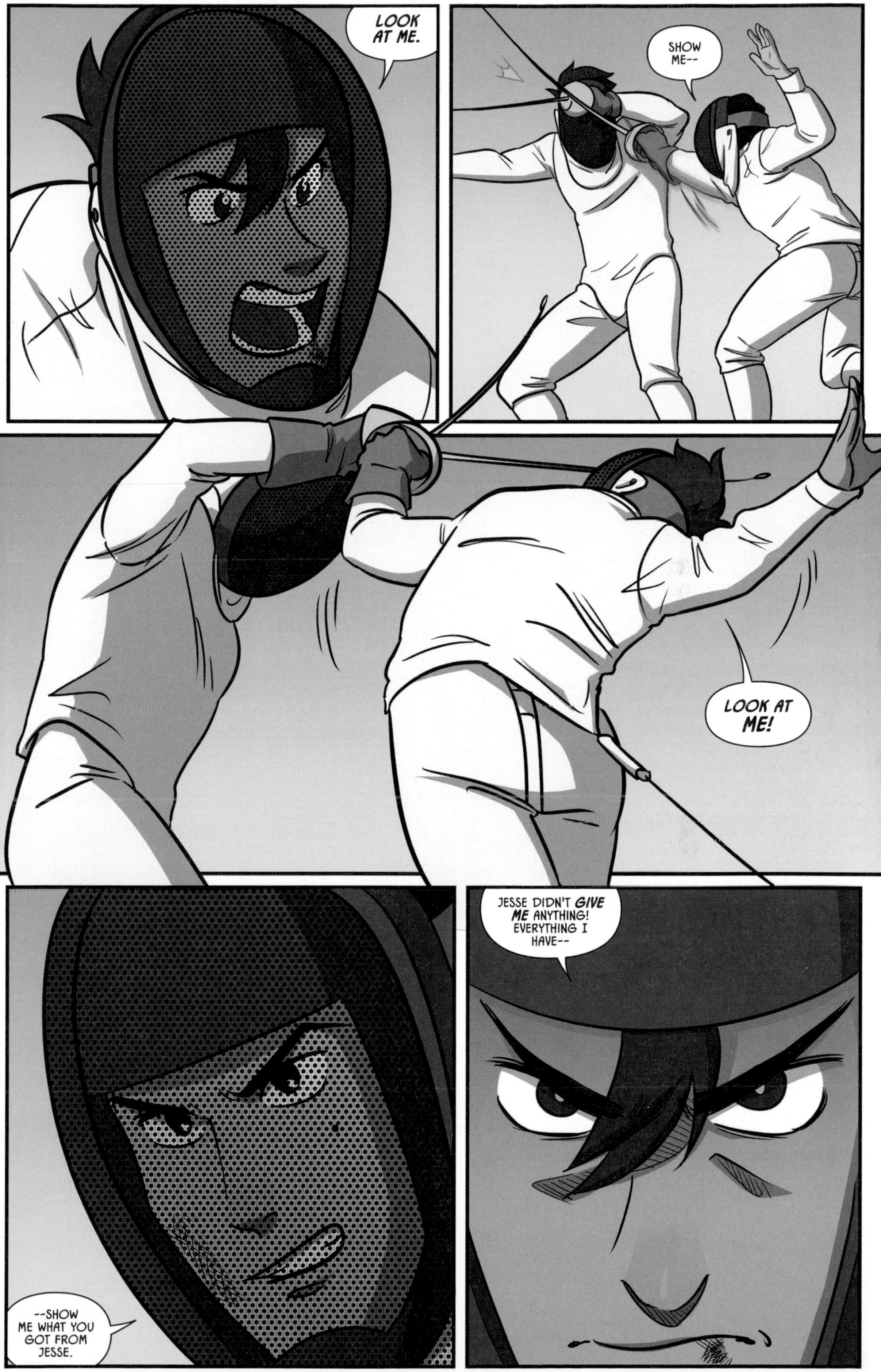
LOOK AT ME.
SHOW ME--
LOOK AT ME!
--SHOW ME WHAT YOU GOT FROM JESSE.
JESSE DIDN'T **GIVE ME** ANYTHING! EVERYTHING I HAVE--

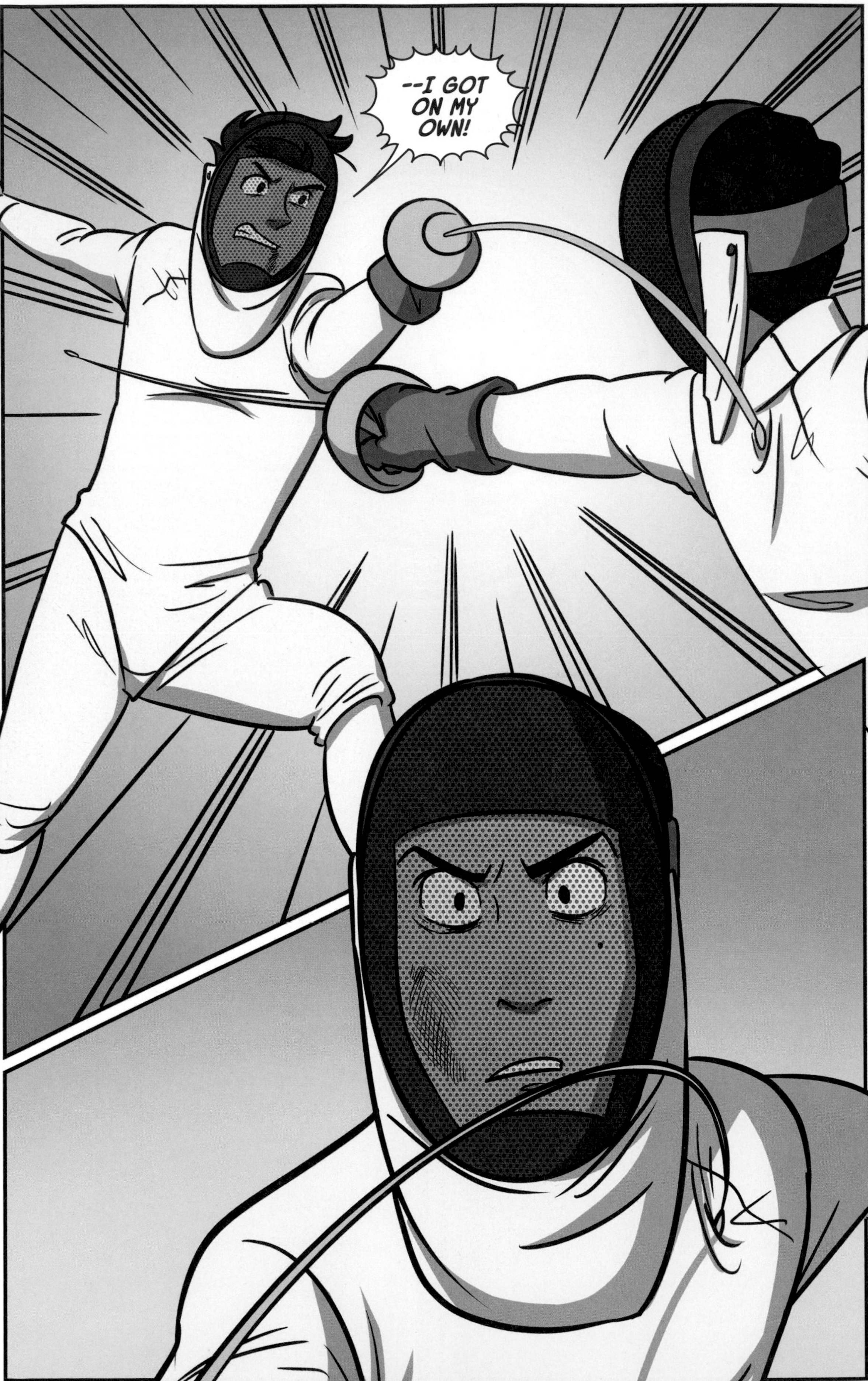
--I GOT ON MY OWN!

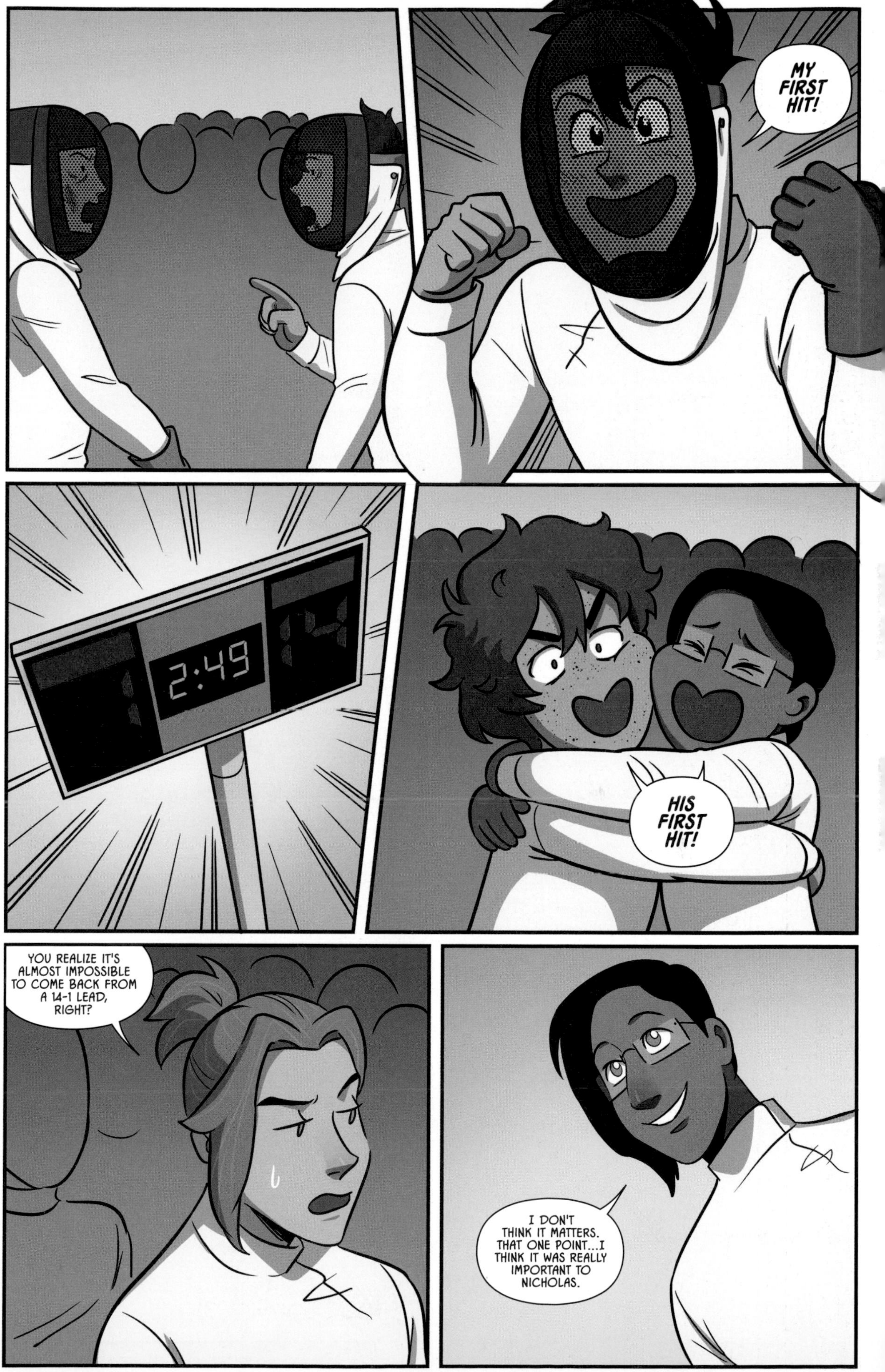
MY FIRST HIT!
2:49
HIS FIRST HIT!
YOU REALIZE IT'S ALMOST IMPOSSIBLE TO COME BACK FROM A 14-1 LEAD, RIGHT?
I DON'T THINK IT MATTERS. THAT ONE POINT...I THINK IT WAS REALLY IMPORTANT TO NICHOLAS.

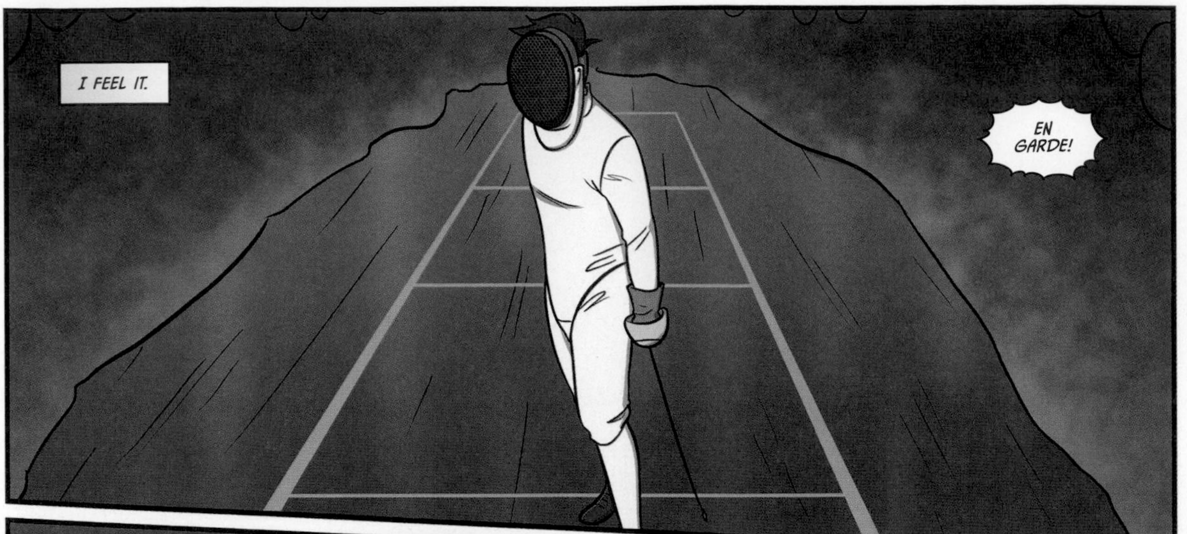
I FEEL IT.
EN GARDE!

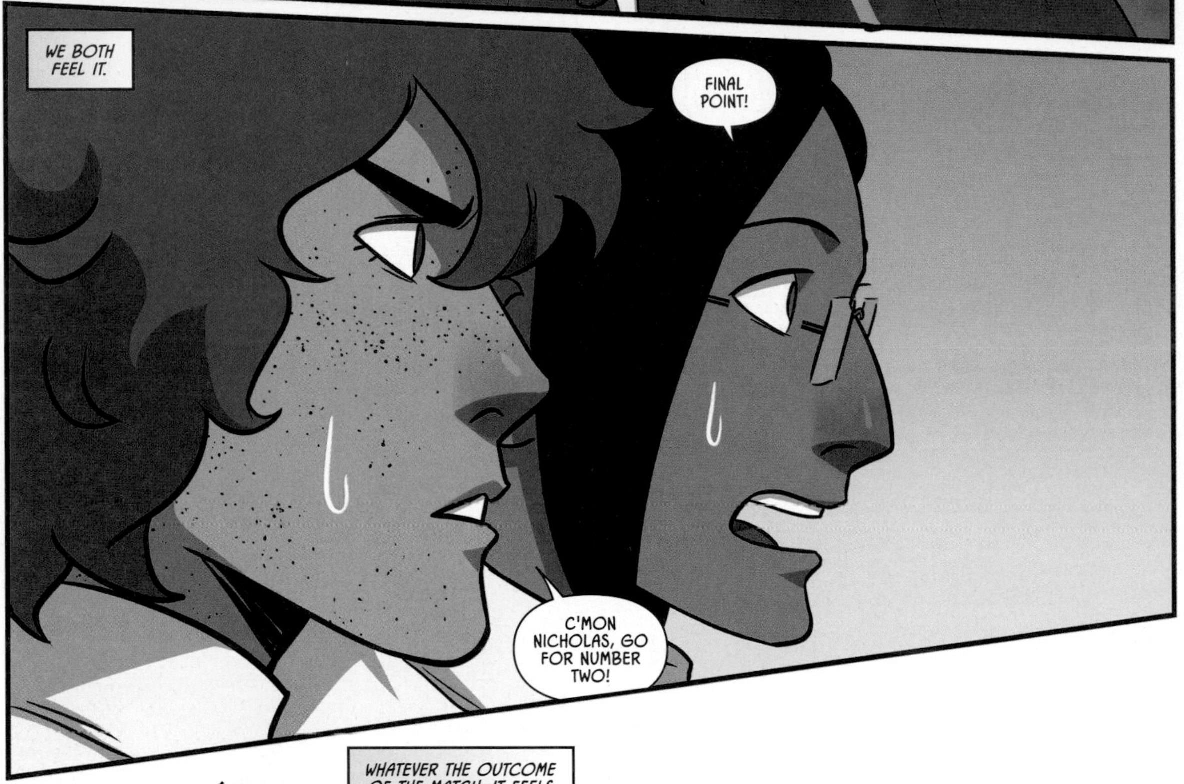
WE BOTH FEEL IT.
FINAL POINT!
C'MON NICHOLAS, GO FOR NUMBER TWO!

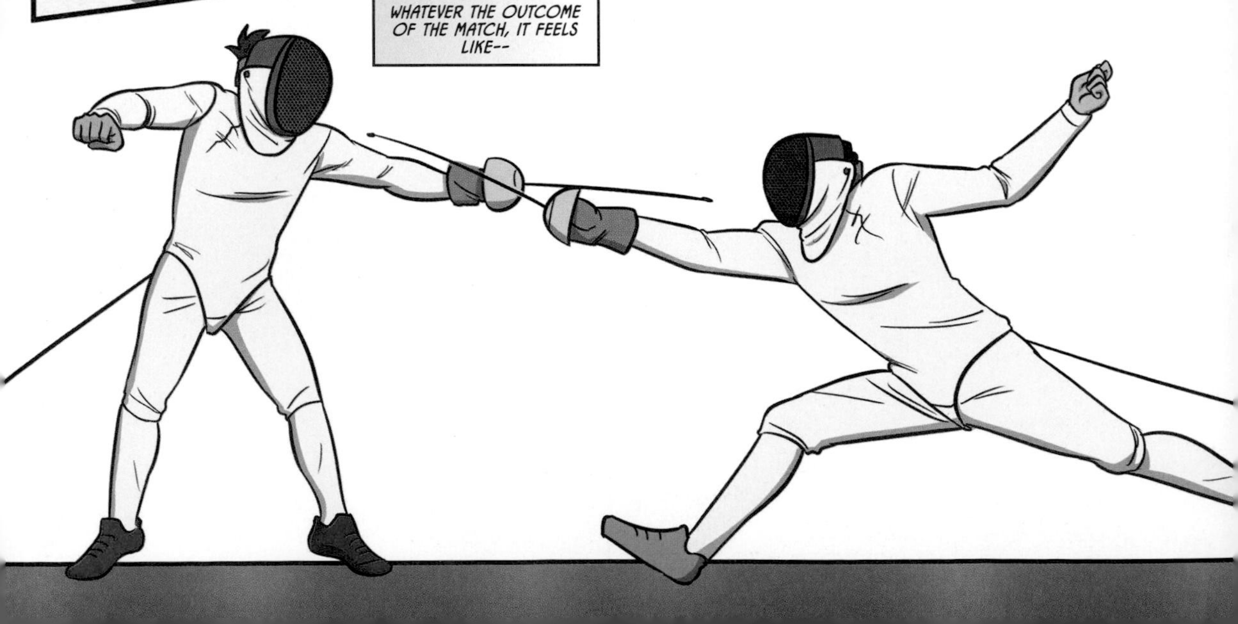
WHATEVER THE OUTCOME OF THE MATCH, IT FEELS LIKE--

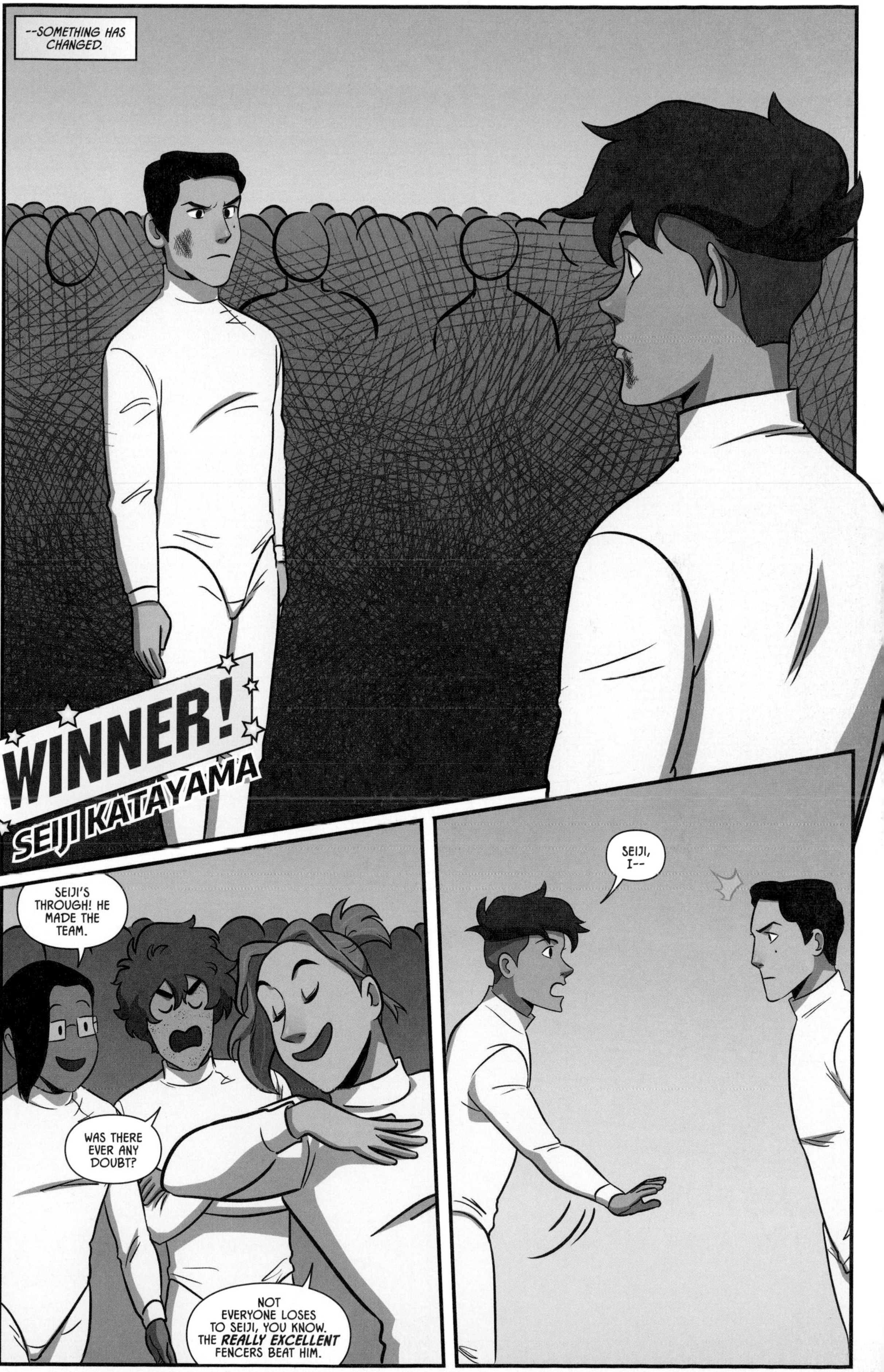
--SOMETHING HAS CHANGED.
WINNER!
SEIJI KATAYAMA
SEIJI'S THROUGH! HE MADE THE TEAM.
WAS THERE EVER ANY DOUBT?
NOT EVERYONE LOSES TO SEIJI, YOU KNOW. THE ***REALLY EXCELLENT*** FENCERS BEAT HIM.
SEIJI, I--

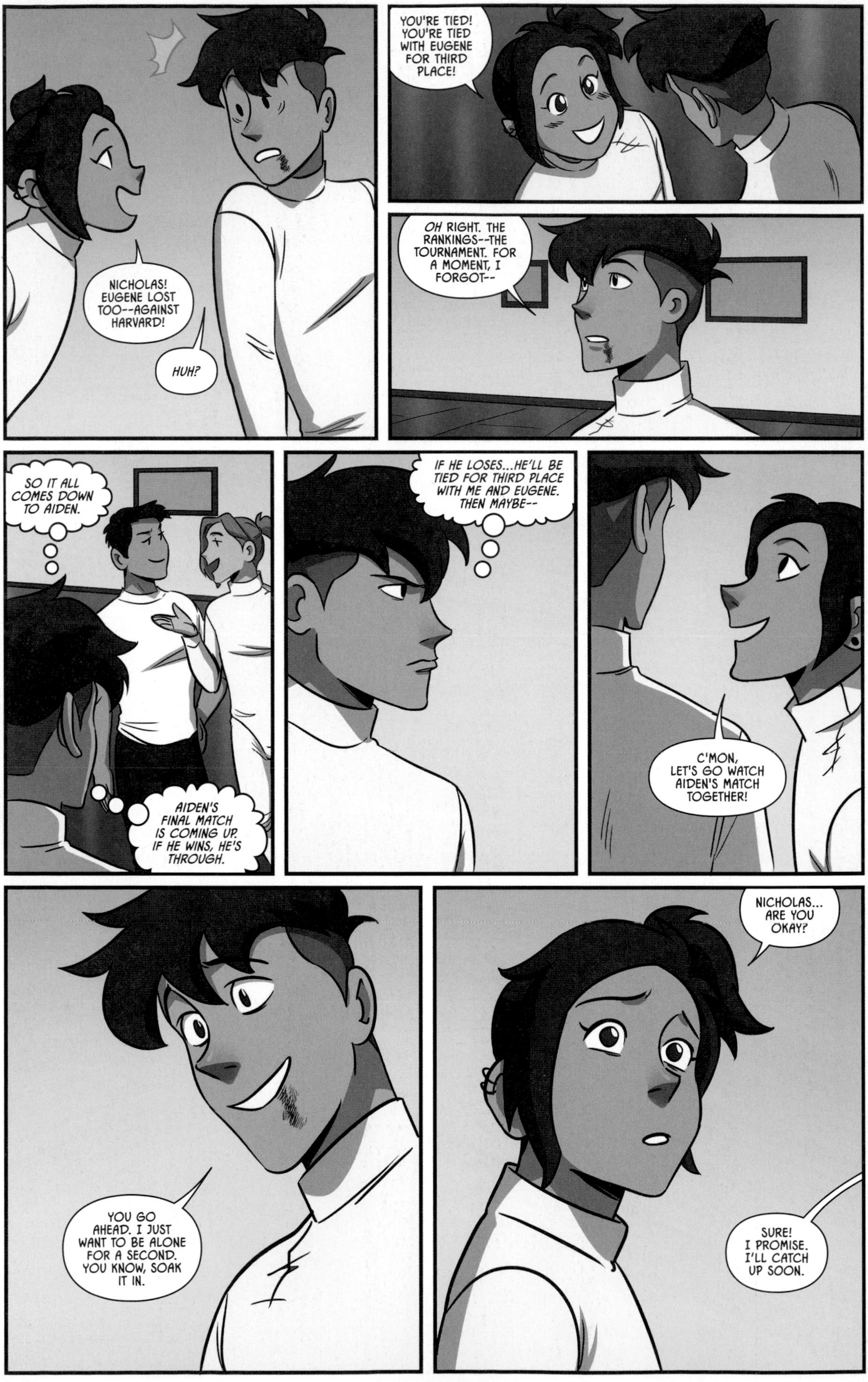
NICHOLAS! EUGENE LOST TOO--AGAINST HARVARD!
HUH?
YOU'RE TIED! YOU'RE TIED WITH EUGENE FOR THIRD PLACE!
OH RIGHT. THE RANKINGS--THE TOURNAMENT. FOR A MOMENT, I FORGOT--
SO IT ALL COMES DOWN TO AIDEN.
AIDEN'S FINAL MATCH IS COMING UP. IF HE WINS, HE'S THROUGH.
IF HE LOSES...HE'LL BE TIED FOR THIRD PLACE WITH ME AND EUGENE. THEN MAYBE--
C'MON, LET'S GO WATCH AIDEN'S MATCH TOGETHER!
YOU GO AHEAD. I JUST WANT TO BE ALONE FOR A SECOND. YOU KNOW, SOAK IT IN.
NICHOLAS... ARE YOU OKAY?
SURE! I PROMISE. I'LL CATCH UP SOON.

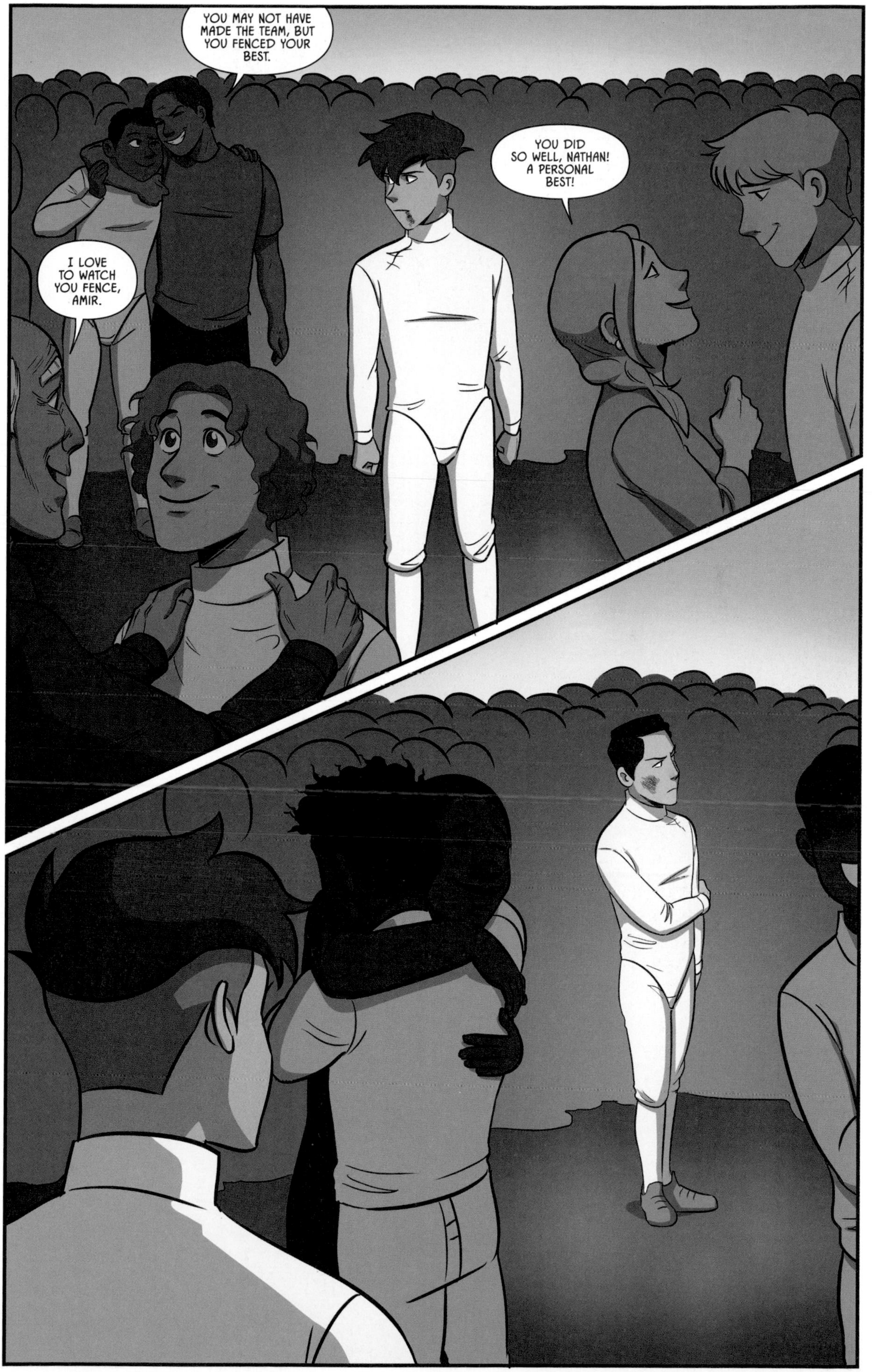
YOU MAY NOT HAVE MADE THE TEAM, BUT YOU FENCED YOUR BEST.
YOU DID SO WELL, NATHAN! A PERSONAL BEST!
I LOVE TO WATCH YOU FENCE, AMIR.

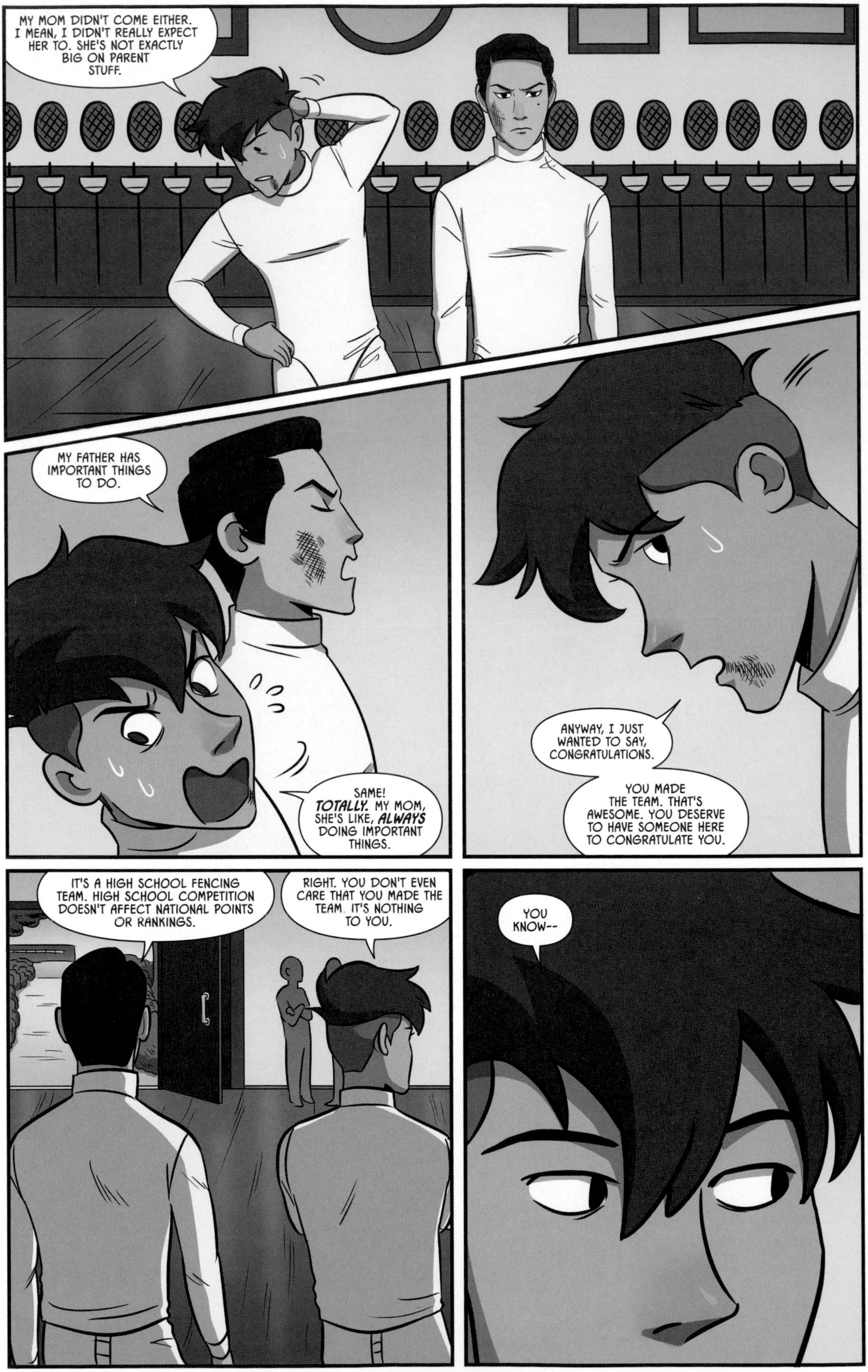
MY MOM DIDN'T COME EITHER. I MEAN, I DIDN'T REALLY EXPECT HER TO. SHE'S NOT EXACTLY BIG ON PARENT STUFF.
MY FATHER HAS IMPORTANT THINGS TO DO.
SAME! ***TOTALLY.*** MY MOM, SHE'S LIKE, ***ALWAYS*** DOING IMPORTANT THINGS.
ANYWAY, I JUST WANTED TO SAY, CONGRATULATIONS.
YOU MADE THE TEAM. THAT'S AWESOME. YOU DESERVE TO HAVE SOMEONE HERE TO CONGRATULATE YOU.
IT'S A HIGH SCHOOL FENCING TEAM. HIGH SCHOOL COMPETITION DOESN'T AFFECT NATIONAL POINTS OR RANKINGS.
RIGHT. YOU DON'T EVEN CARE THAT YOU MADE THE TEAM. IT'S NOTHING TO YOU.
YOU KNOW--

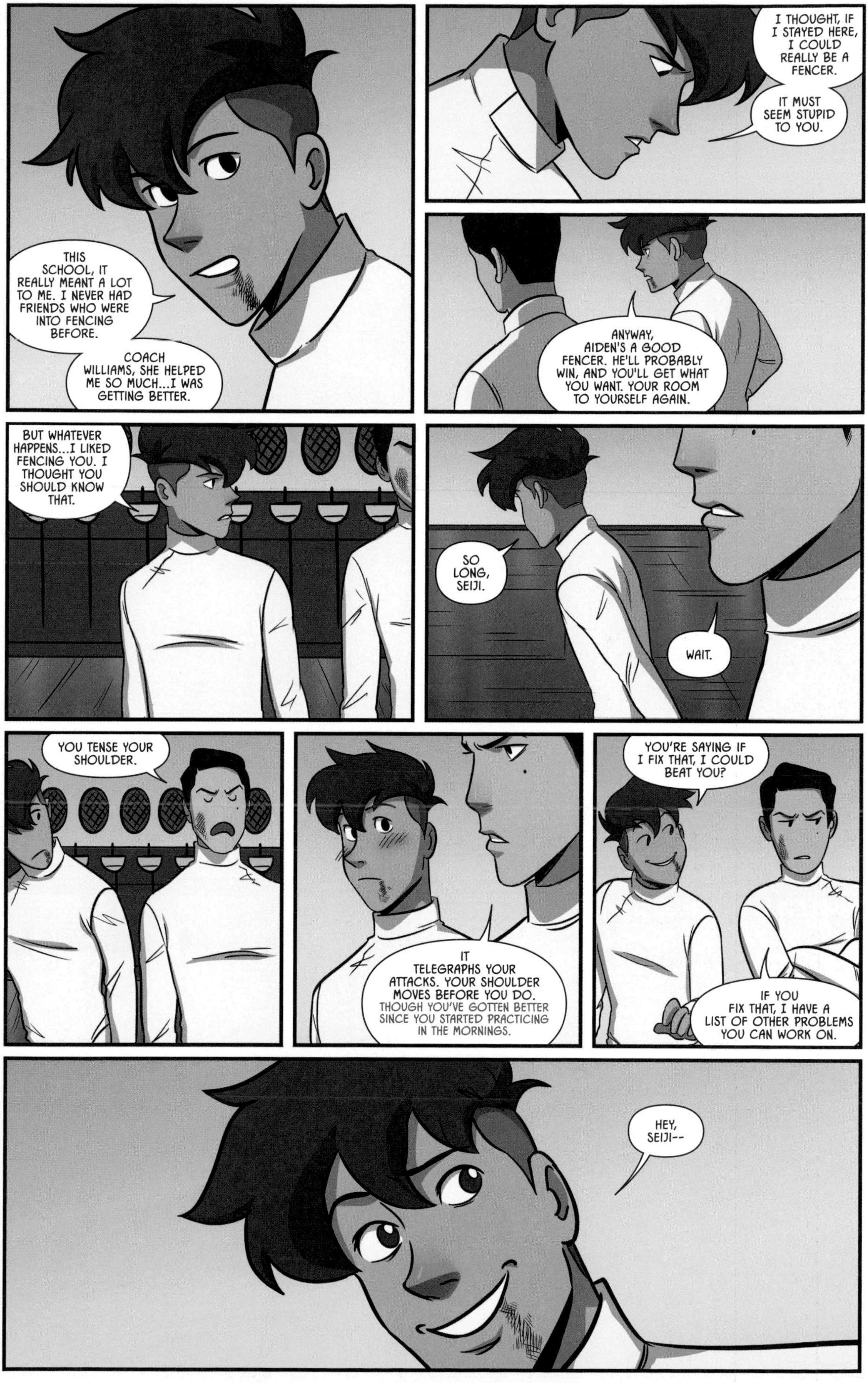
THIS SCHOOL, IT REALLY MEANT A LOT TO ME. I NEVER HAD FRIENDS WHO WERE INTO FENCING BEFORE.
COACH WILLIAMS, SHE HELPED ME SO MUCH...I WAS GETTING BETTER.
I THOUGHT, IF I STAYED HERE, I COULD REALLY BE A FENCER.
IT MUST SEEM STUPID TO YOU.
ANYWAY, AIDEN'S A GOOD FENCER. HE'LL PROBABLY WIN, AND YOU'LL GET WHAT YOU WANT. YOUR ROOM TO YOURSELF AGAIN.
BUT WHATEVER HAPPENS...I LIKED FENCING YOU. I THOUGHT YOU SHOULD KNOW THAT.
SO LONG, SEIJI.
WAIT.
YOU TENSE YOUR SHOULDER.
IT TELEGRAPHS YOUR ATTACKS. YOUR SHOULDER MOVES BEFORE YOU DO. THOUGH YOU'VE GOTTEN BETTER SINCE YOU STARTED PRACTICING IN THE MORNINGS.
YOU'RE SAYING IF I FIX THAT, I COULD BEAT YOU?
IF YOU FIX THAT, I HAVE A LIST OF OTHER PROBLEMS YOU CAN WORK ON.
HEY, SEIJI--

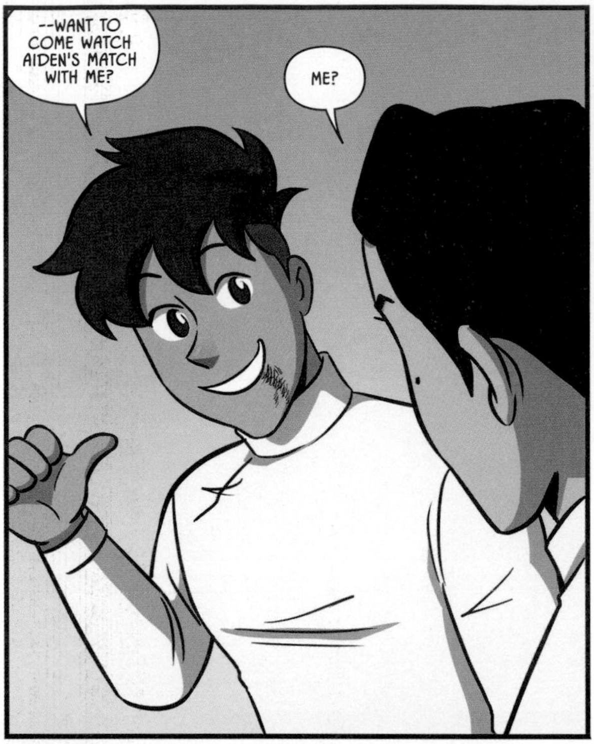
--WANT TO COME WATCH AIDEN'S MATCH WITH ME?
ME?

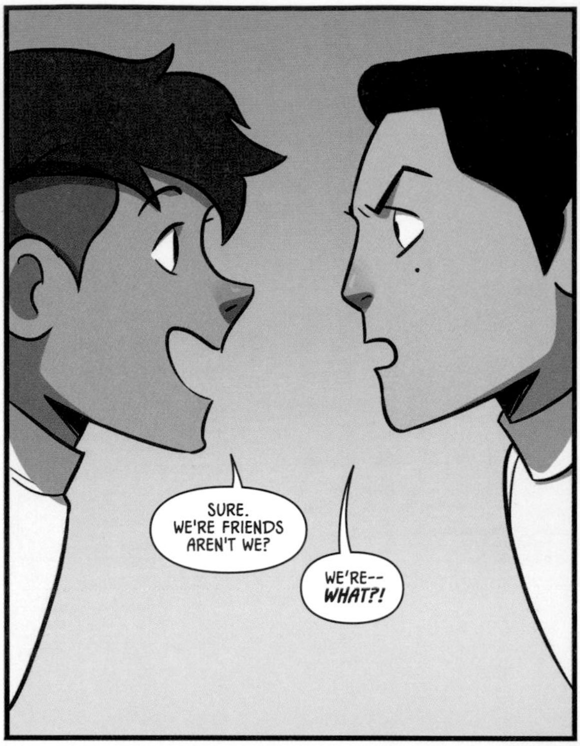
SURE. WE'RE FRIENDS AREN'T WE?
WE'RE-- ***WHAT?!***

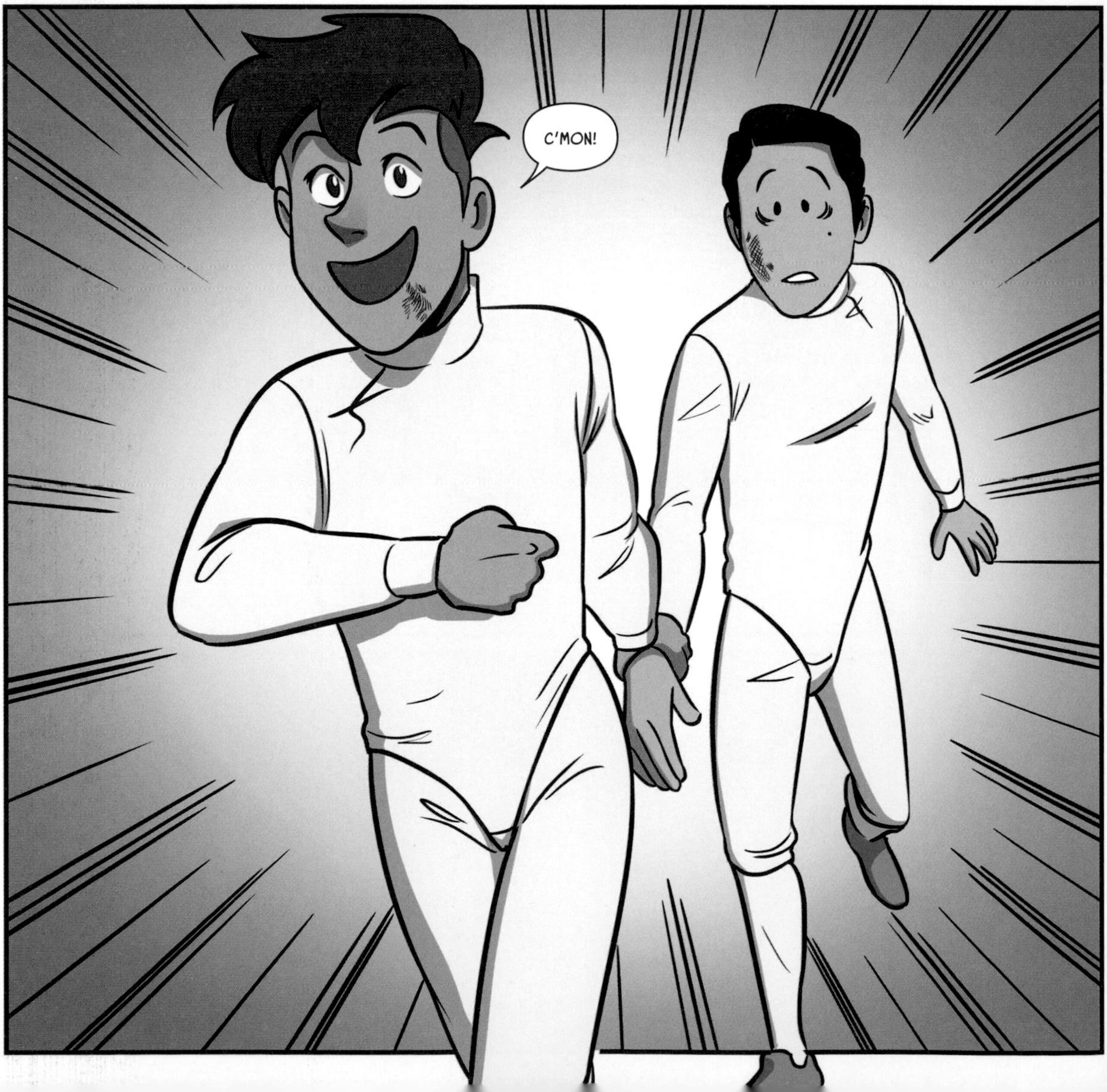
C'MON!

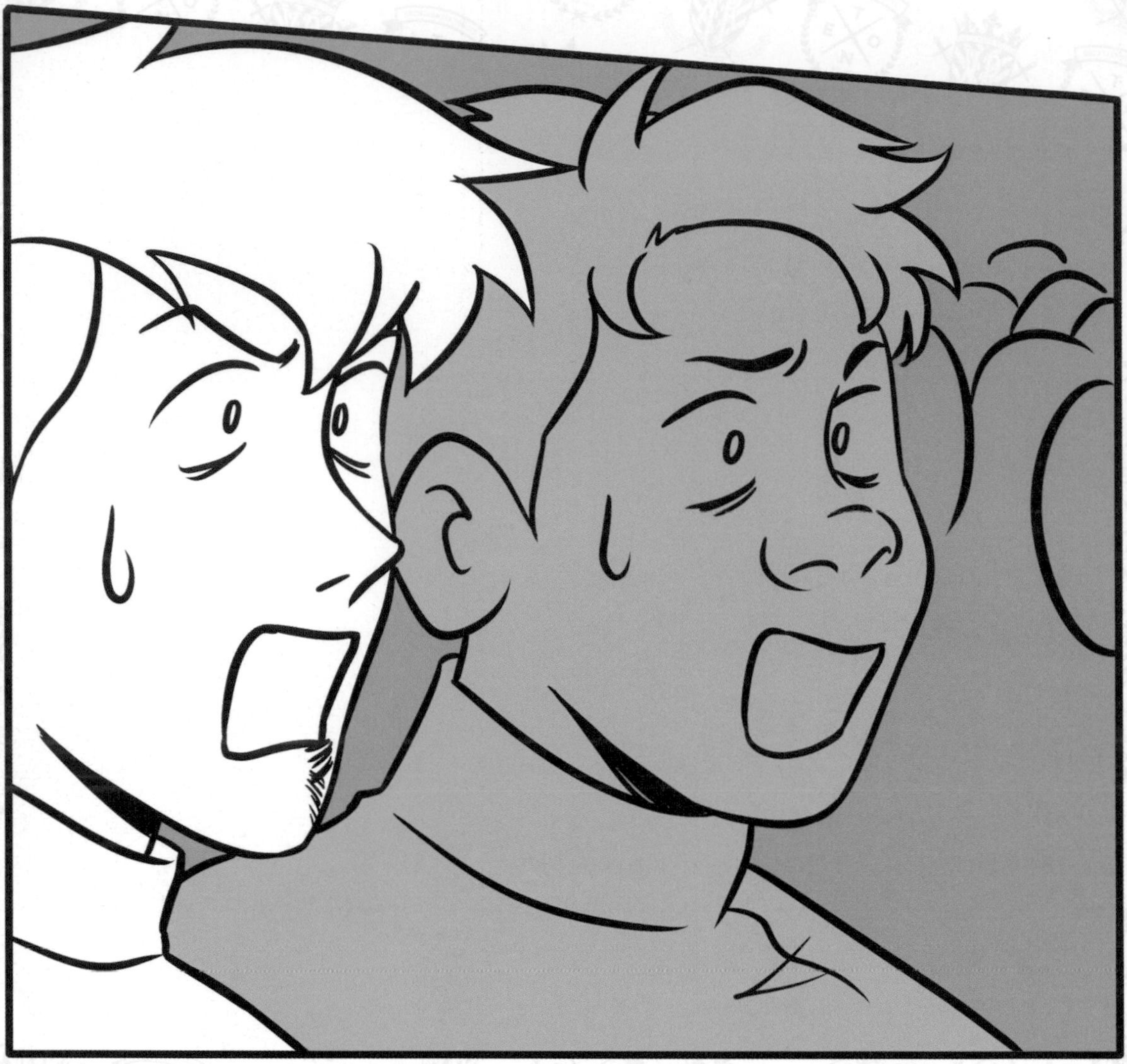

CHAPTER
Eleven

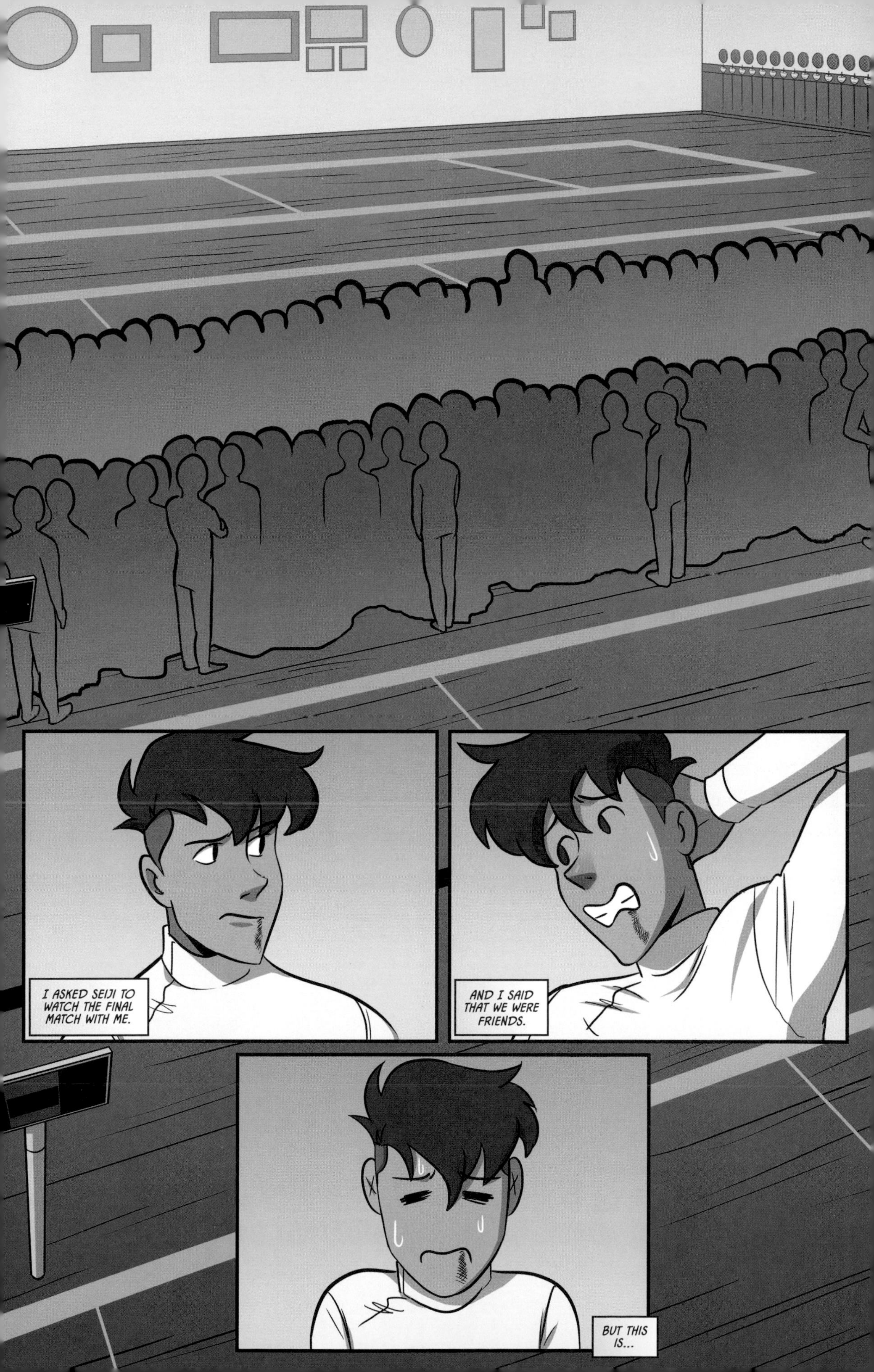
I ASKED SEIJI TO WATCH THE FINAL MATCH WITH ME.
AND I SAID THAT WE WERE FRIENDS.
BUT THIS IS...

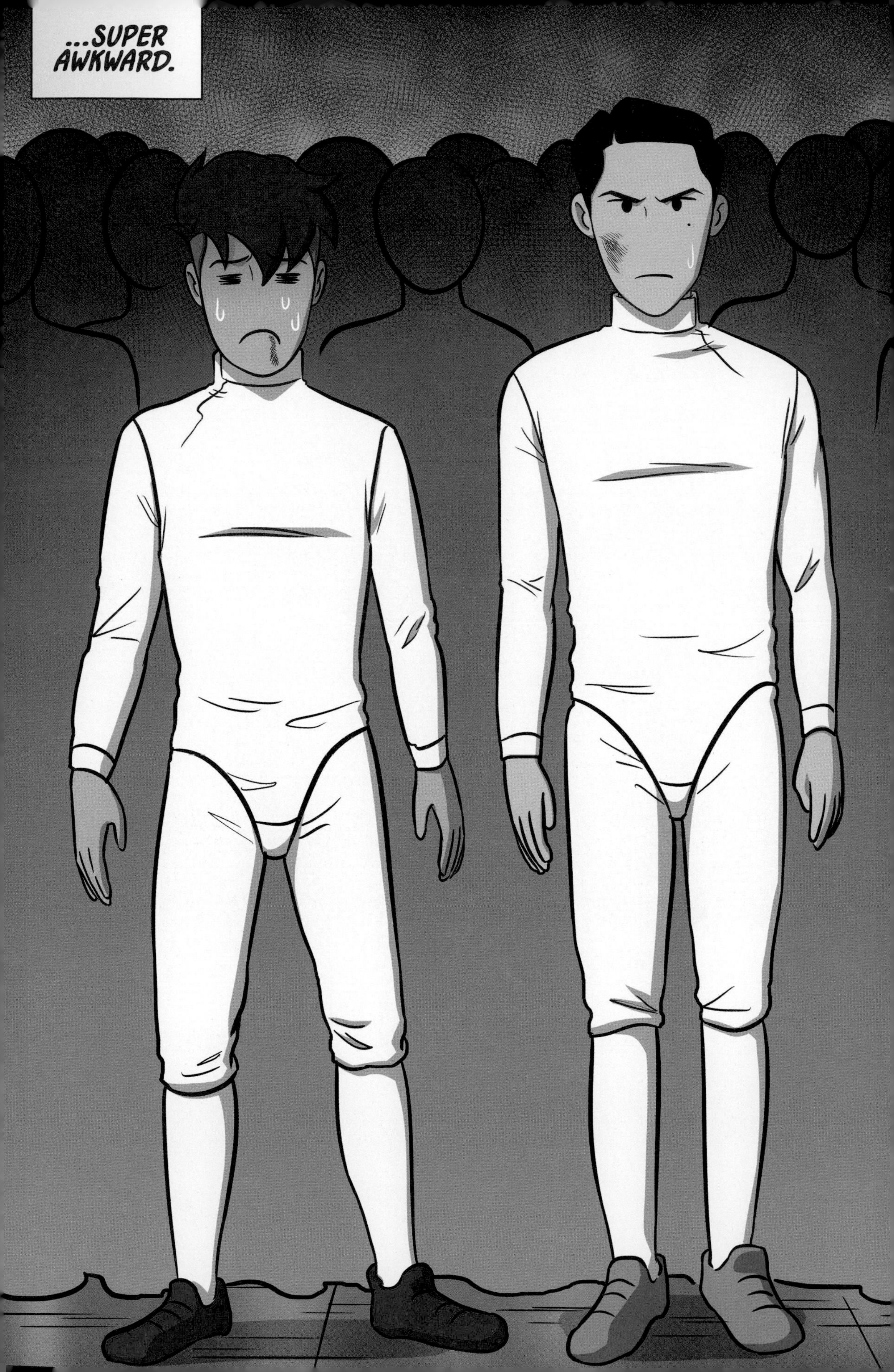
...SUPER AWKWARD.

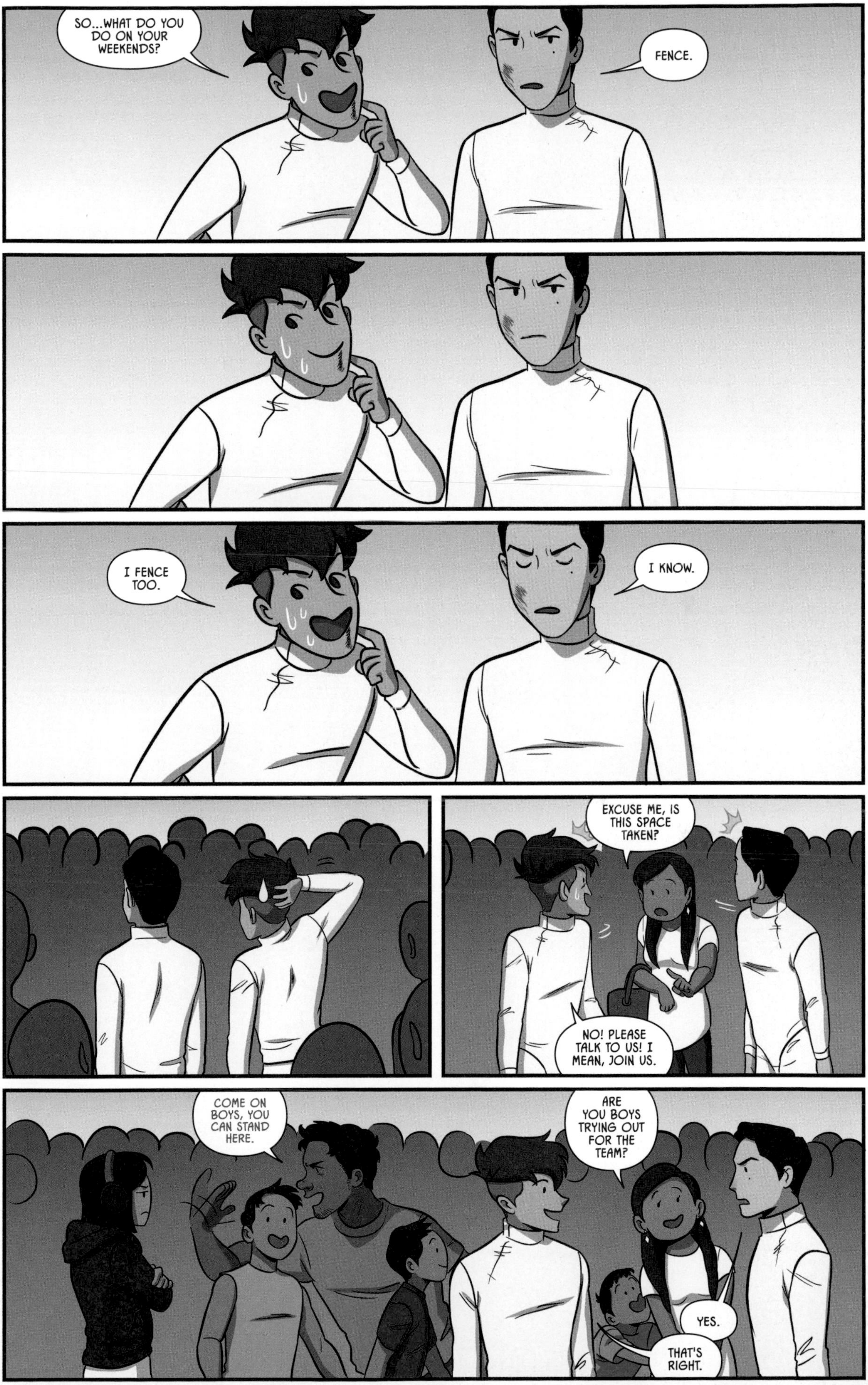
SO...WHAT DO YOU DO ON YOUR WEEKENDS?
FENCE.
I FENCE TOO.
I KNOW.
EXCUSE ME, IS THIS SPACE TAKEN?
NO! PLEASE TALK TO US! I MEAN, JOIN US.
COME ON BOYS, YOU CAN STAND HERE.
ARE YOU BOYS TRYING OUT FOR THE TEAM?
YES.
THAT'S RIGHT.

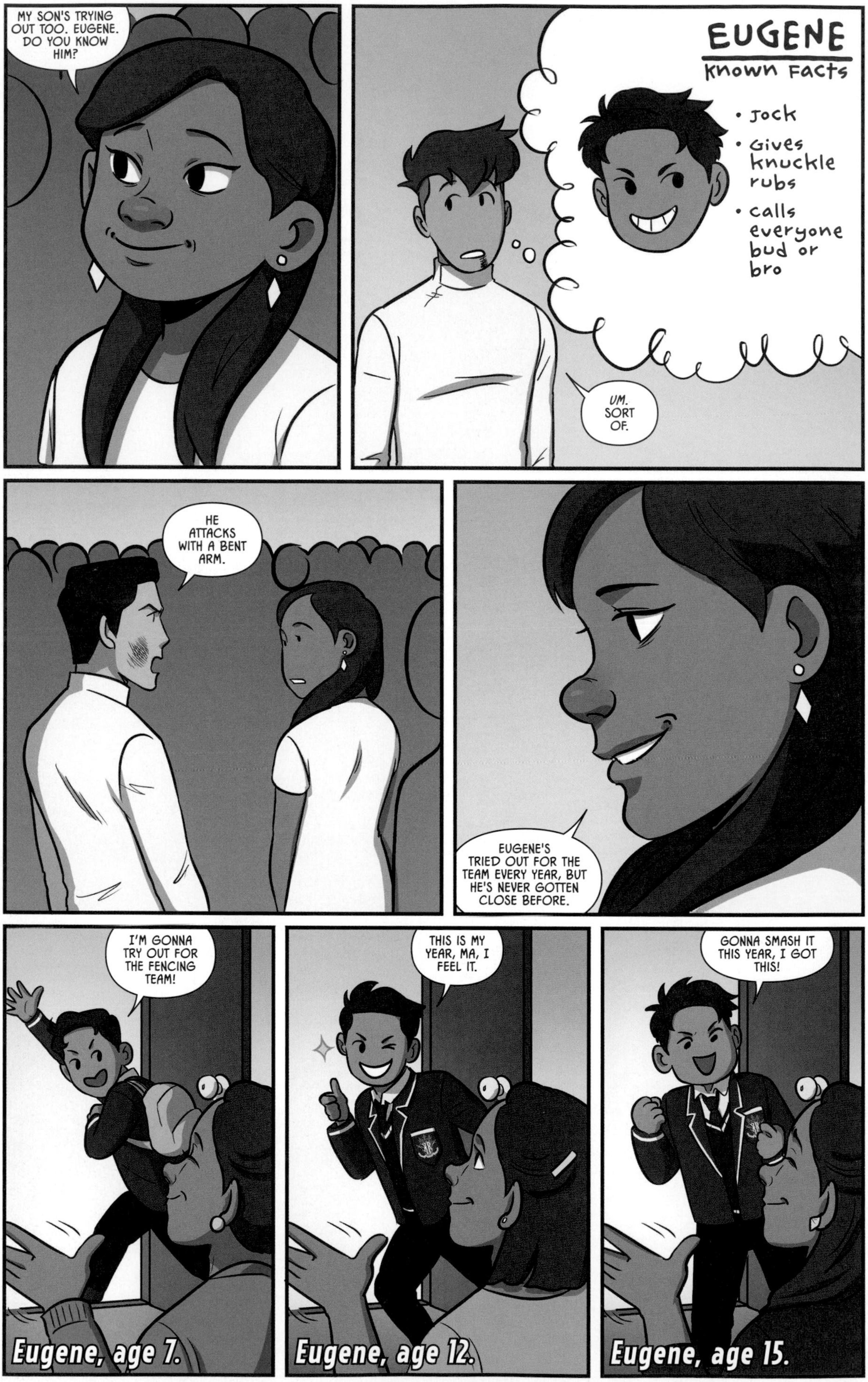
MY SON'S TRYING OUT TOO. EUGENE. DO YOU KNOW HIM?
EUGENE
Known Facts
• Jock
• Gives knuckle rubs
• calls everyone bud or bro
UM. SORT OF.
HE ATTACKS WITH A BENT ARM.
EUGENE'S TRIED OUT FOR THE TEAM EVERY YEAR, BUT HE'S NEVER GOTTEN CLOSE BEFORE.
I'M GONNA TRY OUT FOR THE FENCING TEAM!
Eugene, age 7.
THIS IS MY YEAR, MA, I FEEL IT.
Eugene, age 12.
GONNA SMASH IT THIS YEAR, I GOT THIS!
Eugene, age 15.

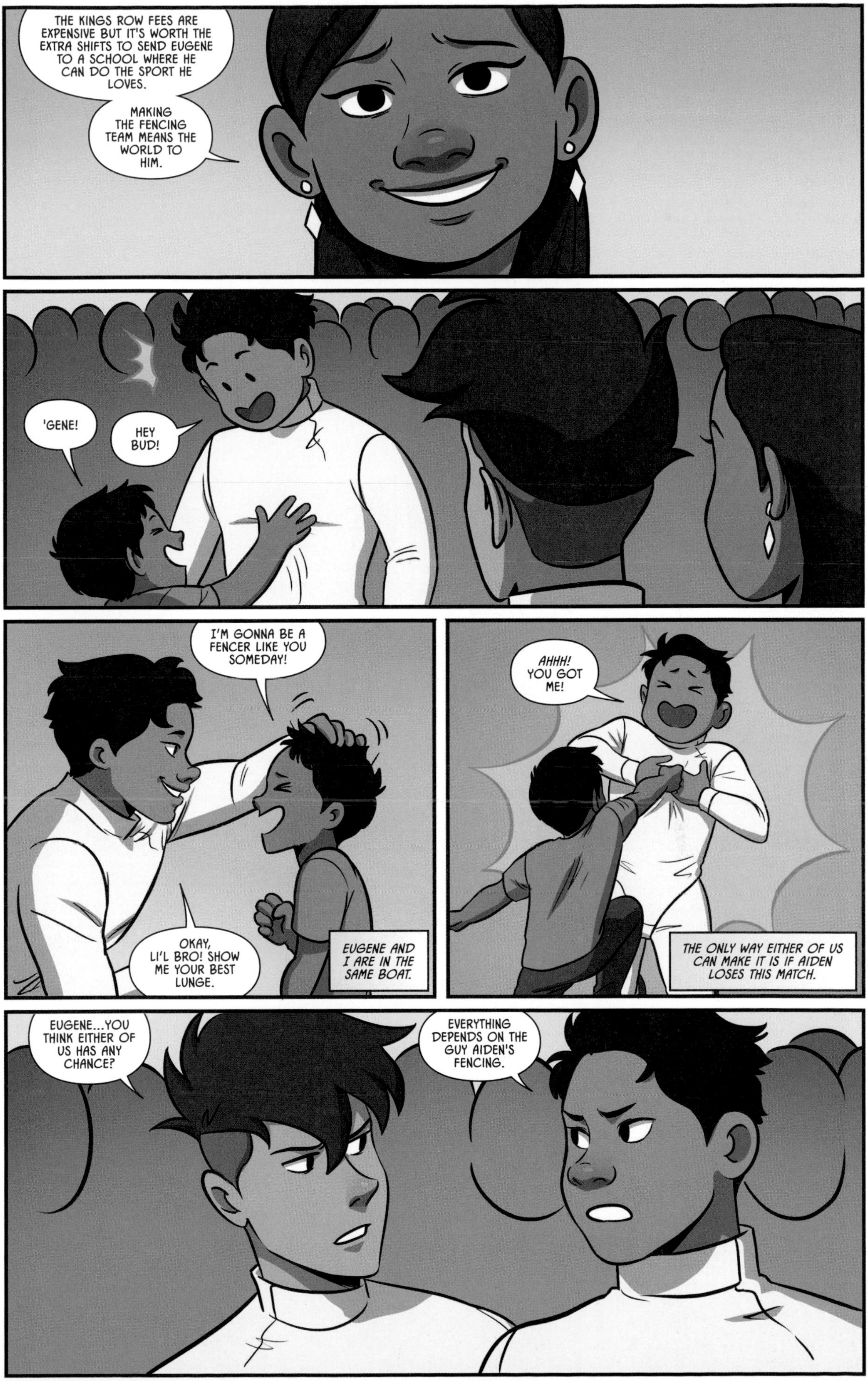
THE KINGS ROW FEES ARE EXPENSIVE BUT IT'S WORTH THE EXTRA SHIFTS TO SEND EUGENE TO A SCHOOL WHERE HE CAN DO THE SPORT HE LOVES.
MAKING THE FENCING TEAM MEANS THE WORLD TO HIM.
'GENE!
HEY BUD!
I'M GONNA BE A FENCER LIKE YOU SOMEDAY!
OKAY, LI'L BRO! SHOW ME YOUR BEST LUNGE.
EUGENE AND I ARE IN THE SAME BOAT.
AHHH! YOU GOT ME!
THE ONLY WAY EITHER OF US CAN MAKE IT IS IF AIDEN LOSES THIS MATCH.
EUGENE...YOU THINK EITHER OF US HAS ANY CHANCE?
EVERYTHING DEPENDS ON THE GUY AIDEN'S FENCING.

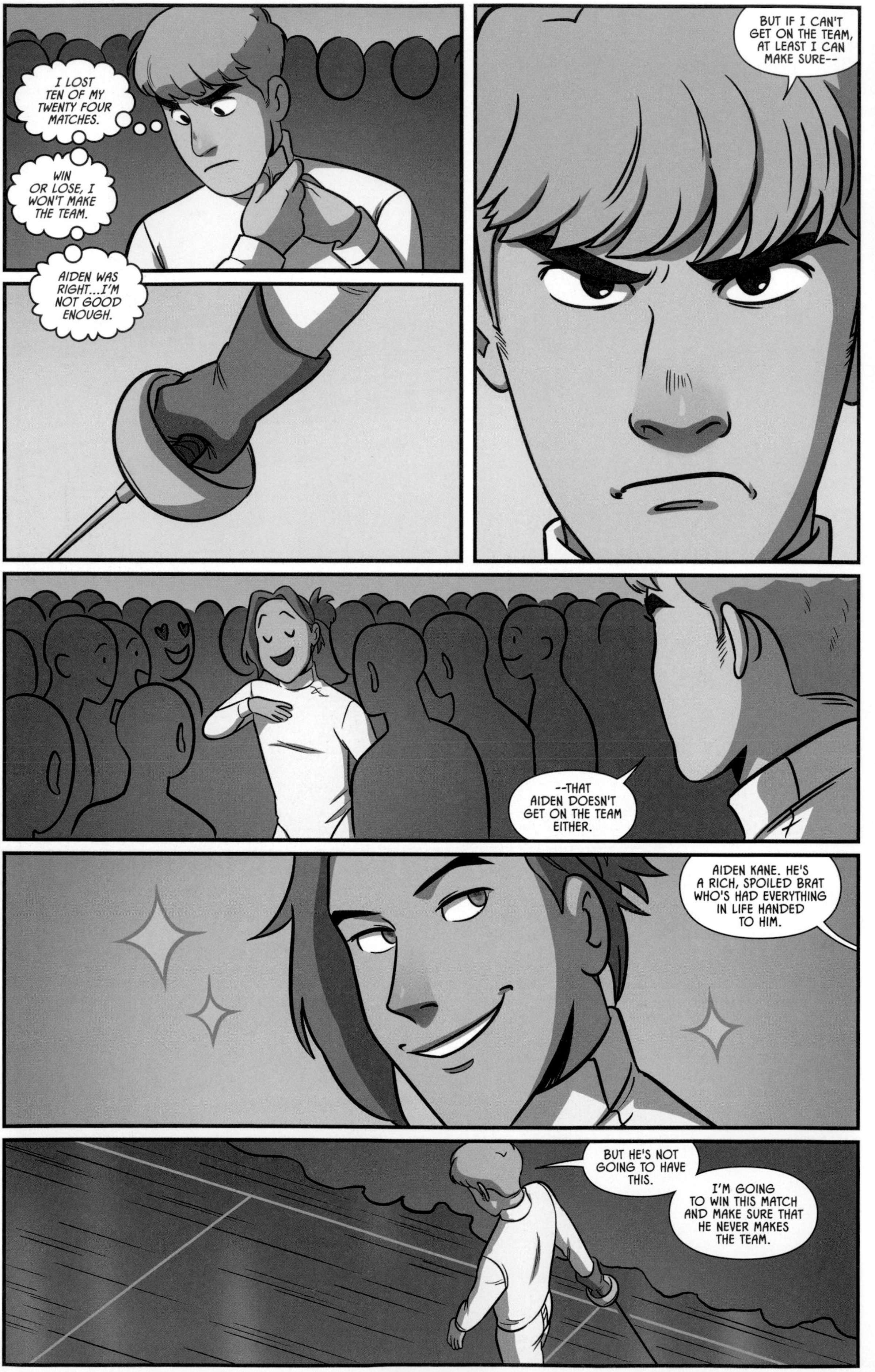
I LOST TEN OF MY TWENTY FOUR MATCHES.
WIN OR LOSE, I WON'T MAKE THE TEAM.
AIDEN WAS RIGHT...I'M NOT GOOD ENOUGH.
BUT IF I CAN'T GET ON THE TEAM, AT LEAST I CAN MAKE SURE--
--THAT AIDEN DOESN'T GET ON THE TEAM EITHER.
AIDEN KANE. HE'S A RICH, SPOILED BRAT WHO'S HAD EVERYTHING IN LIFE HANDED TO HIM.
BUT HE'S NOT GOING TO HAVE THIS.
I'M GOING TO WIN THIS MATCH AND MAKE SURE THAT HE NEVER MAKES THE TEAM.

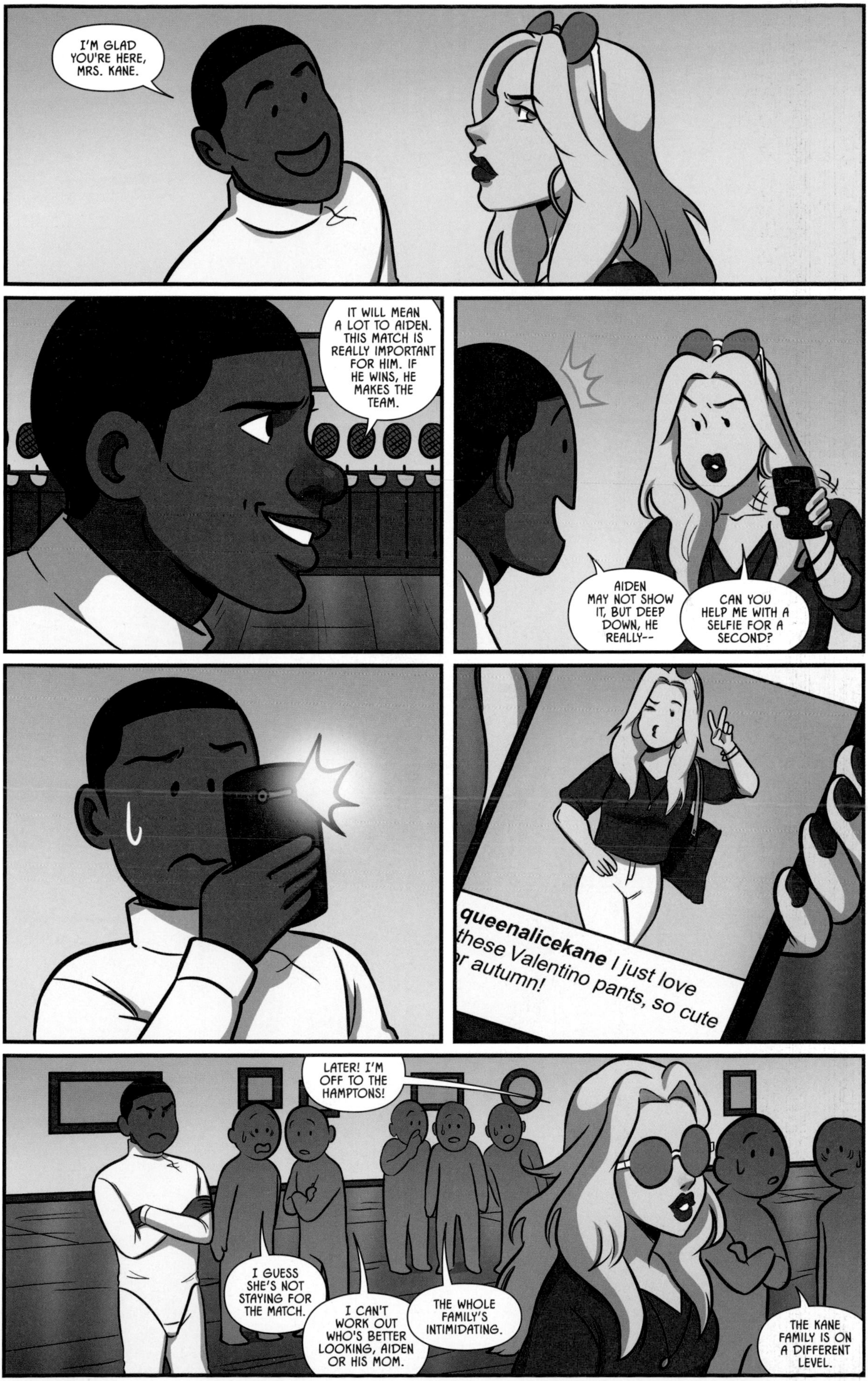
I'M GLAD YOU'RE HERE, MRS. KANE.
IT WILL MEAN A LOT TO AIDEN. THIS MATCH IS REALLY IMPORTANT FOR HIM. IF HE WINS, HE MAKES THE TEAM.
AIDEN MAY NOT SHOW IT, BUT DEEP DOWN, HE REALLY--
CAN YOU HELP ME WITH A SELFIE FOR A SECOND?
queenalicekane I just love these Valentino pants, so cute r autumn!
LATER! I'M OFF TO THE HAMPTONS!
I GUESS SHE'S NOT STAYING FOR THE MATCH.
I CAN'T WORK OUT WHO'S BETTER LOOKING, AIDEN OR HIS MOM.
THE WHOLE FAMILY'S INTIMIDATING.
THE KANE FAMILY IS ON A DIFFERENT LEVEL.

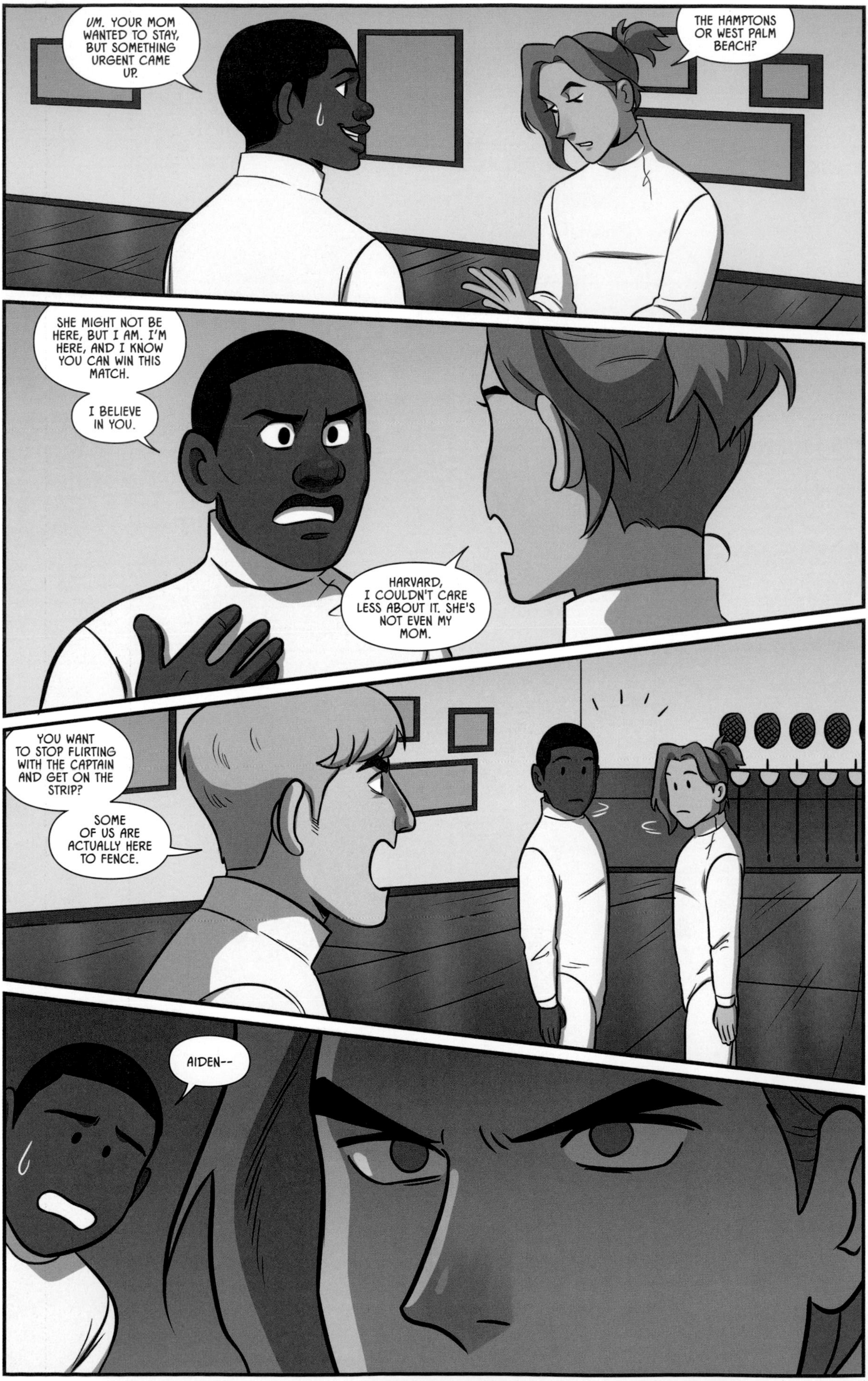

UM. YOUR MOM WANTED TO STAY, BUT SOMETHING URGENT CAME UP.
THE HAMPTONS OR WEST PALM BEACH?
SHE MIGHT NOT BE HERE, BUT I AM. I'M HERE, AND I KNOW YOU CAN WIN THIS MATCH.
I BELIEVE IN YOU.
HARVARD, I COULDN'T CARE LESS ABOUT IT. SHE'S NOT EVEN MY MOM.
YOU WANT TO STOP FLIRTING WITH THE CAPTAIN AND GET ON THE STRIP?
SOME OF US ARE ACTUALLY HERE TO FENCE.
AIDEN--

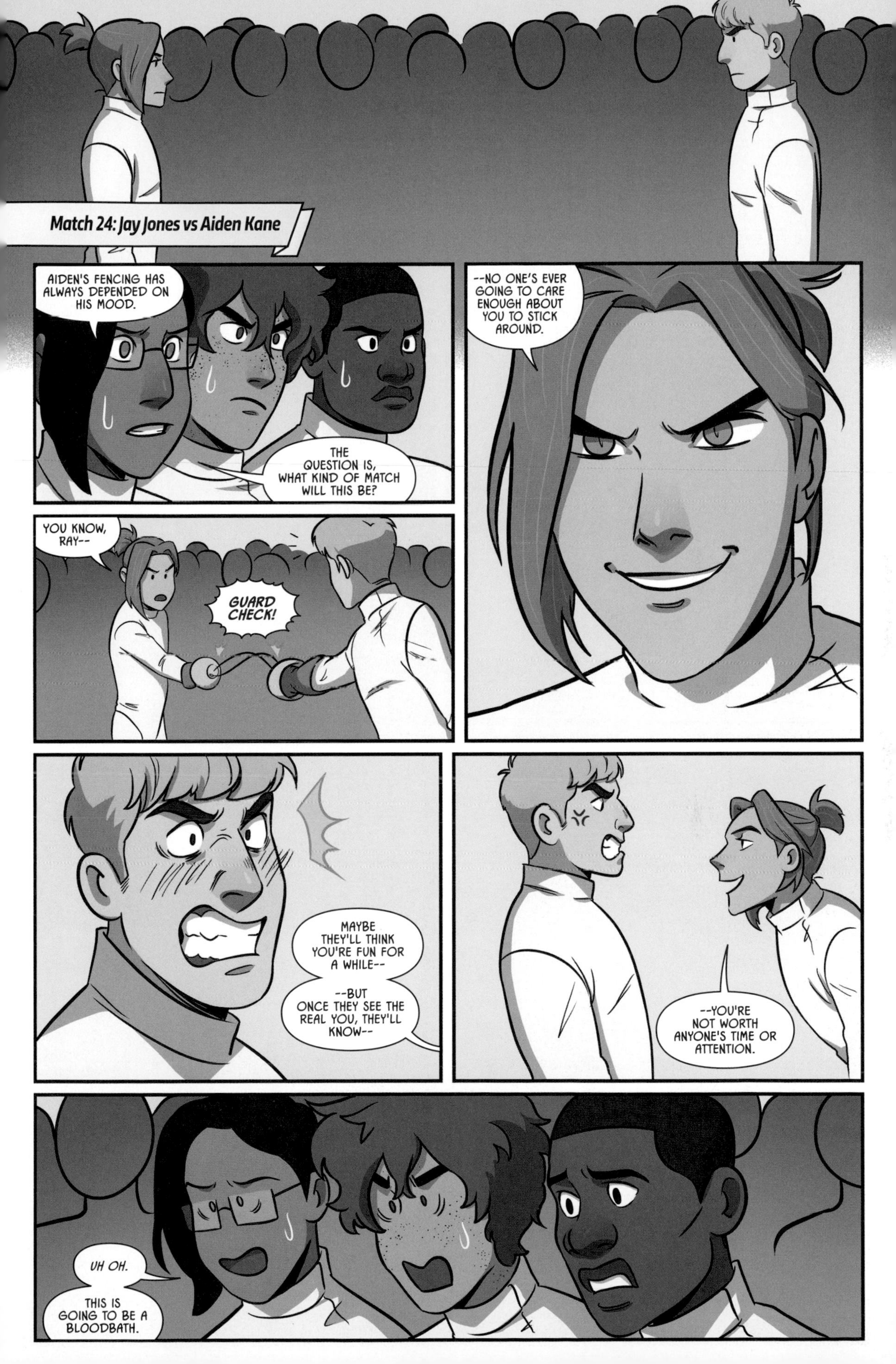
Match 24: Jay Jones vs Aiden Kane
AIDEN'S FENCING HAS ALWAYS DEPENDED ON HIS MOOD.
THE QUESTION IS, WHAT KIND OF MATCH WILL THIS BE?
YOU KNOW, RAY--
GUARD CHECK!
--NO ONE'S EVER GOING TO CARE ENOUGH ABOUT YOU TO STICK AROUND.
MAYBE THEY'LL THINK YOU'RE FUN FOR A WHILE--
--BUT ONCE THEY SEE THE REAL YOU, THEY'LL KNOW--
--YOU'RE NOT WORTH ANYONE'S TIME OR ATTENTION.
UH OH.
THIS IS GOING TO BE A BLOODBATH.

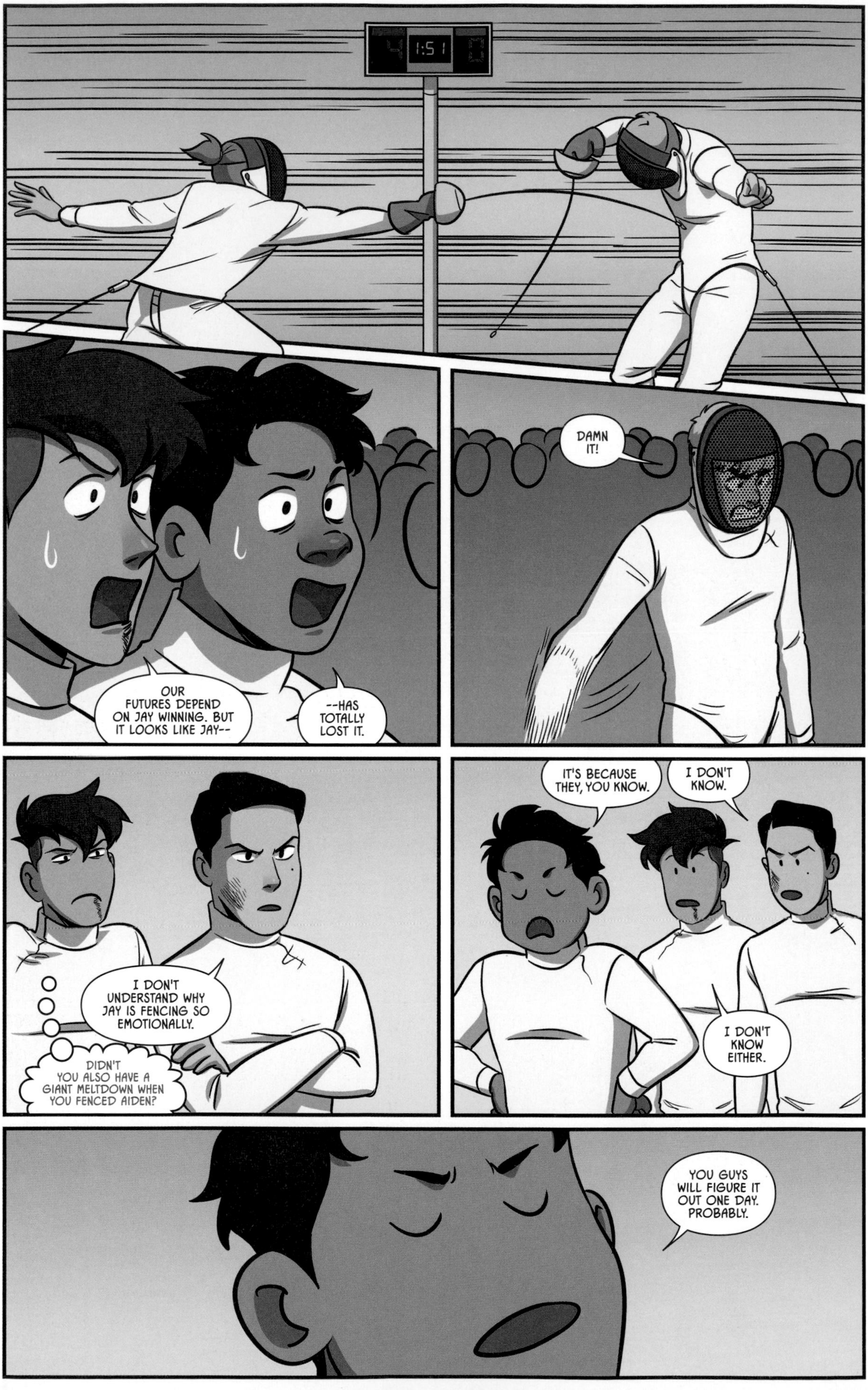

4 1:51 0
OUR FUTURES DEPEND ON JAY WINNING. BUT IT LOOKS LIKE JAY--
--HAS TOTALLY LOST IT.
DAMN IT!
I DON'T UNDERSTAND WHY JAY IS FENCING SO EMOTIONALLY.
DIDN'T YOU ALSO HAVE A GIANT MELTDOWN WHEN YOU FENCED AIDEN?
IT'S BECAUSE THEY, YOU KNOW.
I DON'T KNOW.
I DON'T KNOW EITHER.
YOU GUYS WILL FIGURE IT OUT ONE DAY. PROBABLY.

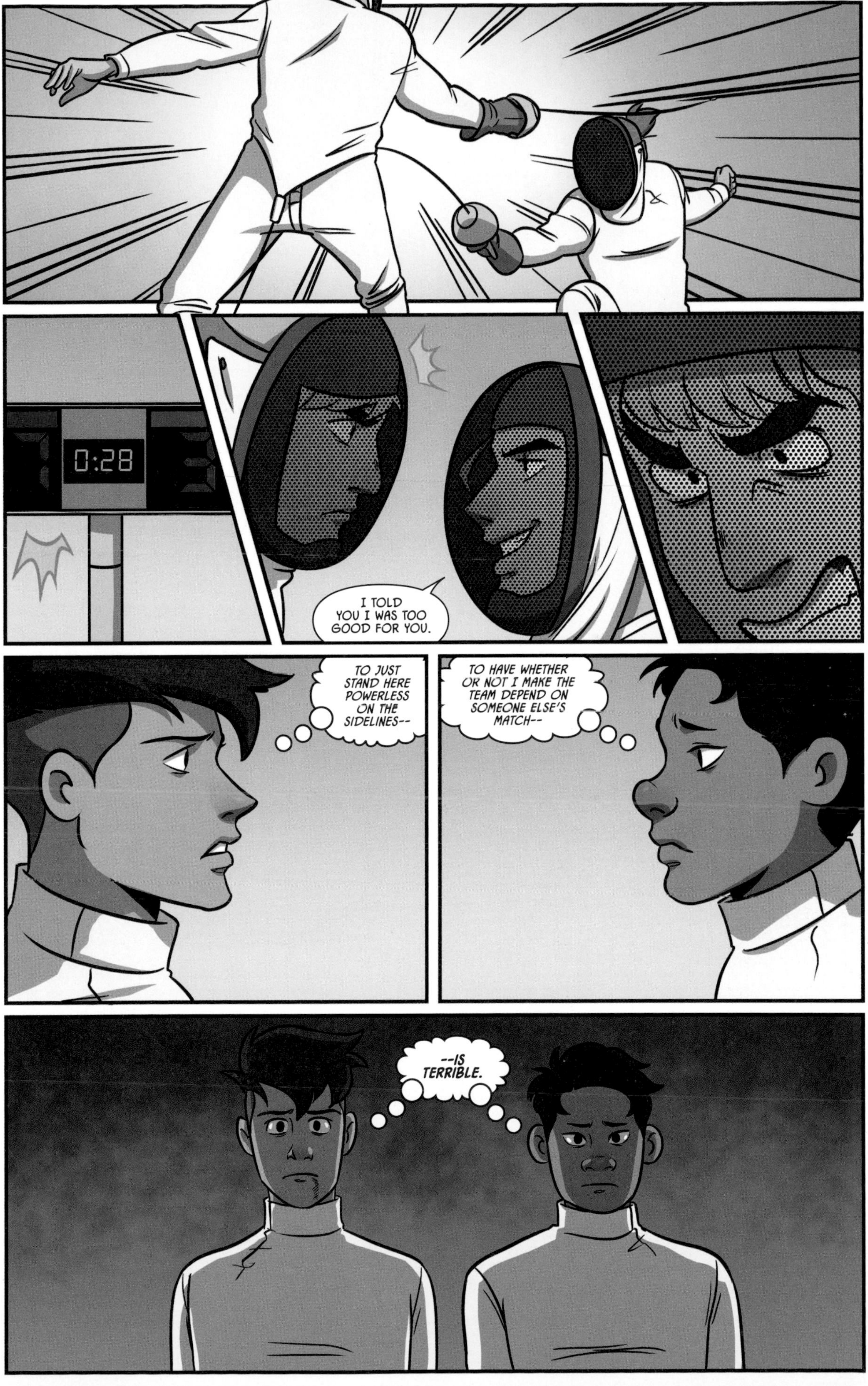
0:28
I TOLD YOU I WAS TOO GOOD FOR YOU.
TO JUST STAND HERE POWERLESS ON THE SIDELINES--
TO HAVE WHETHER OR NOT I MAKE THE TEAM DEPEND ON SOMEONE ELSE'S MATCH--
--IS TERRIBLE.

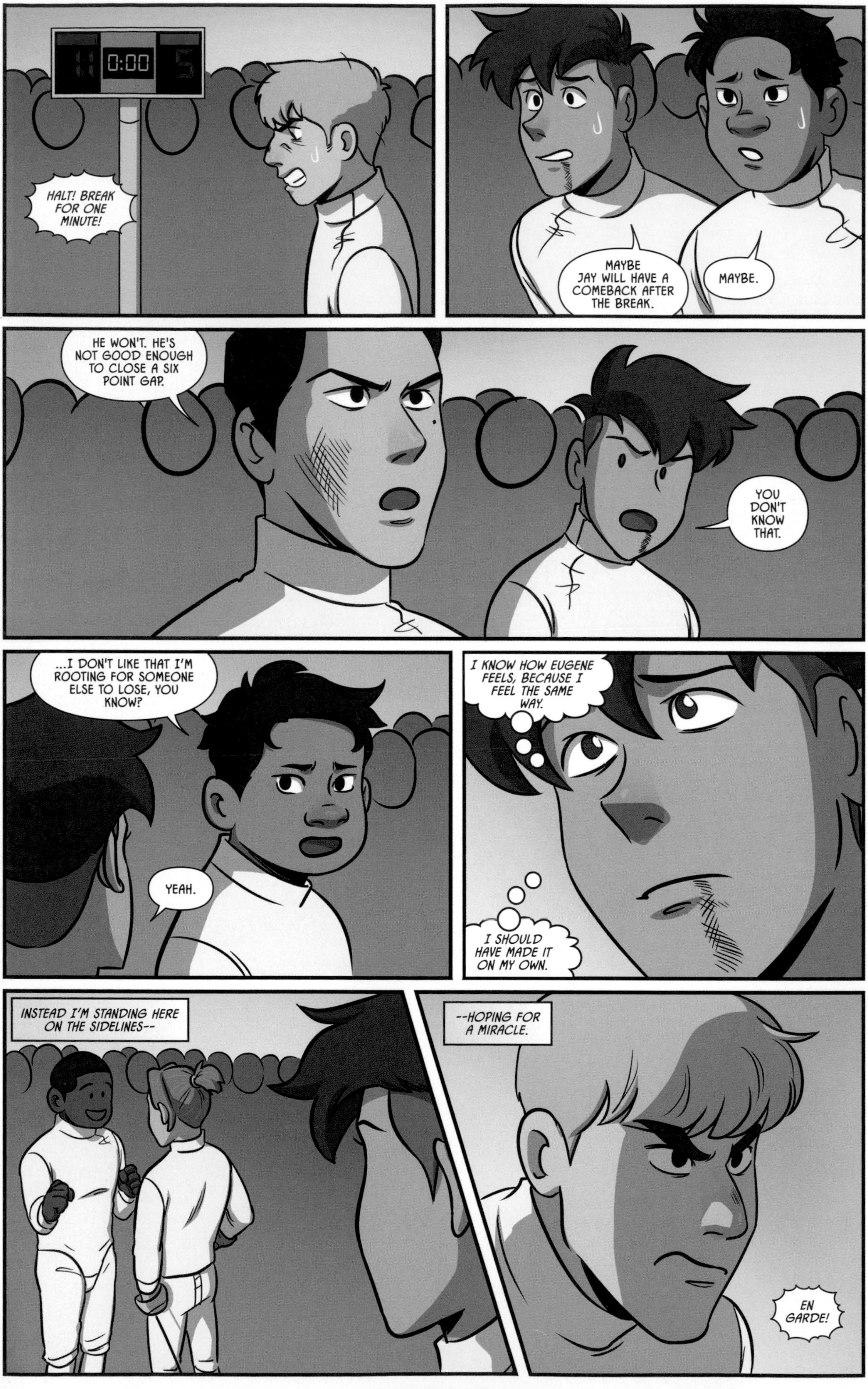
0:00
HALT! BREAK FOR ONE MINUTE!
MAYBE JAY WILL HAVE A COMEBACK AFTER THE BREAK.
MAYBE.
HE WON'T. HE'S NOT GOOD ENOUGH TO CLOSE A SIX POINT GAP.
YOU DON'T KNOW THAT.
...I DON'T LIKE THAT I'M ROOTING FOR SOMEONE ELSE TO LOSE, YOU KNOW?
YEAH.
I KNOW HOW EUGENE FEELS, BECAUSE I FEEL THE SAME WAY.
I SHOULD HAVE MADE IT ON MY OWN.
INSTEAD I'M STANDING HERE ON THE SIDELINES--
--HOPING FOR A MIRACLE.
EN GARDE!

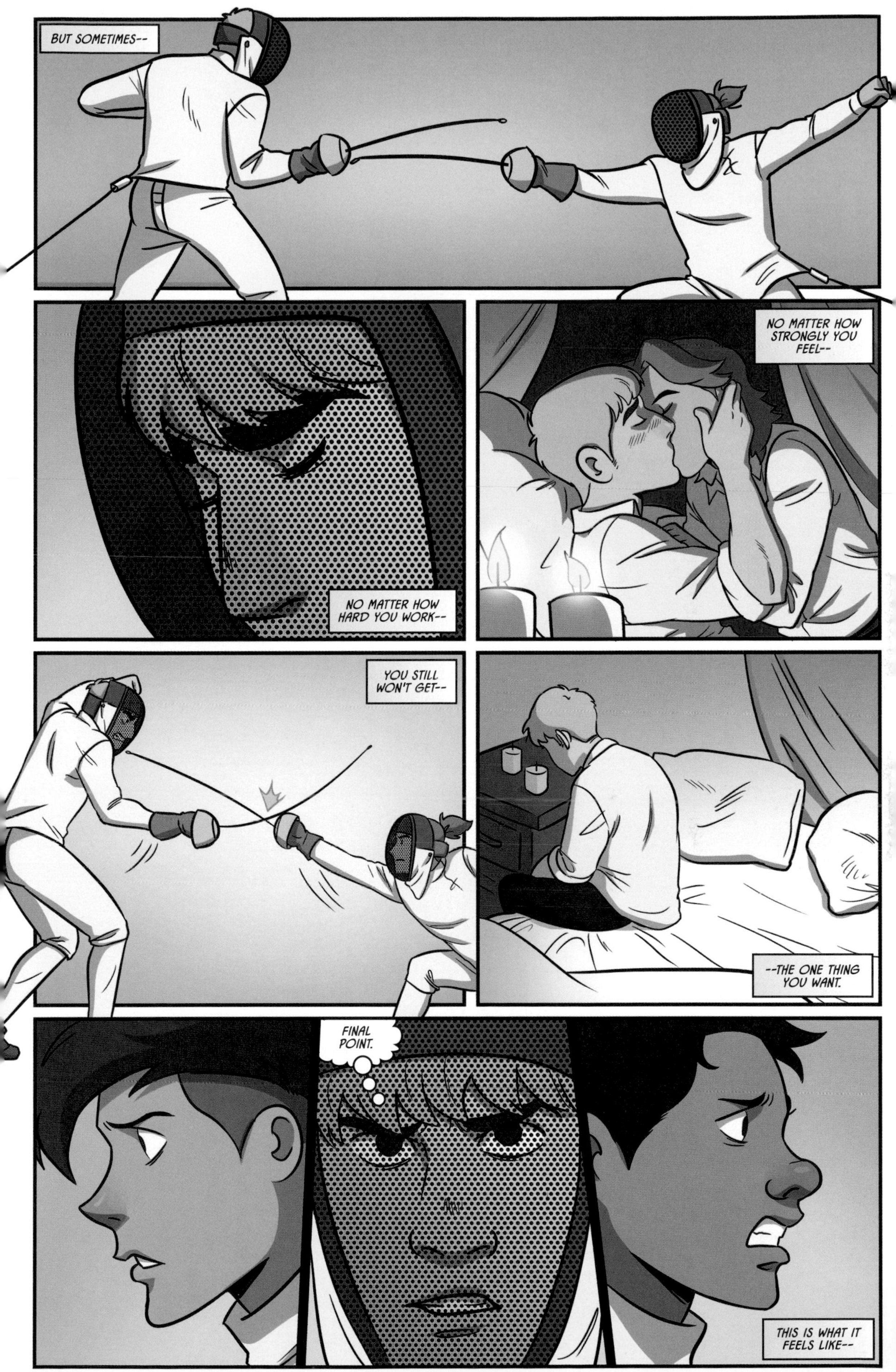
BUT SOMETIMES--
NO MATTER HOW HARD YOU WORK--
NO MATTER HOW STRONGLY YOU FEEL--
YOU STILL WON'T GET--
--THE ONE THING YOU WANT.
FINAL POINT.
THIS IS WHAT IT FEELS LIKE--

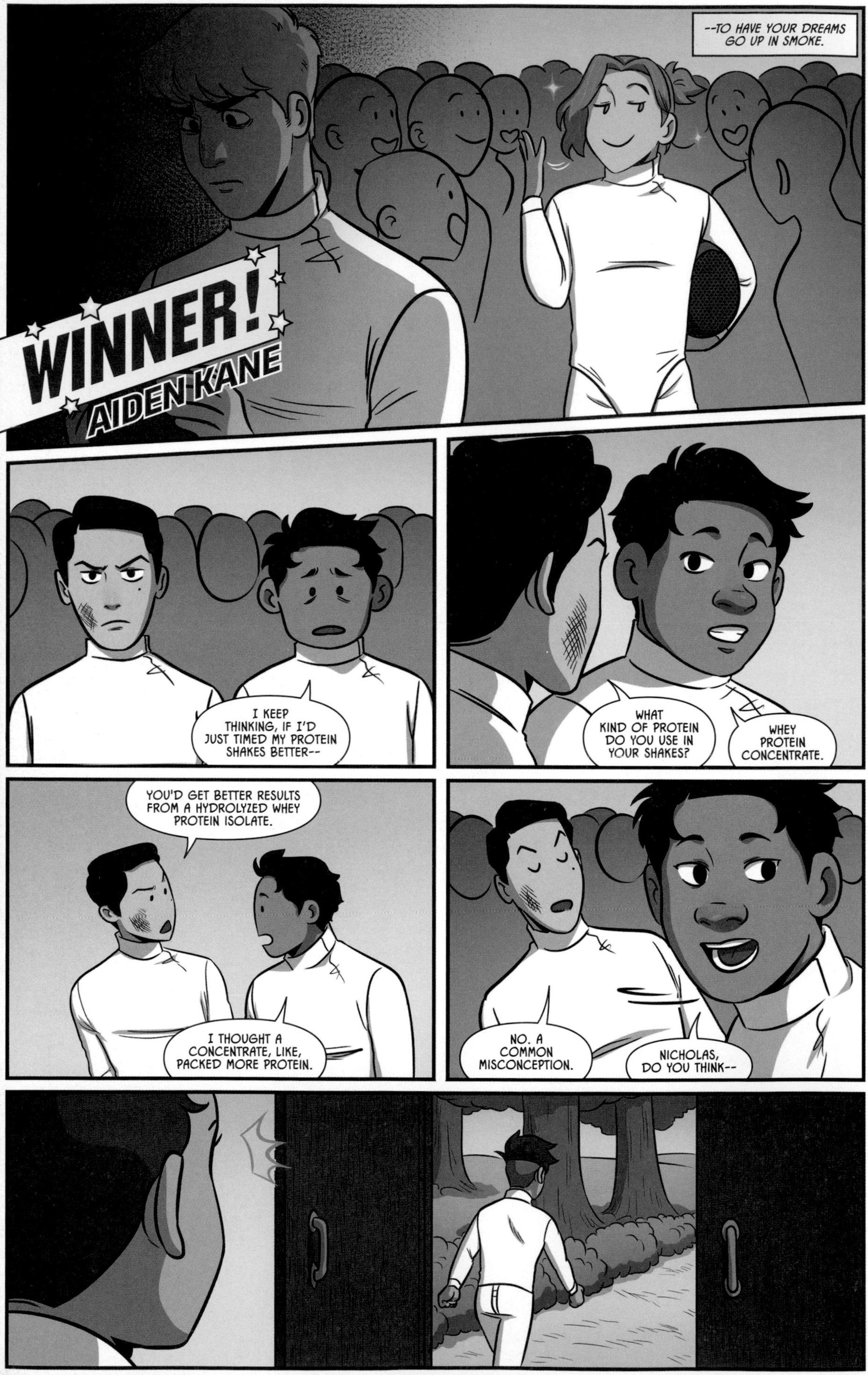
--TO HAVE YOUR DREAMS GO UP IN SMOKE.
WINNER!
AIDEN KANE
I KEEP THINKING, IF I'D JUST TIMED MY PROTEIN SHAKES BETTER--
WHAT KIND OF PROTEIN DO YOU USE IN YOUR SHAKES?
WHEY PROTEIN CONCENTRATE.
YOU'D GET BETTER RESULTS FROM A HYDROLYZED WHEY PROTEIN ISOLATE.
I THOUGHT A CONCENTRATE, LIKE, PACKED MORE PROTEIN.
NO. A COMMON MISCONCEPTION.
NICHOLAS, DO YOU THINK--

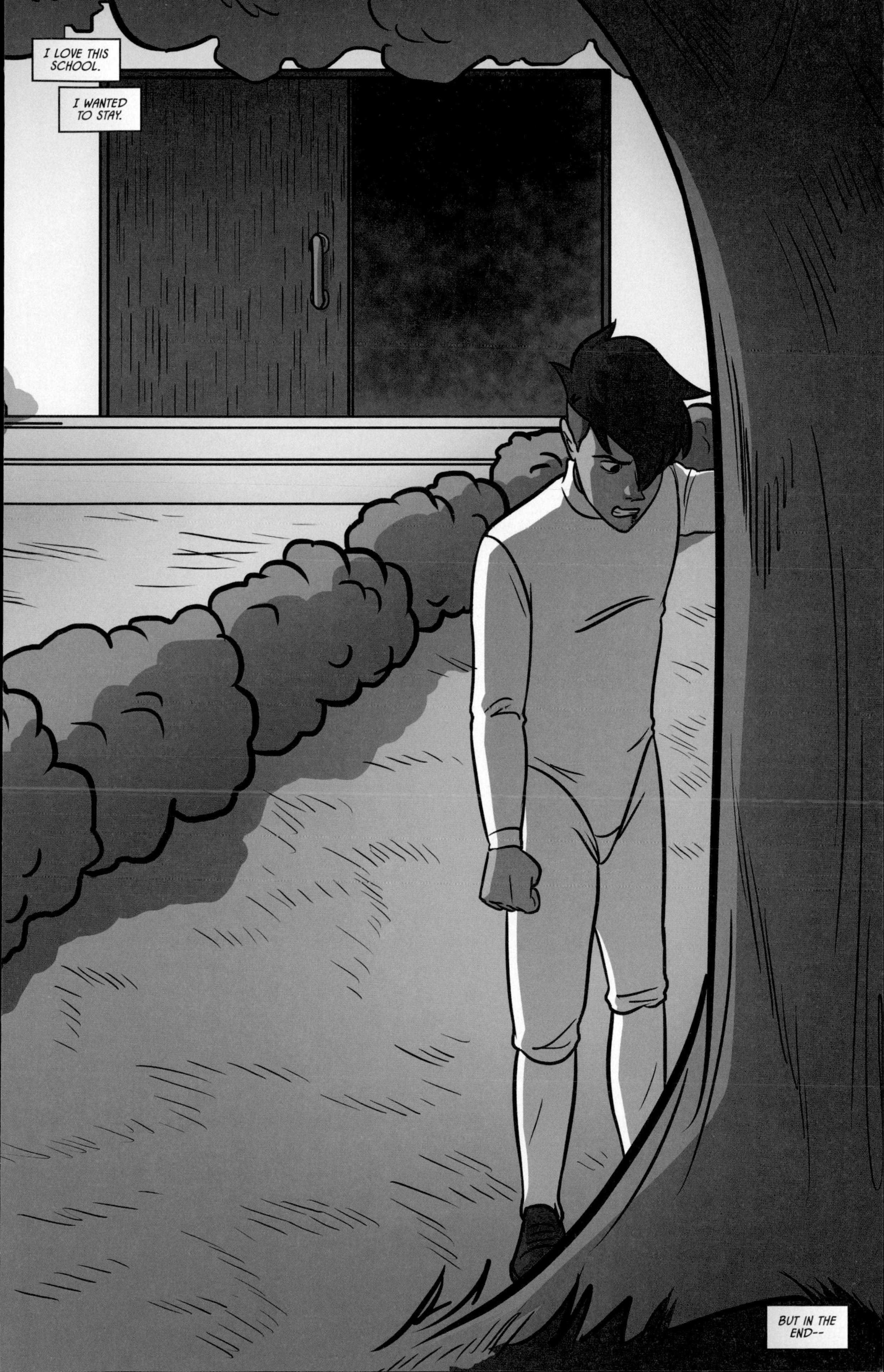
I LOVE THIS SCHOOL.
I WANTED TO STAY.
BUT IN THE END--

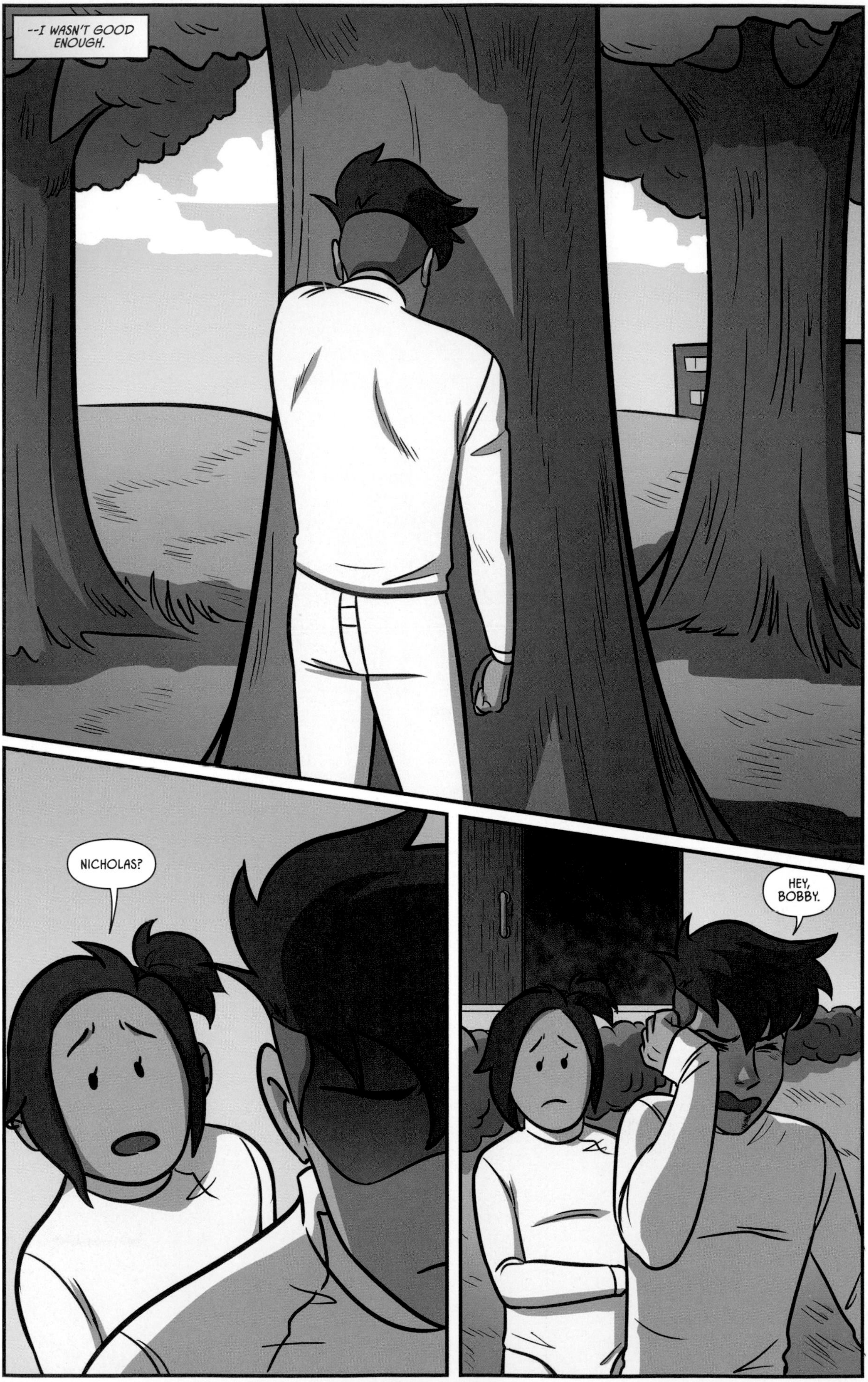
--I WASN'T GOOD ENOUGH.
NICHOLAS?
HEY, BOBBY.

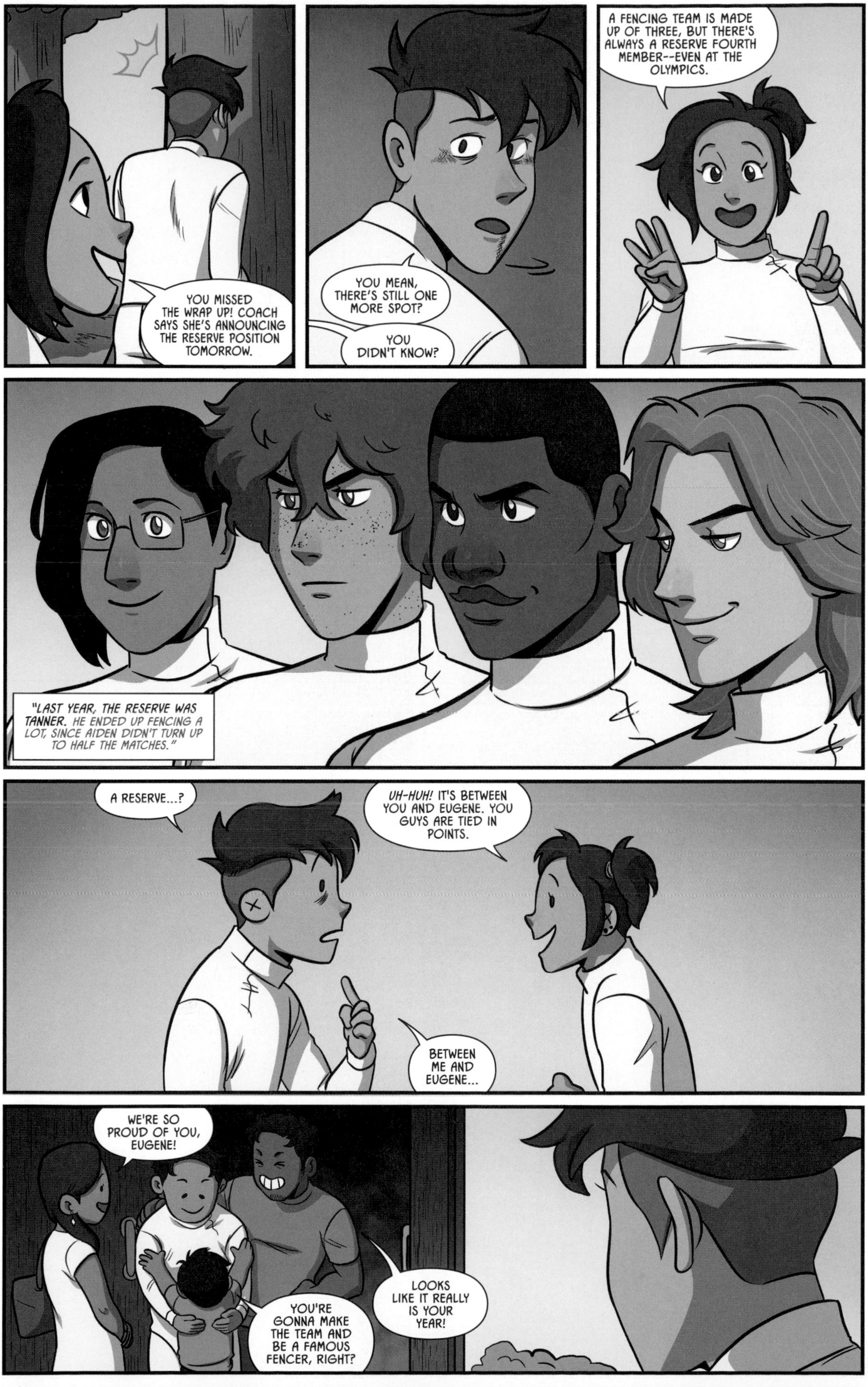
YOU MISSED THE WRAP UP! COACH SAYS SHE'S ANNOUNCING THE RESERVE POSITION TOMORROW.
YOU MEAN, THERE'S STILL ONE MORE SPOT?
YOU DIDN'T KNOW?
A FENCING TEAM IS MADE UP OF THREE, BUT THERE'S ALWAYS A RESERVE FOURTH MEMBER--EVEN AT THE OLYMPICS.
"LAST YEAR, THE RESERVE WAS TANNER. HE ENDED UP FENCING A LOT, SINCE AIDEN DIDN'T TURN UP TO HALF THE MATCHES."
A RESERVE...?
UH-HUH! IT'S BETWEEN YOU AND EUGENE. YOU GUYS ARE TIED IN POINTS.
BETWEEN ME AND EUGENE...
WE'RE SO PROUD OF YOU, EUGENE!
YOU'RE GONNA MAKE THE TEAM AND BE A FAMOUS FENCER, RIGHT?
LOOKS LIKE IT REALLY IS YOUR YEAR!

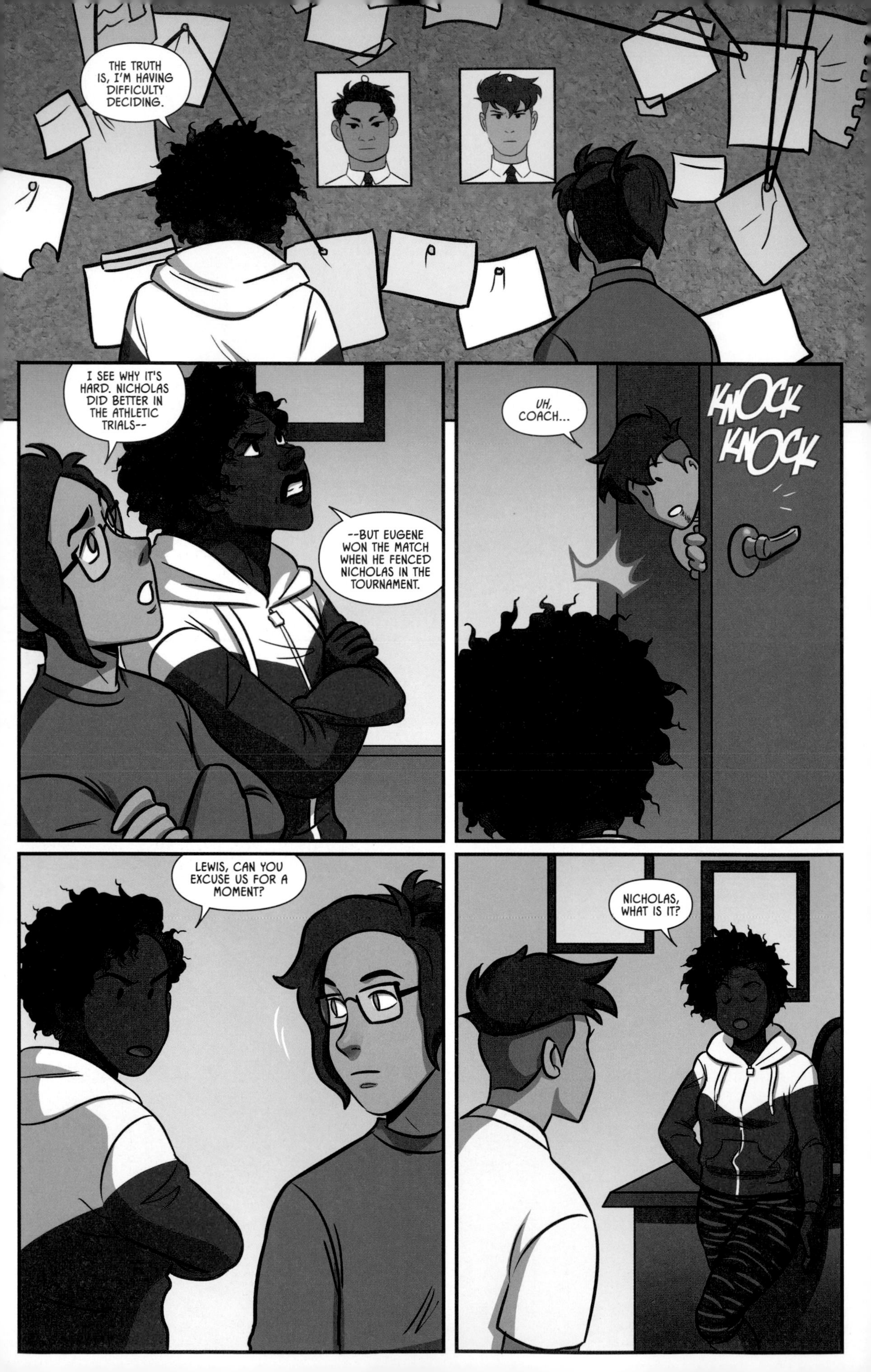
THE TRUTH IS, I'M HAVING DIFFICULTY DECIDING.
I SEE WHY IT'S HARD. NICHOLAS DID BETTER IN THE ATHLETIC TRIALS--
--BUT EUGENE WON THE MATCH WHEN HE FENCED NICHOLAS IN THE TOURNAMENT.
KNOCK KNOCK
UH, COACH...
LEWIS, CAN YOU EXCUSE US FOR A MOMENT?
NICHOLAS, WHAT IS IT?

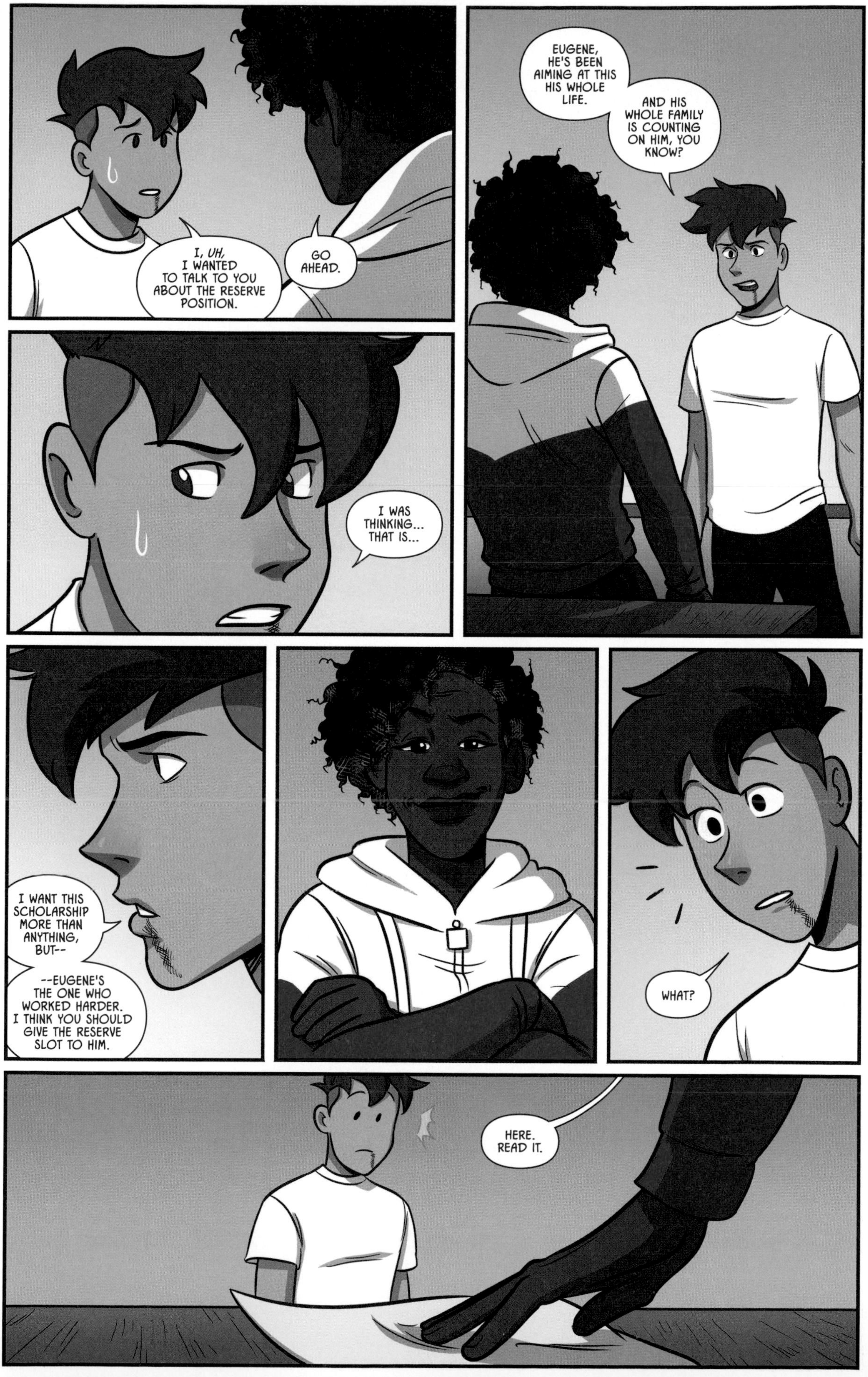
I, UH, I WANTED TO TALK TO YOU ABOUT THE RESERVE POSITION.
GO AHEAD.
EUGENE, HE'S BEEN AIMING AT THIS HIS WHOLE LIFE.
AND HIS WHOLE FAMILY IS COUNTING ON HIM, YOU KNOW?
I WAS THINKING... THAT IS...
I WANT THIS SCHOLARSHIP MORE THAN ANYTHING, BUT--
--EUGENE'S THE ONE WHO WORKED HARDER. I THINK YOU SHOULD GIVE THE RESERVE SLOT TO HIM.
WHAT?
HERE. READ IT.

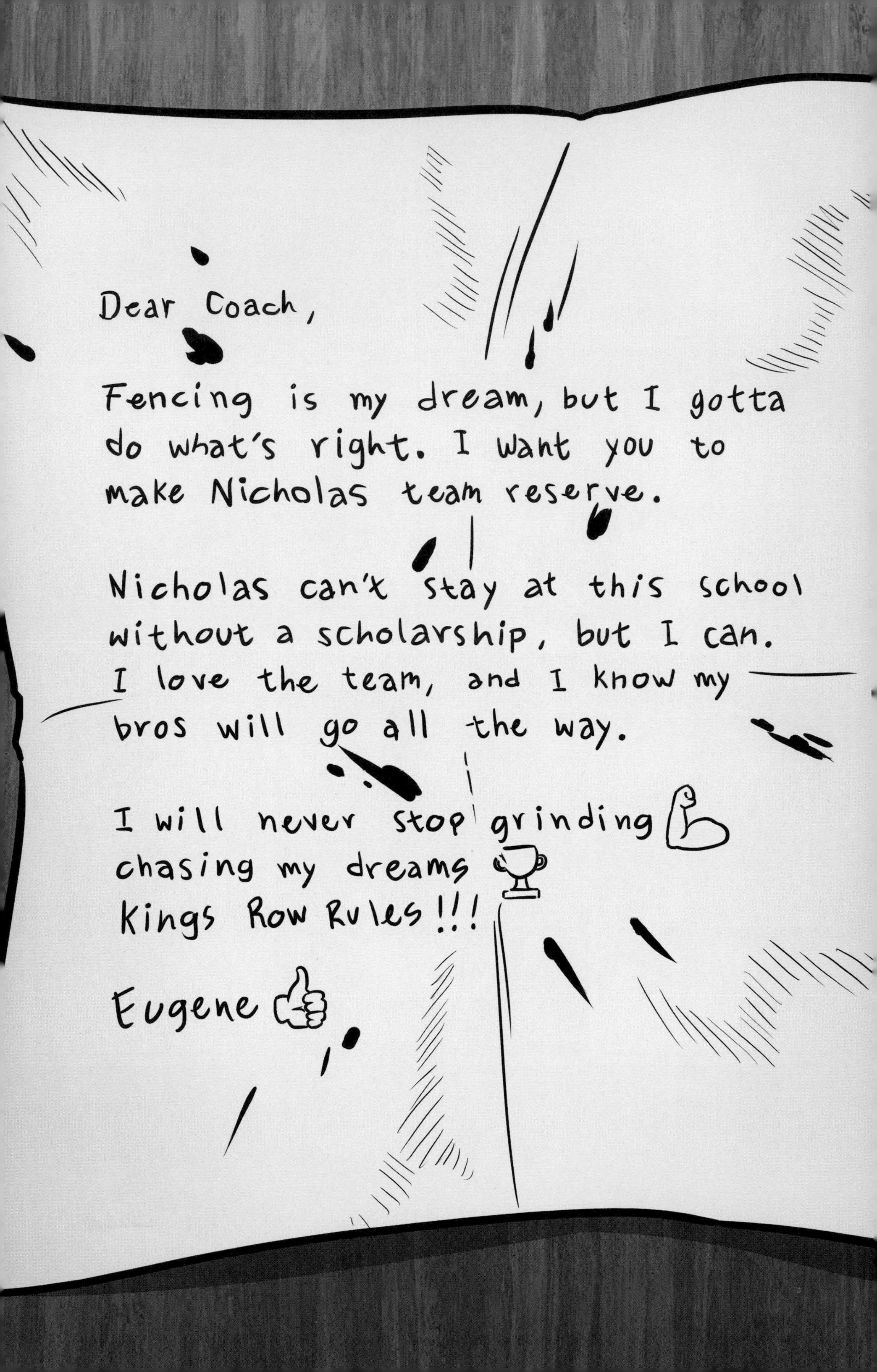
Dear Coach,
Fencing is my dream, but I gotta do what's right. I want you to make Nicholas team reserve.
Nicholas can't stay at this school without a scholarship, but I can. I love the team, and I know my bros will go all the way.
I will never stop grinding
chasing my dreams
Kings Row Rules!!!
Eugene

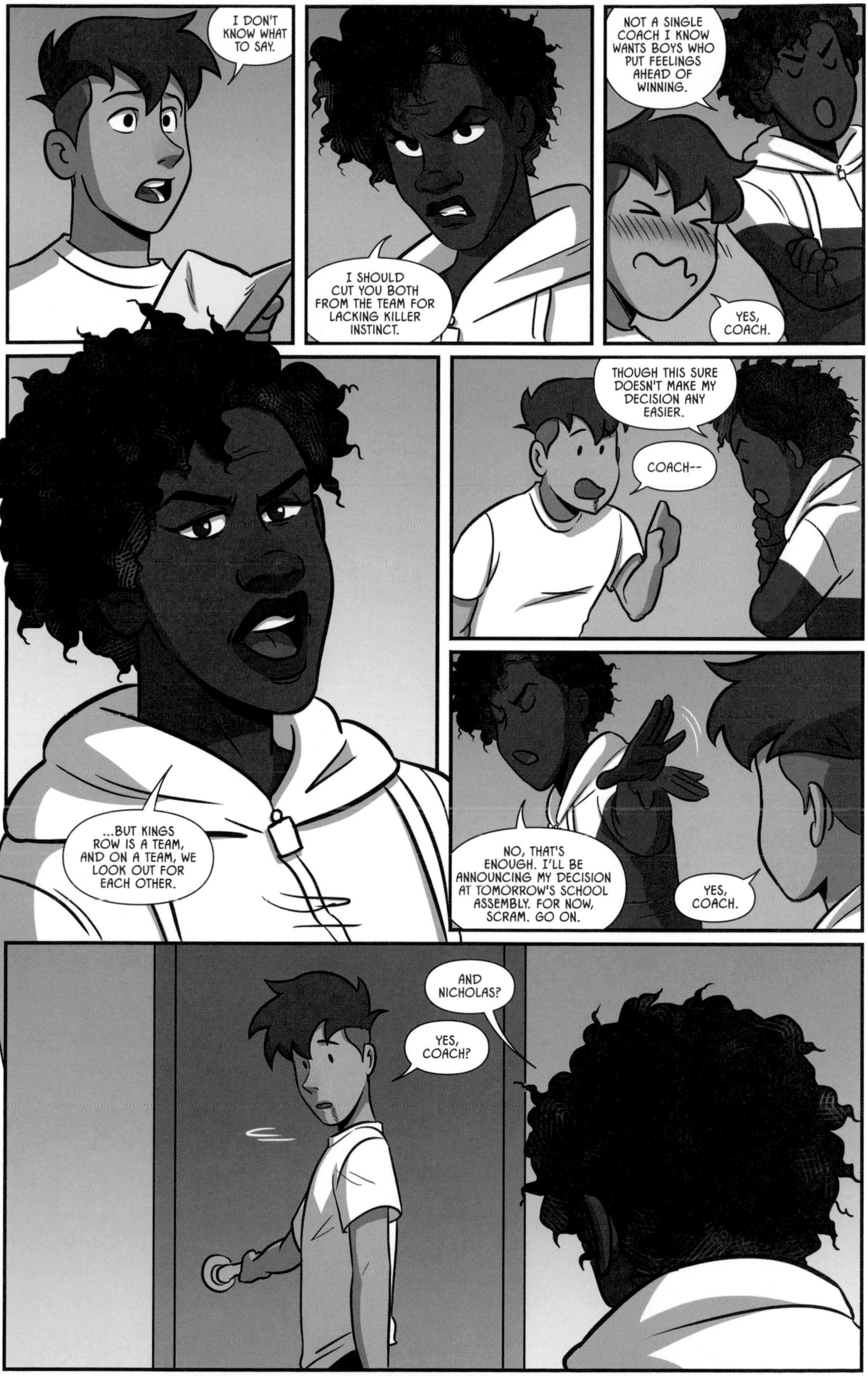
I DON'T KNOW WHAT TO SAY.
I SHOULD CUT YOU BOTH FROM THE TEAM FOR LACKING KILLER INSTINCT.
NOT A SINGLE COACH I KNOW WANTS BOYS WHO PUT FEELINGS AHEAD OF WINNING.
YES, COACH.
...BUT KINGS ROW IS A TEAM, AND ON A TEAM, WE LOOK OUT FOR EACH OTHER.
THOUGH THIS SURE DOESN'T MAKE MY DECISION ANY EASIER.
COACH--
NO, THAT'S ENOUGH. I'LL BE ANNOUNCING MY DECISION AT TOMORROW'S SCHOOL ASSEMBLY. FOR NOW, SCRAM. GO ON.
YES, COACH.
AND NICHOLAS?
YES, COACH?

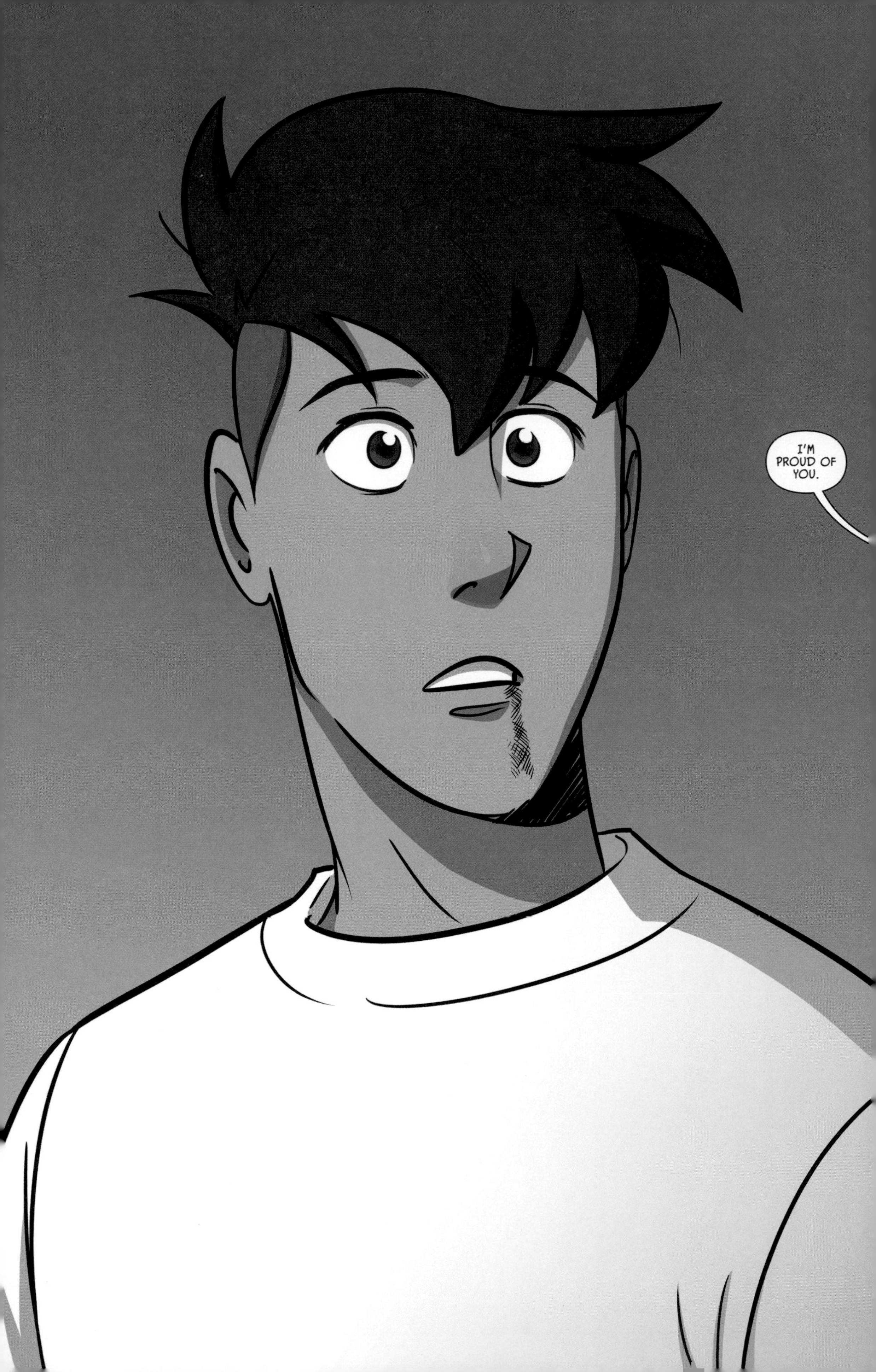
I'M PROUD OF YOU.

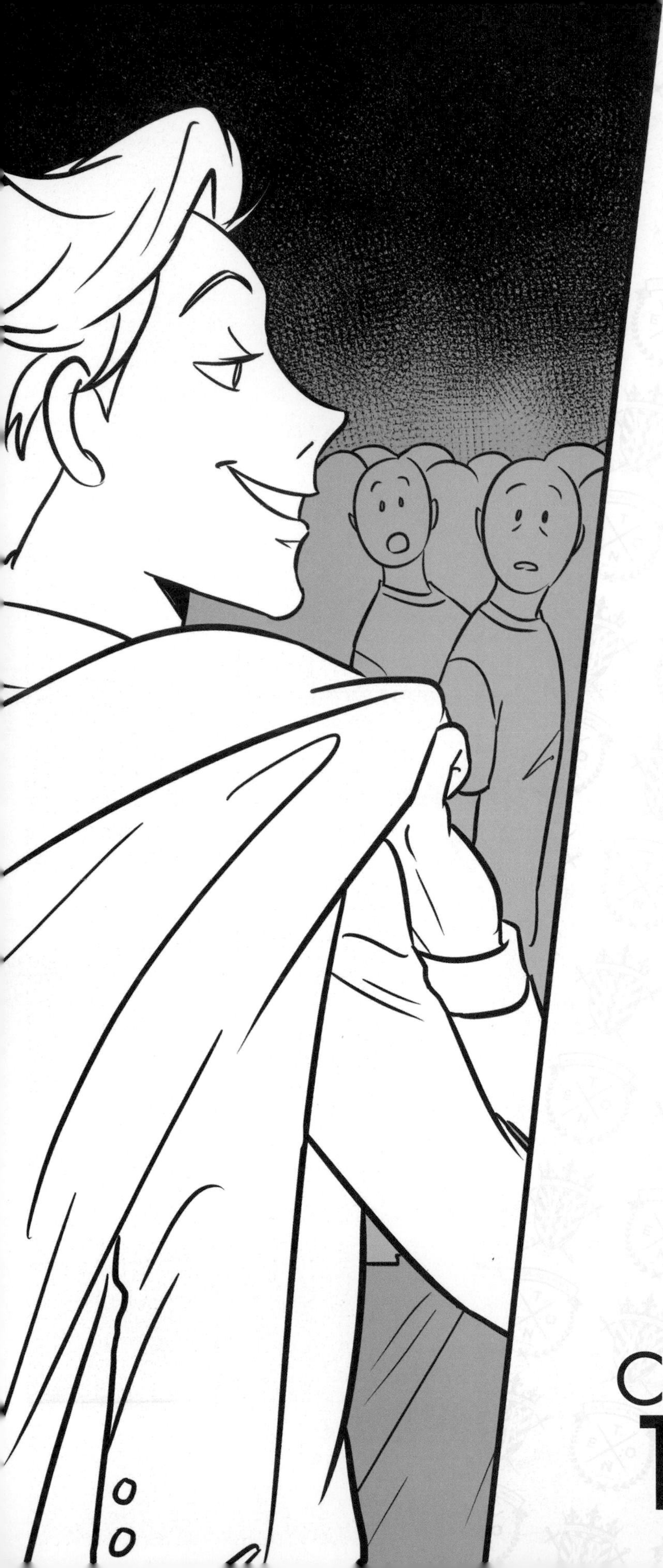

CHAPTER Twelve

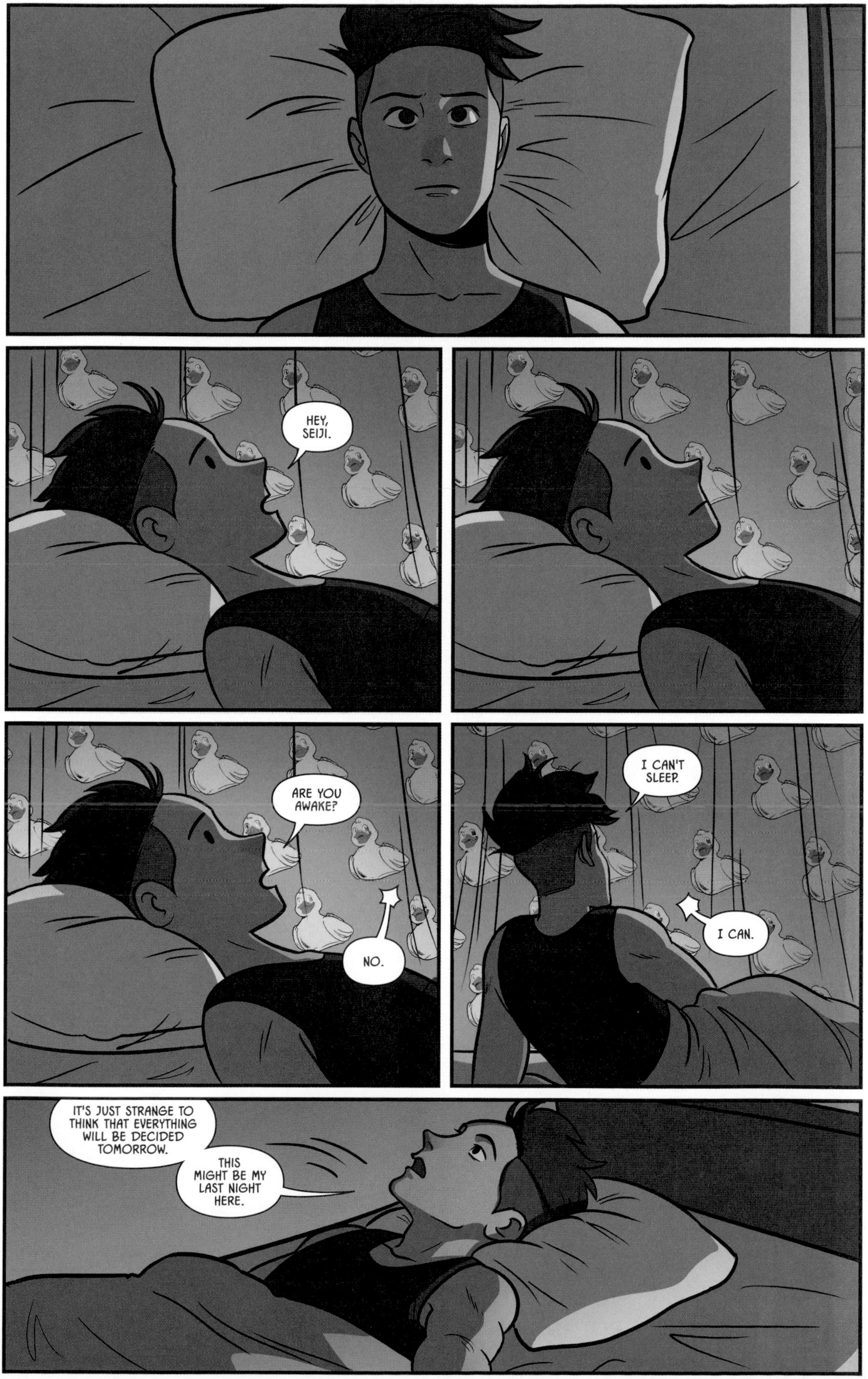
HEY, SEIJI.
ARE YOU AWAKE?
NO.
I CAN'T SLEEP.
I CAN.
IT'S JUST STRANGE TO THINK THAT EVERYTHING WILL BE DECIDED TOMORROW.
THIS MIGHT BE MY LAST NIGHT HERE.

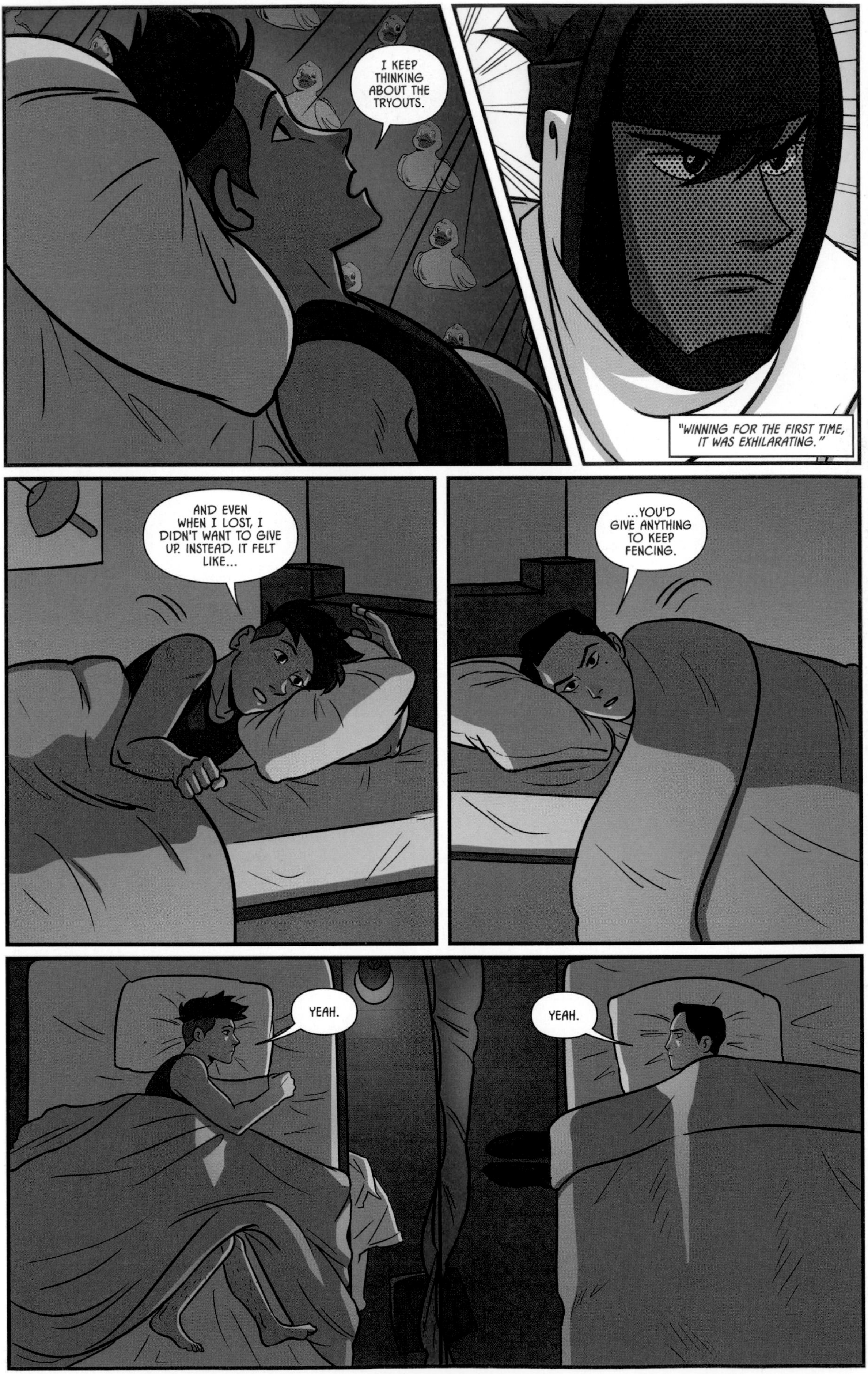
I KEEP THINKING ABOUT THE TRYOUTS.
"WINNING FOR THE FIRST TIME, IT WAS EXHILARATING."
AND EVEN WHEN I LOST, I DIDN'T WANT TO GIVE UP. INSTEAD, IT FELT LIKE...
...YOU'D GIVE ANYTHING TO KEEP FENCING.
YEAH.
YEAH.

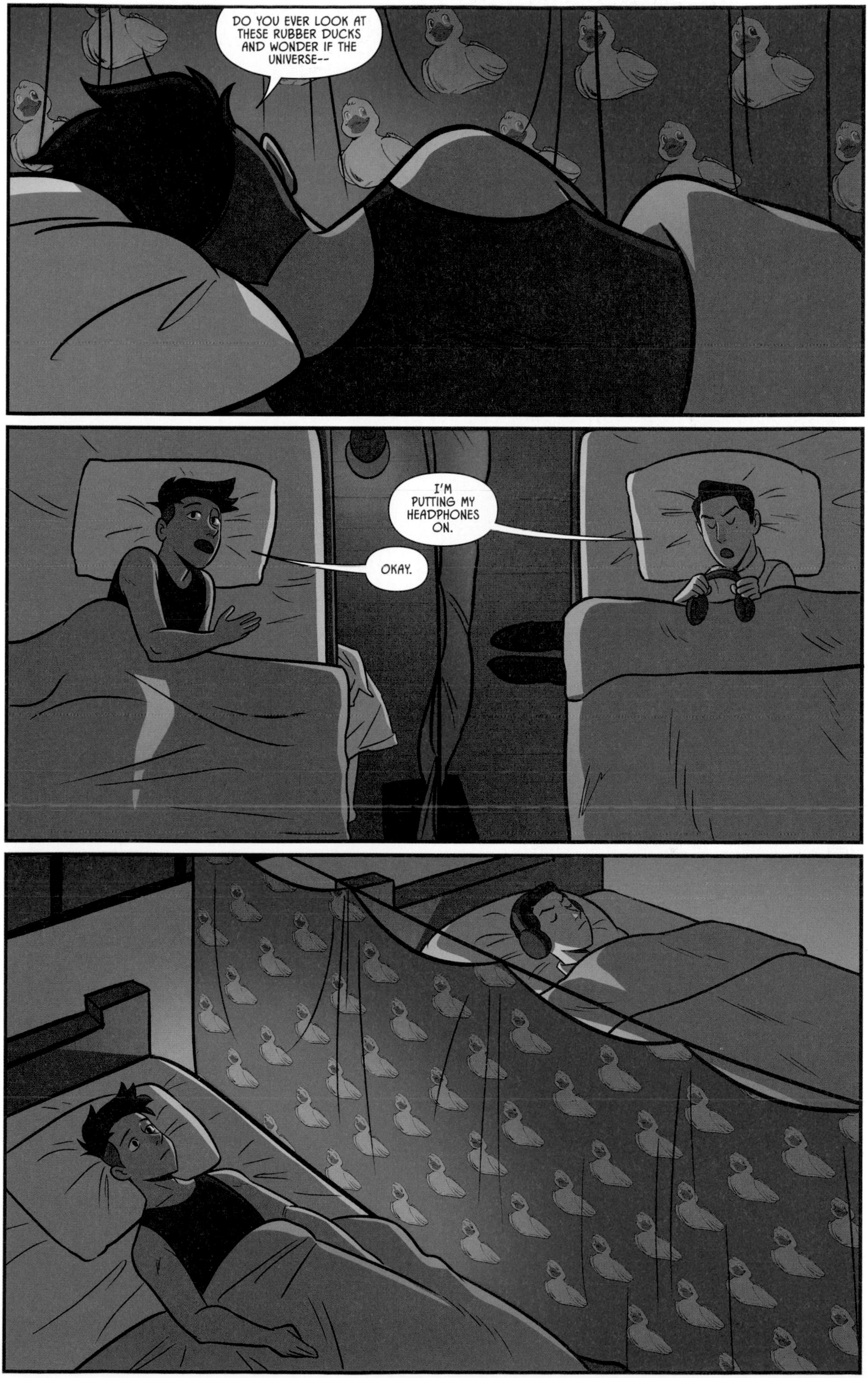
DO YOU EVER LOOK AT THESE RUBBER DUCKS AND WONDER IF THE UNIVERSE--
I'M PUTTING MY HEADPHONES ON.
OKAY.

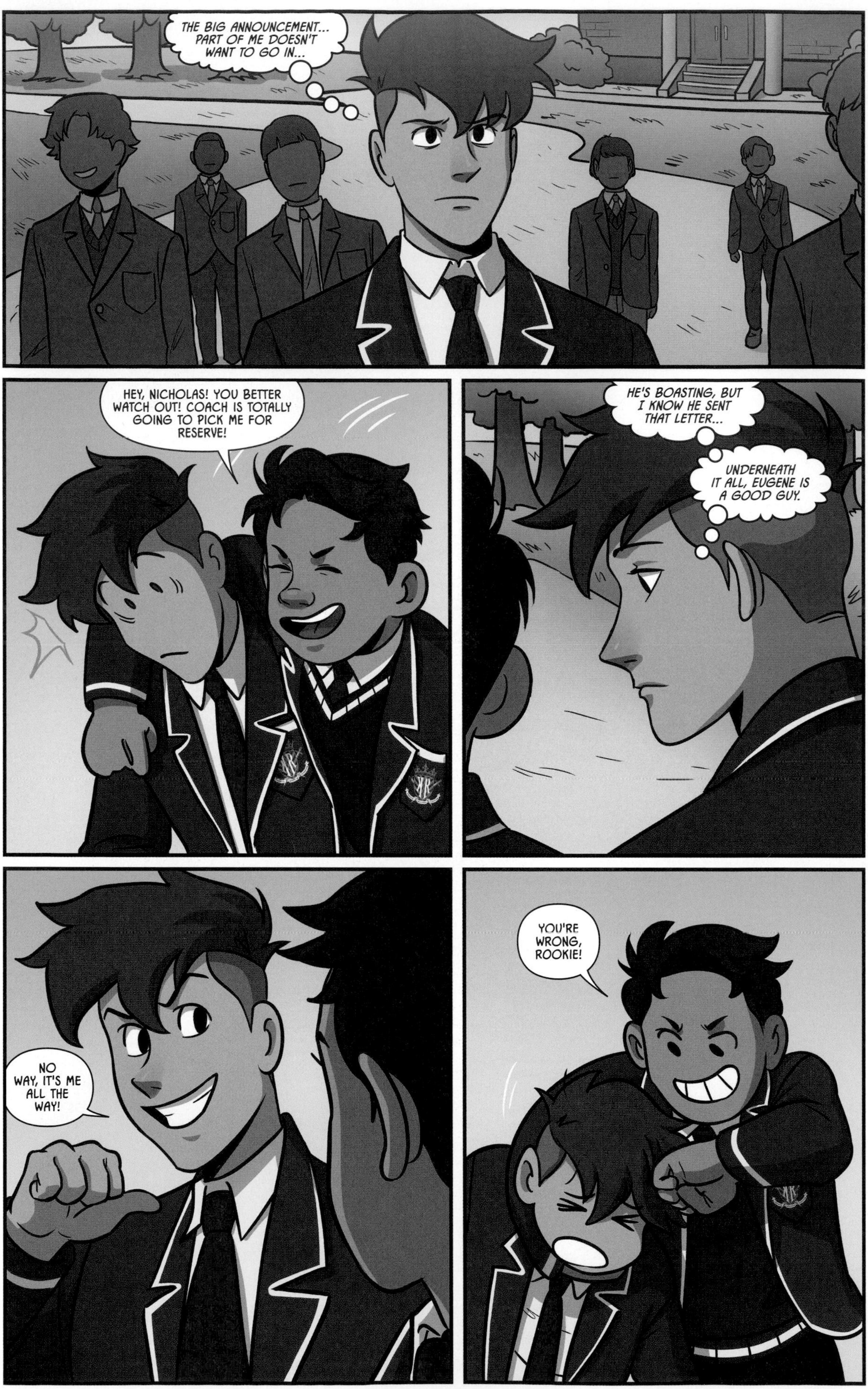
THE BIG ANNOUNCEMENT... PART OF ME DOESN'T WANT TO GO IN...
HEY, NICHOLAS! YOU BETTER WATCH OUT! COACH IS TOTALLY GOING TO PICK ME FOR RESERVE!
HE'S BOASTING, BUT I KNOW HE SENT THAT LETTER...
UNDERNEATH IT ALL, EUGENE IS A GOOD GUY.
NO WAY, IT'S ME ALL THE WAY!
YOU'RE WRONG, ROOKIE!

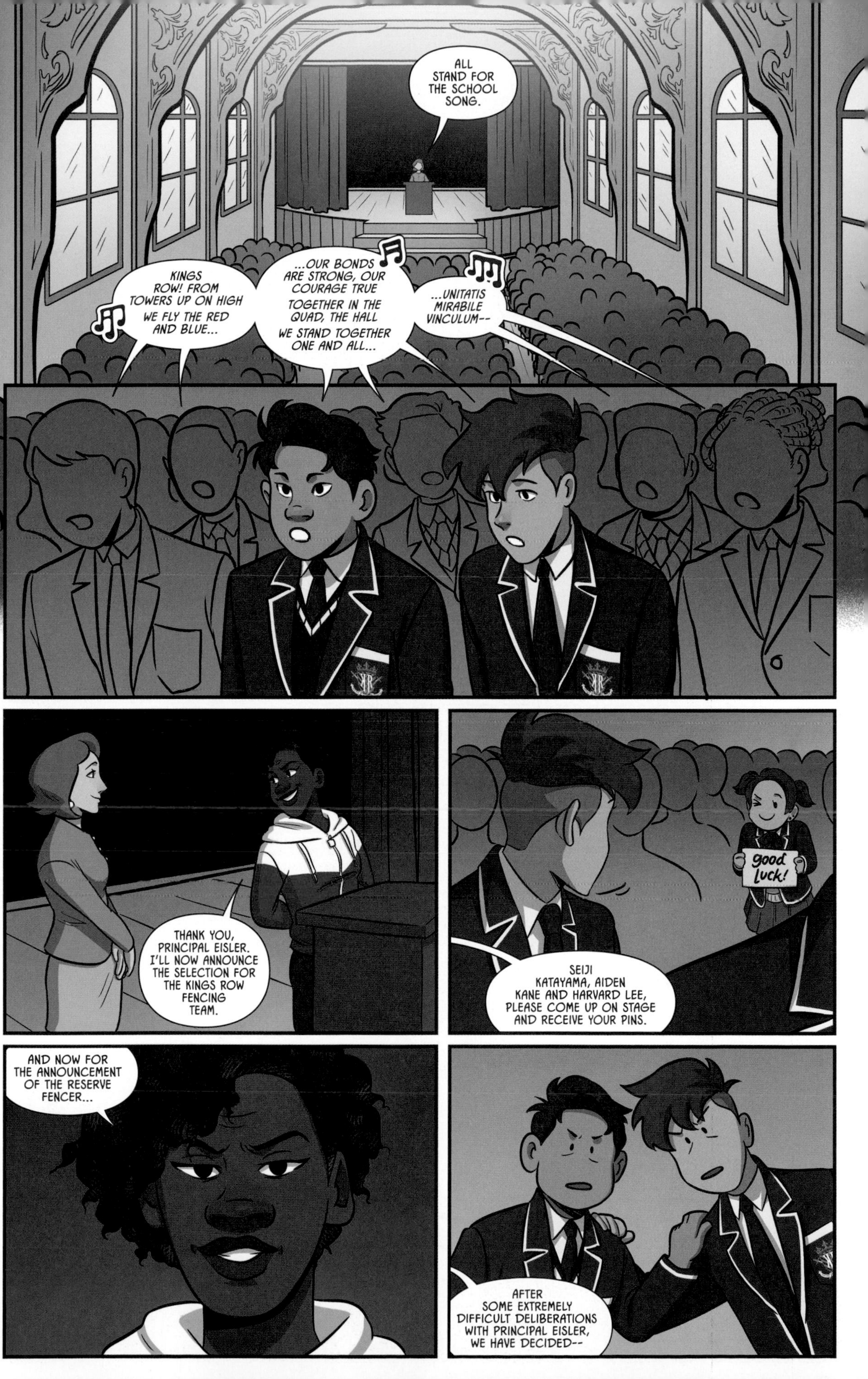
ALL STAND FOR THE SCHOOL SONG.
KINGS ROW! FROM TOWERS UP ON HIGH WE FLY THE RED AND BLUE...
...OUR BONDS ARE STRONG, OUR COURAGE TRUE TOGETHER IN THE QUAD, THE HALL WE STAND TOGETHER ONE AND ALL...
...UNITATIS MIRABILE VINCULUM--
THANK YOU, PRINCIPAL EISLER. I'LL NOW ANNOUNCE THE SELECTION FOR THE KINGS ROW FENCING TEAM.
good luck!
SEIJI KATAYAMA, AIDEN KANE AND HARVARD LEE, PLEASE COME UP ON STAGE AND RECEIVE YOUR PINS.
AND NOW FOR THE ANNOUNCEMENT OF THE RESERVE FENCER...
AFTER SOME EXTREMELY DIFFICULT DELIBERATIONS WITH PRINCIPAL EISLER, WE HAVE DECIDED--

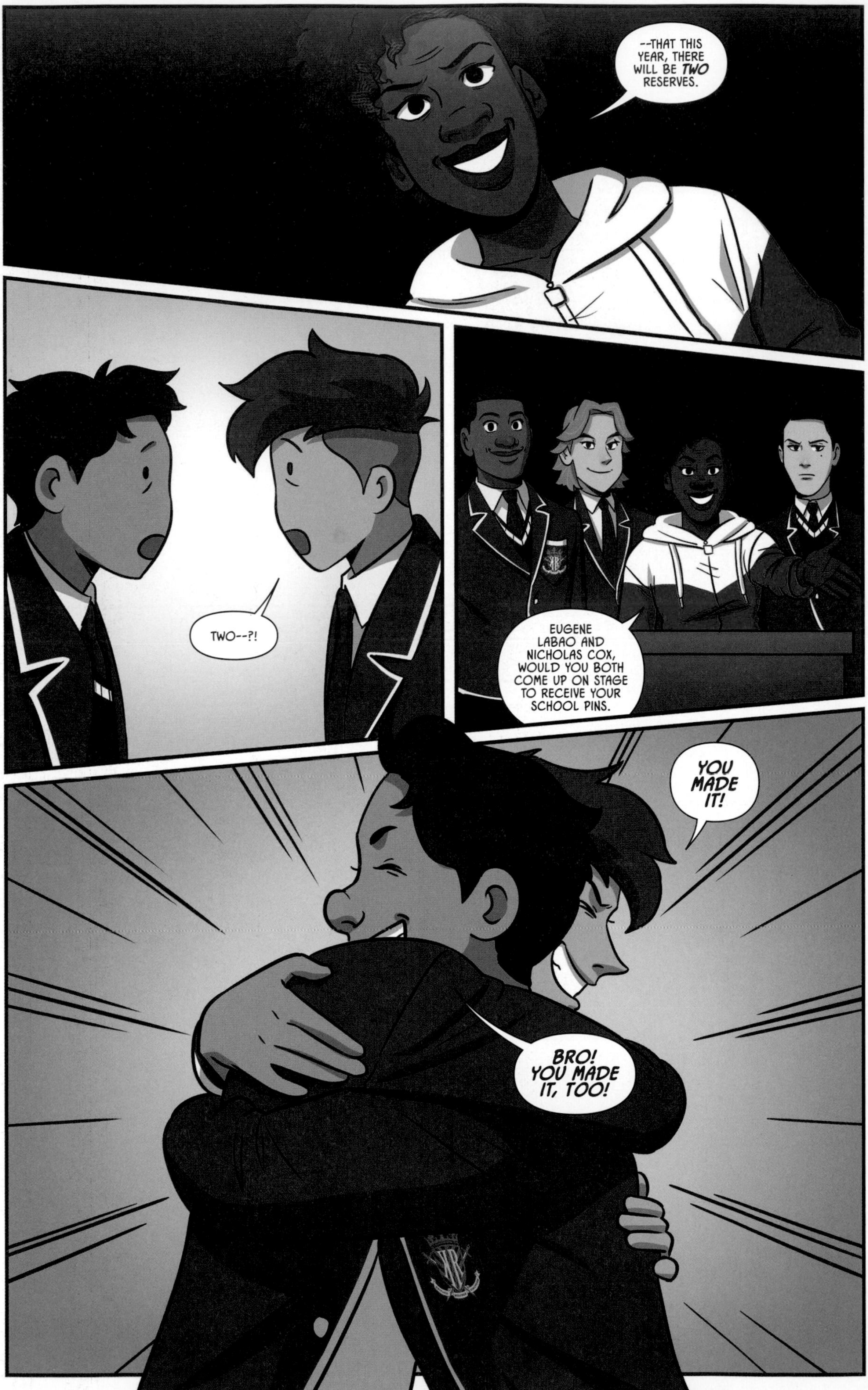
--THAT THIS YEAR, THERE WILL BE *TWO* RESERVES.
TWO--?!
EUGENE LABAO AND NICHOLAS COX, WOULD YOU BOTH COME UP ON STAGE TO RECEIVE YOUR SCHOOL PINS.
YOU MADE IT!
BRO! YOU MADE IT, TOO!

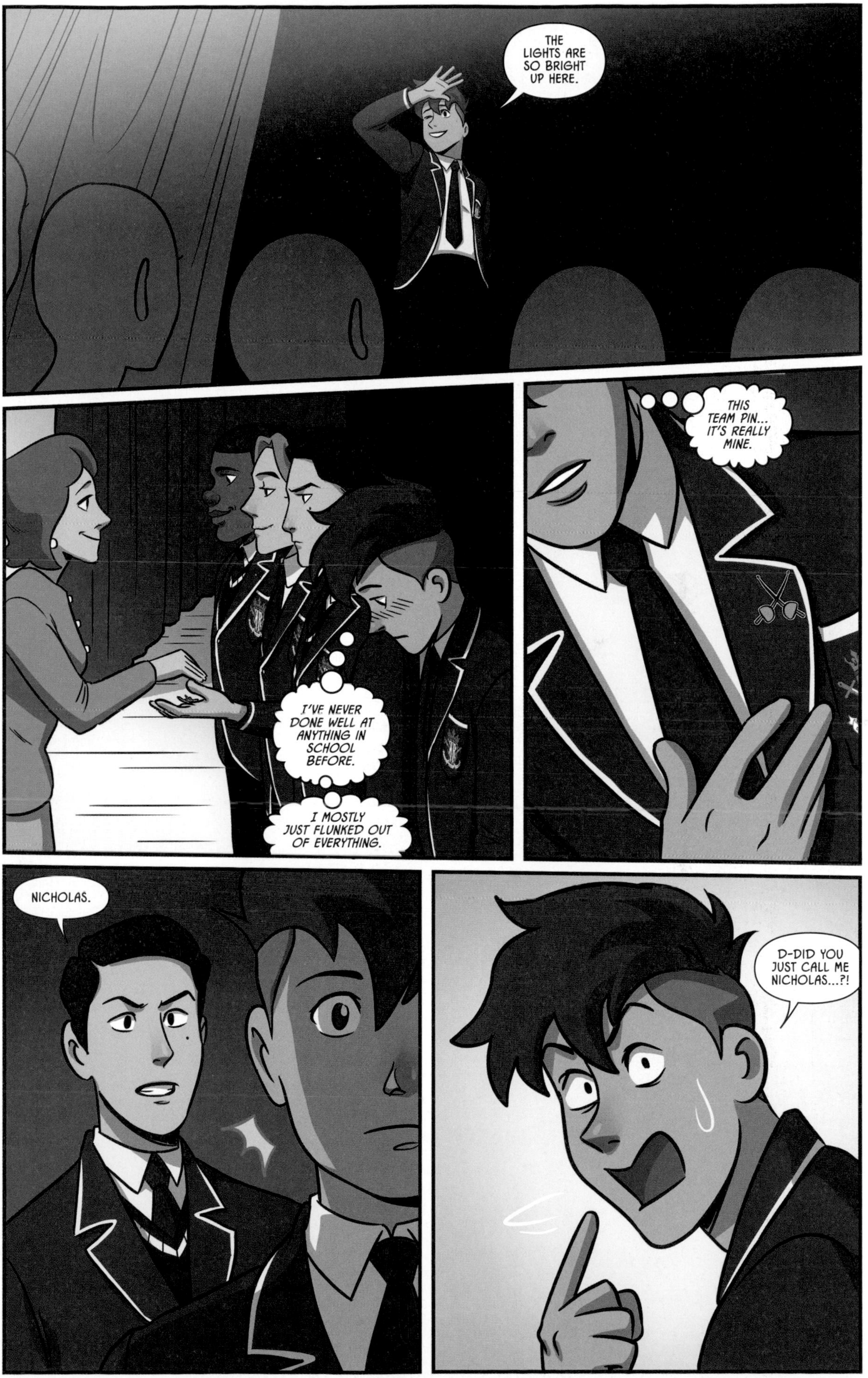
THE LIGHTS ARE SO BRIGHT UP HERE.
I'VE NEVER DONE WELL AT ANYTHING IN SCHOOL BEFORE.
I MOSTLY JUST FLUNKED OUT OF EVERYTHING.
THIS TEAM PIN... IT'S REALLY MINE.
NICHOLAS.
D-DID YOU JUST CALL ME NICHOLAS...?!

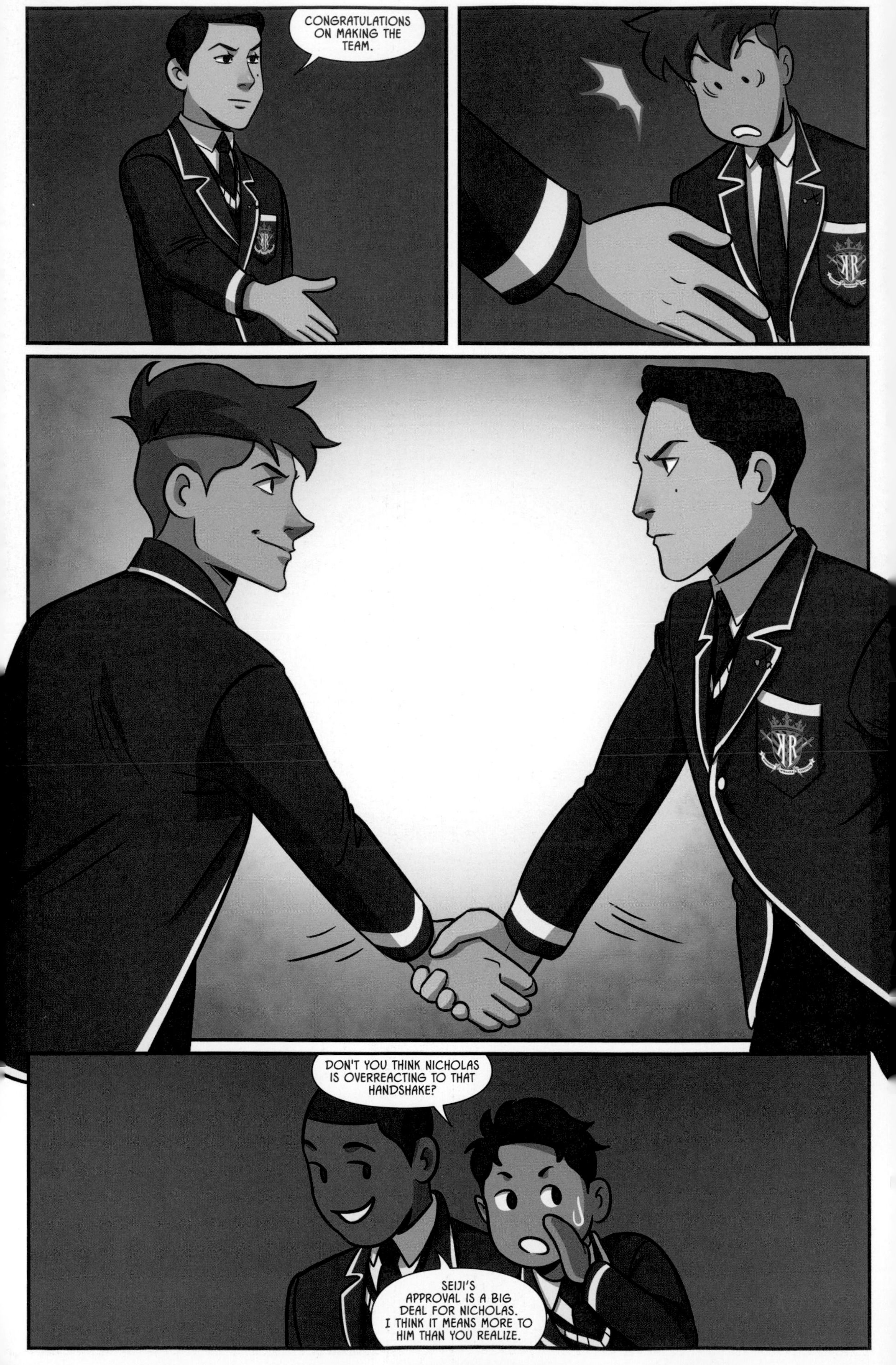
CONGRATULATIONS ON MAKING THE TEAM.
DON'T YOU THINK NICHOLAS IS OVERREACTING TO THAT HANDSHAKE?
SEIJI'S APPROVAL IS A BIG DEAL FOR NICHOLAS. I THINK IT MEANS MORE TO HIM THAN YOU REALIZE.

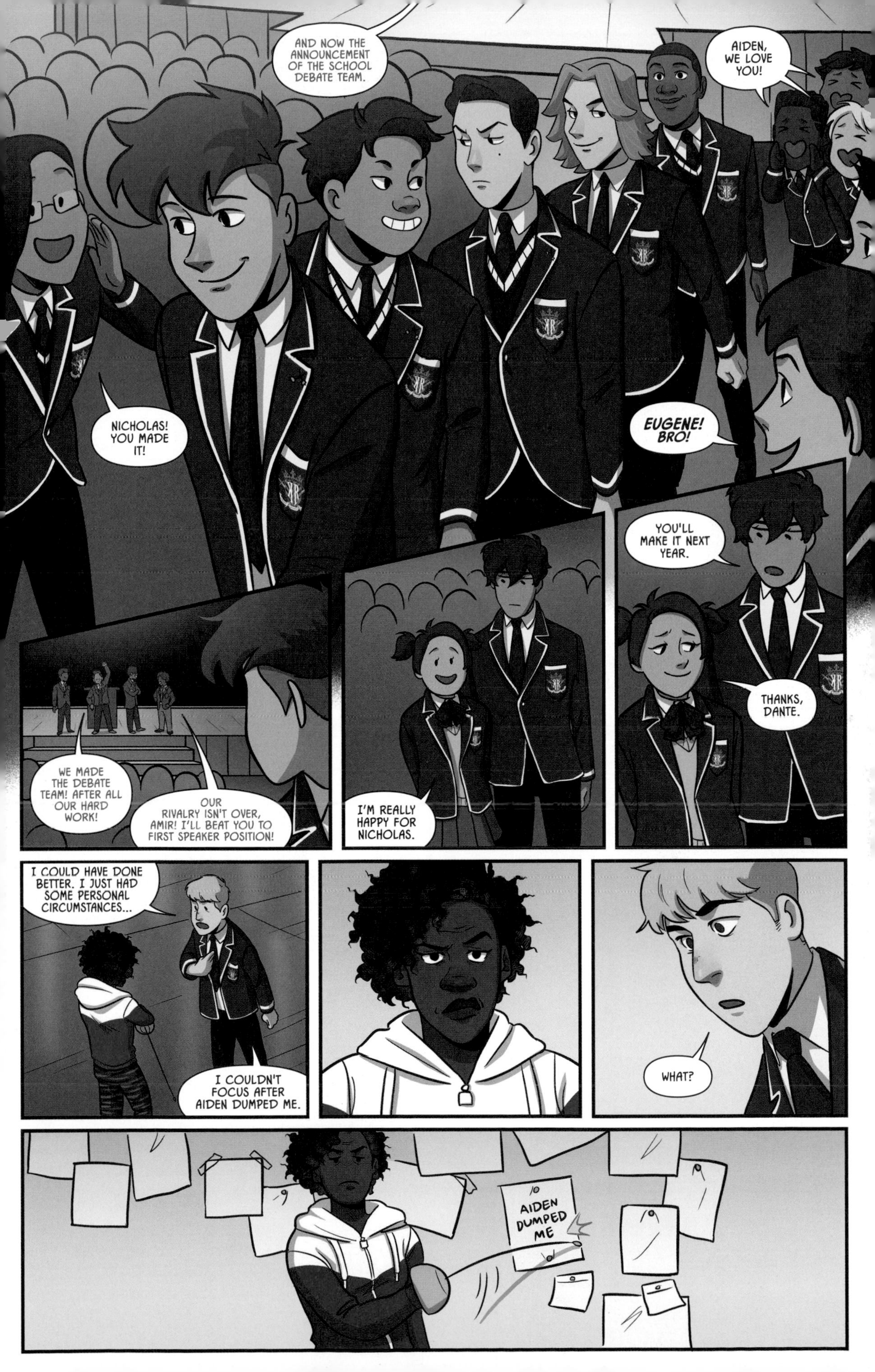

AND NOW THE ANNOUNCEMENT OF THE SCHOOL DEBATE TEAM.
AIDEN, WE LOVE YOU!
NICHOLAS! YOU MADE IT!
EUGENE! BRO!
WE MADE THE DEBATE TEAM! AFTER ALL OUR HARD WORK!
OUR RIVALRY ISN'T OVER, AMIR! I'LL BEAT YOU TO FIRST SPEAKER POSITION!
I'M REALLY HAPPY FOR NICHOLAS.
YOU'LL MAKE IT NEXT YEAR.
THANKS, DANTE.
I COULD HAVE DONE BETTER. I JUST HAD SOME PERSONAL CIRCUMSTANCES...
I COULDN'T FOCUS AFTER AIDEN DUMPED ME.
WHAT?
10
AIDEN DUMPED ME

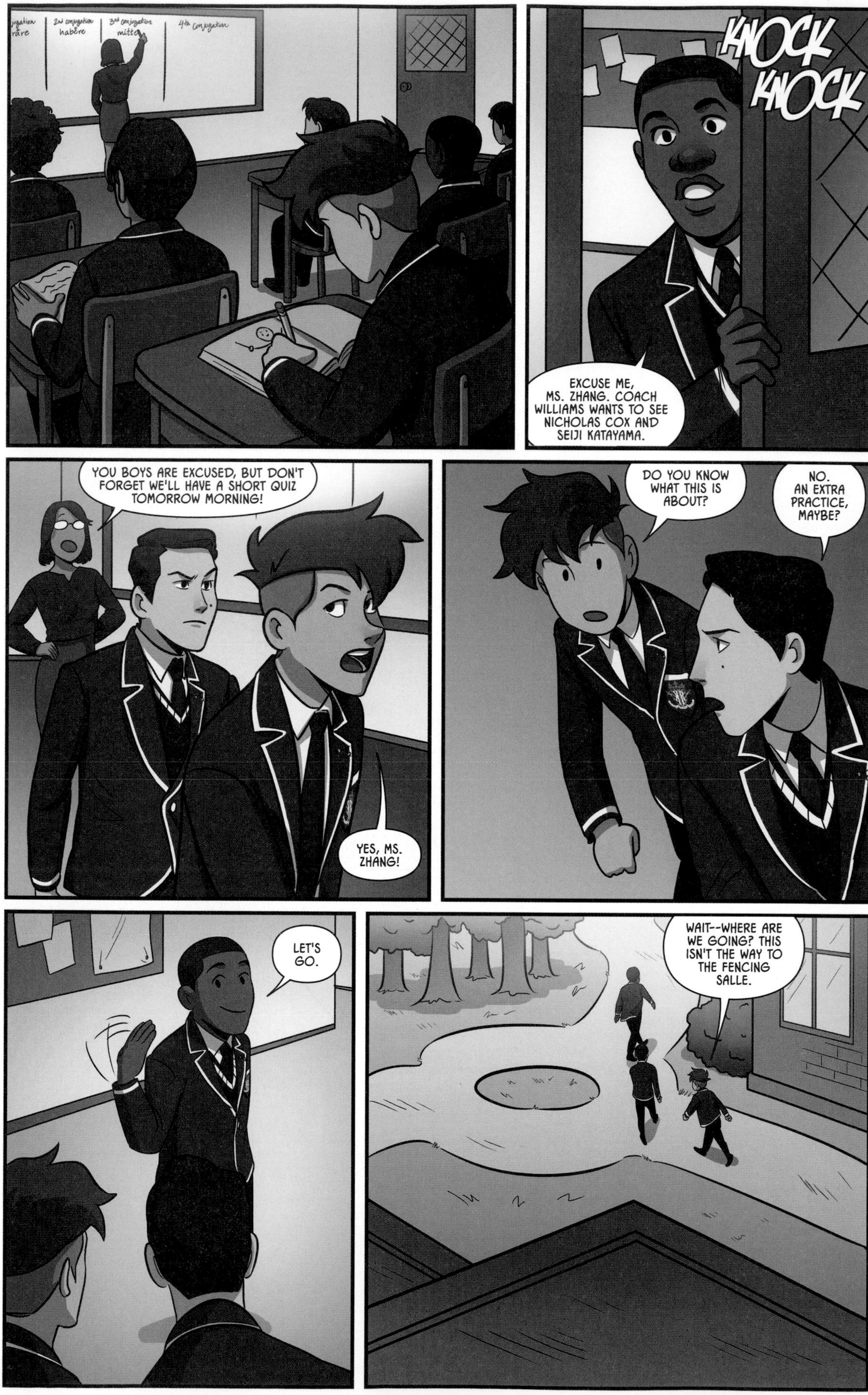
2nd conjugation habēre
3rd conjugation
4th conjugation
KNOCK KNOCK
EXCUSE ME, MS. ZHANG. COACH WILLIAMS WANTS TO SEE NICHOLAS COX AND SEIJI KATAYAMA.
YOU BOYS ARE EXCUSED, BUT DON'T FORGET WE'LL HAVE A SHORT QUIZ TOMORROW MORNING!
YES, MS. ZHANG!
DO YOU KNOW WHAT THIS IS ABOUT?
NO. AN EXTRA PRACTICE, MAYBE?
LET'S GO.
WAIT--WHERE ARE WE GOING? THIS ISN'T THE WAY TO THE FENCING SALLE.

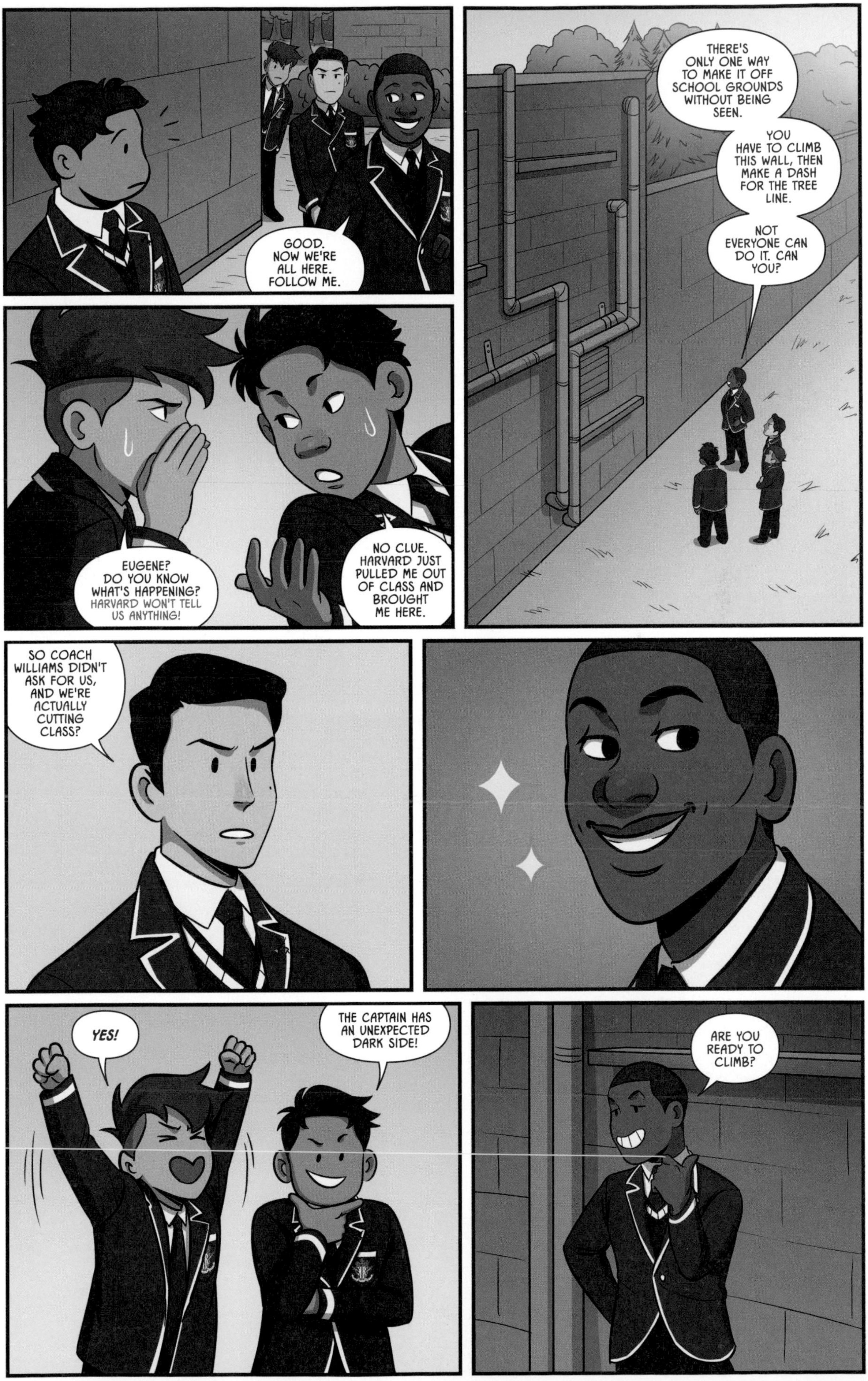
GOOD. NOW WE'RE ALL HERE. FOLLOW ME.
EUGENE? DO YOU KNOW WHAT'S HAPPENING? HARVARD WON'T TELL US ANYTHING!
NO CLUE. HARVARD JUST PULLED ME OUT OF CLASS AND BROUGHT ME HERE.
THERE'S ONLY ONE WAY TO MAKE IT OFF SCHOOL GROUNDS WITHOUT BEING SEEN.
YOU HAVE TO CLIMB THIS WALL, THEN MAKE A DASH FOR THE TREE LINE.
NOT EVERYONE CAN DO IT. CAN YOU?
SO COACH WILLIAMS DIDN'T ASK FOR US, AND WE'RE ACTUALLY CUTTING CLASS?
YES!
THE CAPTAIN HAS AN UNEXPECTED DARK SIDE!
ARE YOU READY TO CLIMB?

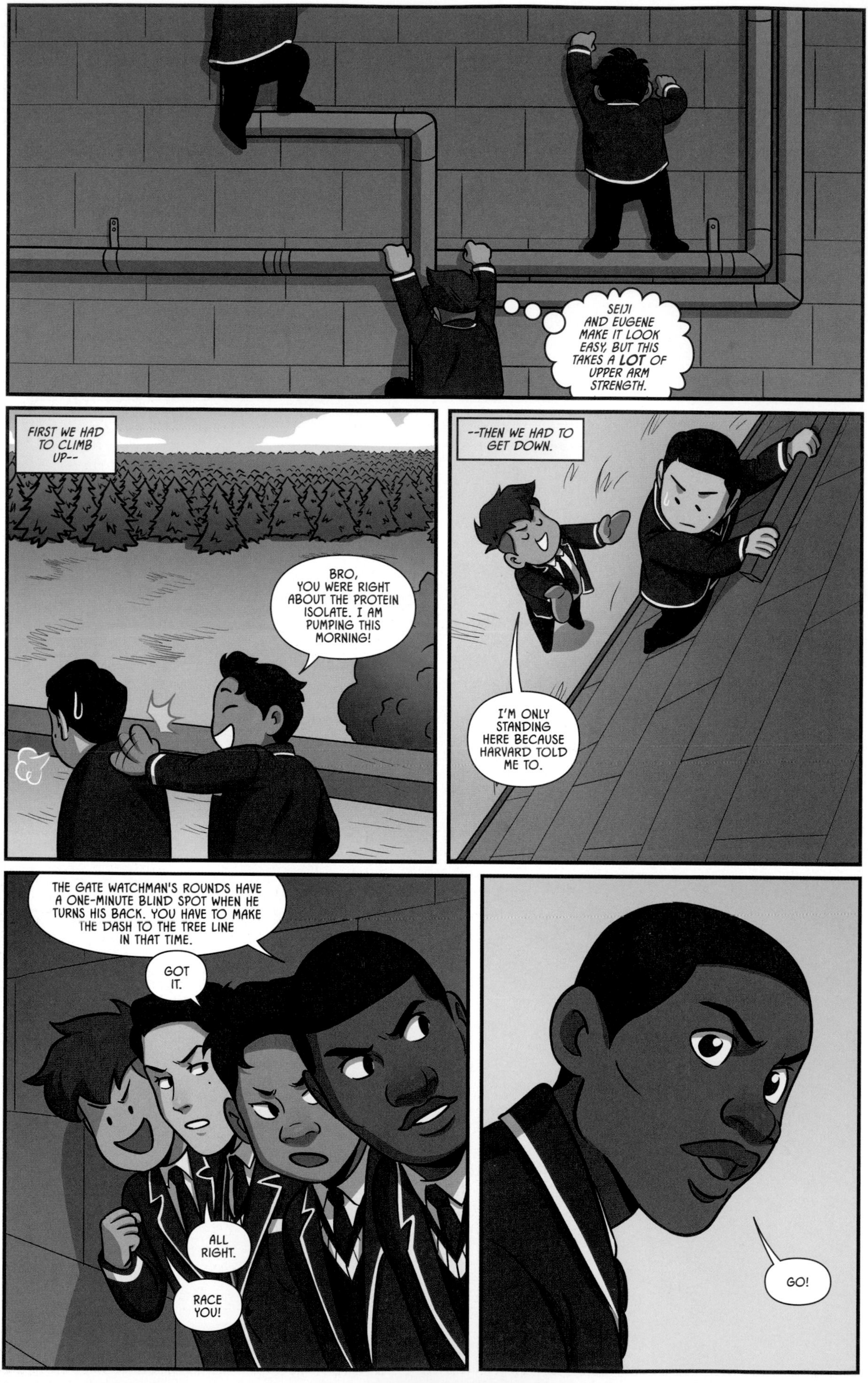
SEIJI AND EUGENE MAKE IT LOOK EASY, BUT THIS TAKES A **LOT** OF UPPER ARM STRENGTH.
FIRST WE HAD TO CLIMB UP--
BRO, YOU WERE RIGHT ABOUT THE PROTEIN ISOLATE. I AM PUMPING THIS MORNING!
--THEN WE HAD TO GET DOWN.
I'M ONLY STANDING HERE BECAUSE HARVARD TOLD ME TO.
THE GATE WATCHMAN'S ROUNDS HAVE A ONE-MINUTE BLIND SPOT WHEN HE TURNS HIS BACK. YOU HAVE TO MAKE THE DASH TO THE TREE LINE IN THAT TIME.
GOT IT.
ALL RIGHT.
RACE YOU!
GO!

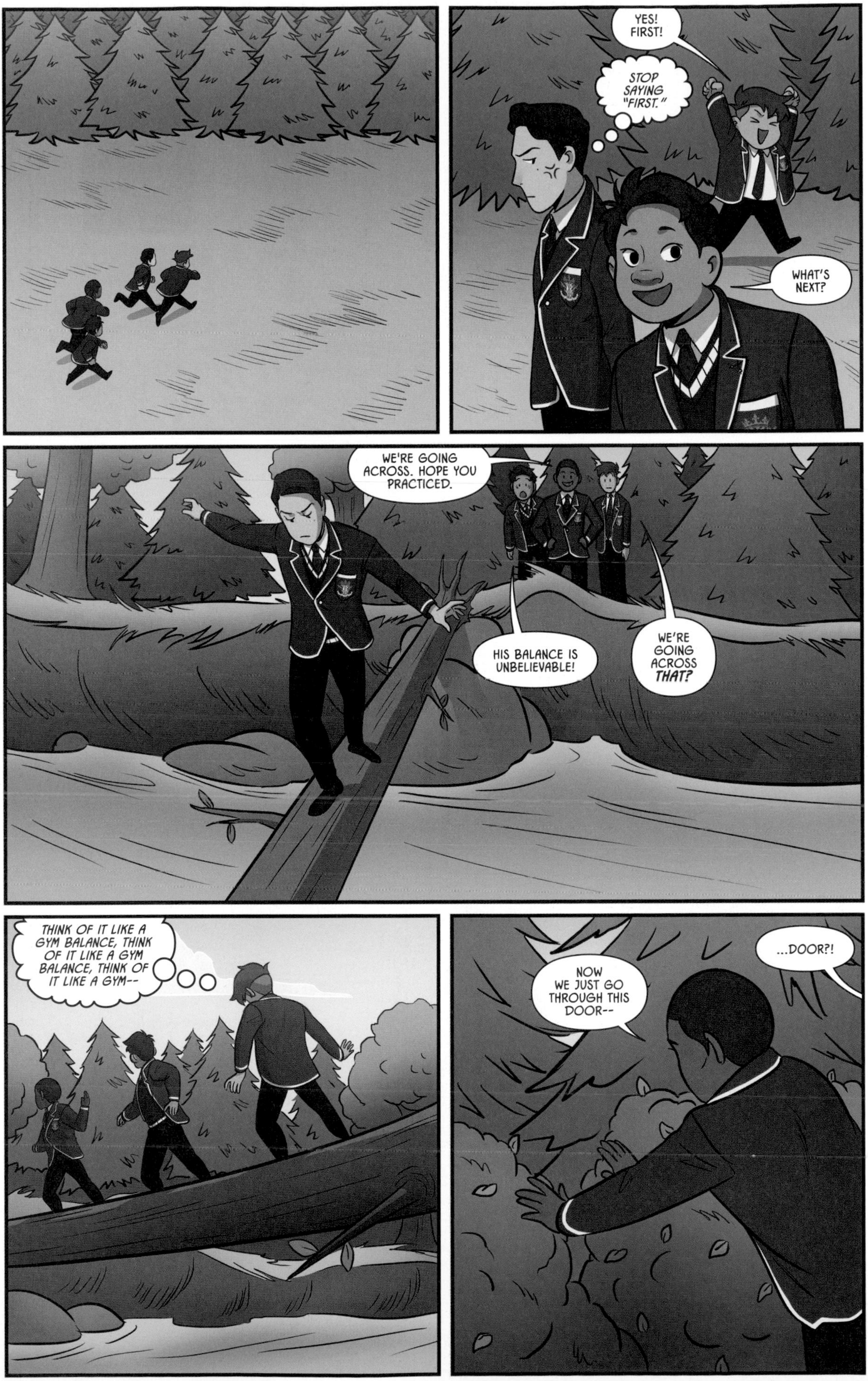
YES! FIRST!
STOP SAYING "FIRST."
WHAT'S NEXT?
WE'RE GOING ACROSS. HOPE YOU PRACTICED.
HIS BALANCE IS UNBELIEVABLE!
WE'RE GOING ACROSS THAT?
THINK OF IT LIKE A GYM BALANCE, THINK OF IT LIKE A GYM BALANCE, THINK OF IT LIKE A GYM--
NOW WE JUST GO THROUGH THIS DOOR--
...DOOR?!

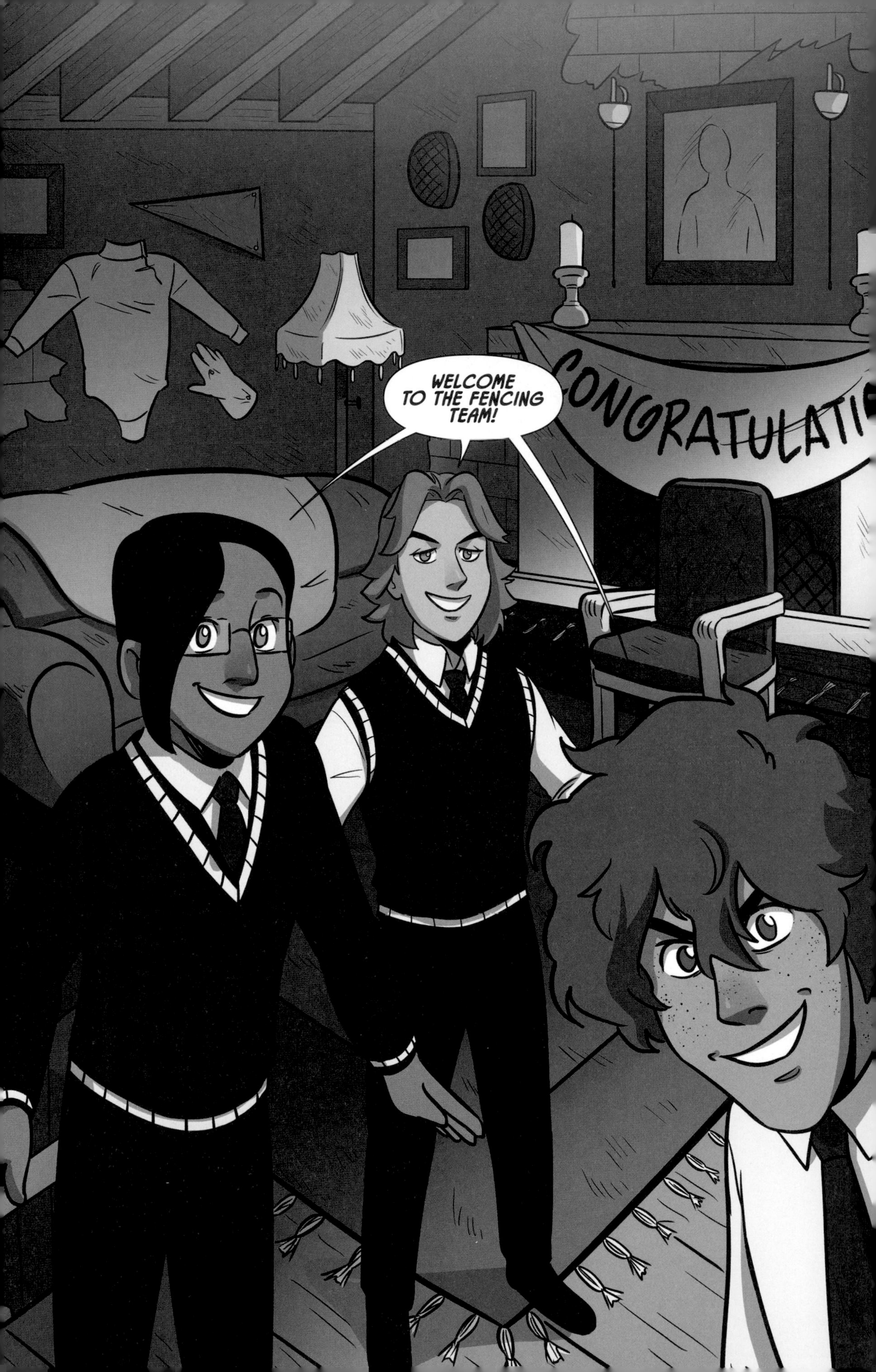
WELCOME TO THE FENCING TEAM!
CONGRATULATI

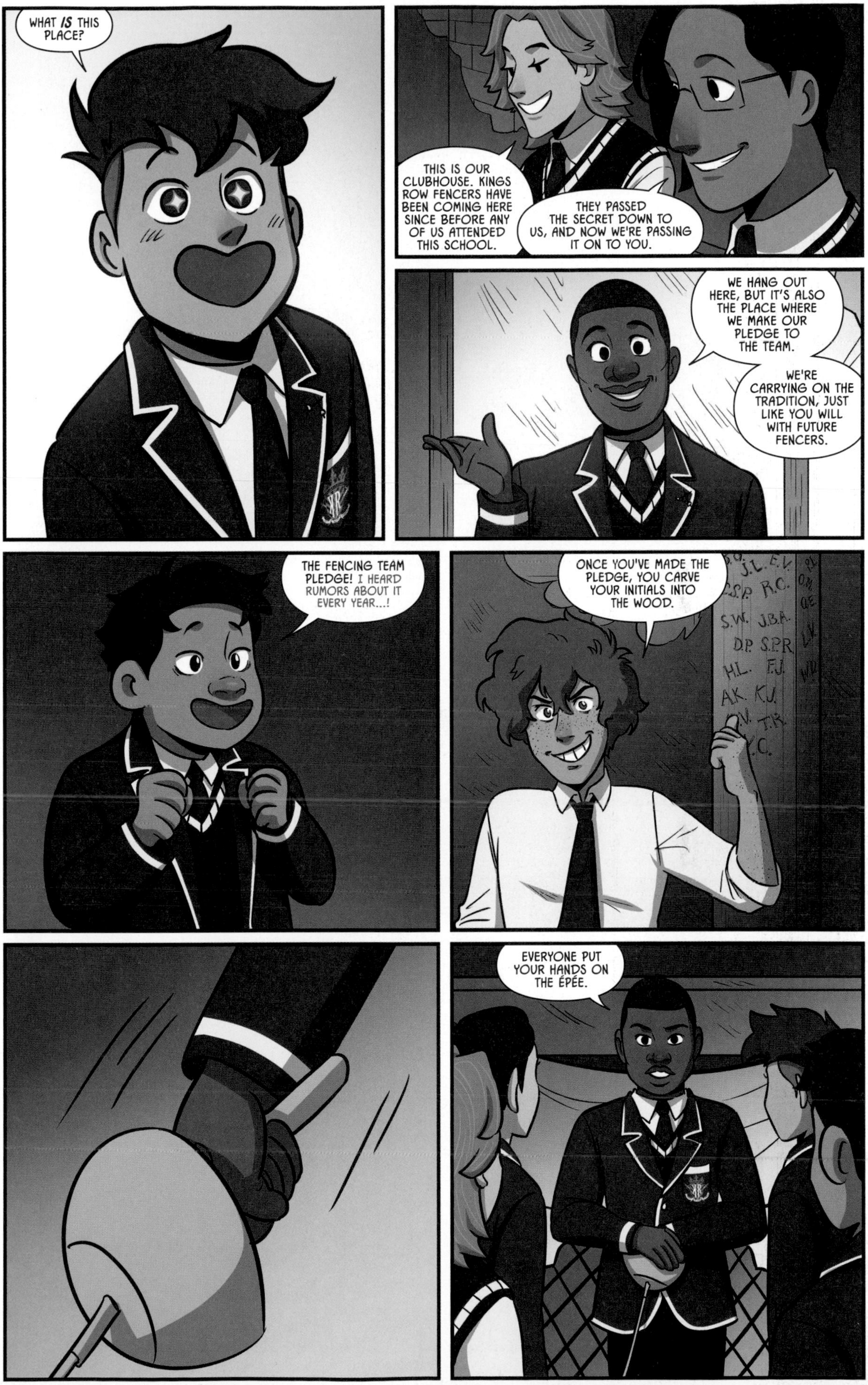
WHAT IS THIS PLACE?
THIS IS OUR CLUBHOUSE. KINGS ROW FENCERS HAVE BEEN COMING HERE SINCE BEFORE ANY OF US ATTENDED THIS SCHOOL.
THEY PASSED THE SECRET DOWN TO US, AND NOW WE'RE PASSING IT ON TO YOU.
WE HANG OUT HERE, BUT IT'S ALSO THE PLACE WHERE WE MAKE OUR PLEDGE TO THE TEAM.
WE'RE CARRYING ON THE TRADITION, JUST LIKE YOU WILL WITH FUTURE FENCERS.
THE FENCING TEAM PLEDGE! I HEARD RUMORS ABOUT IT EVERY YEAR...!
ONCE YOU'VE MADE THE PLEDGE, YOU CARVE YOUR INITIALS INTO THE WOOD.
EVERYONE PUT YOUR HANDS ON THE ÉPÉE.

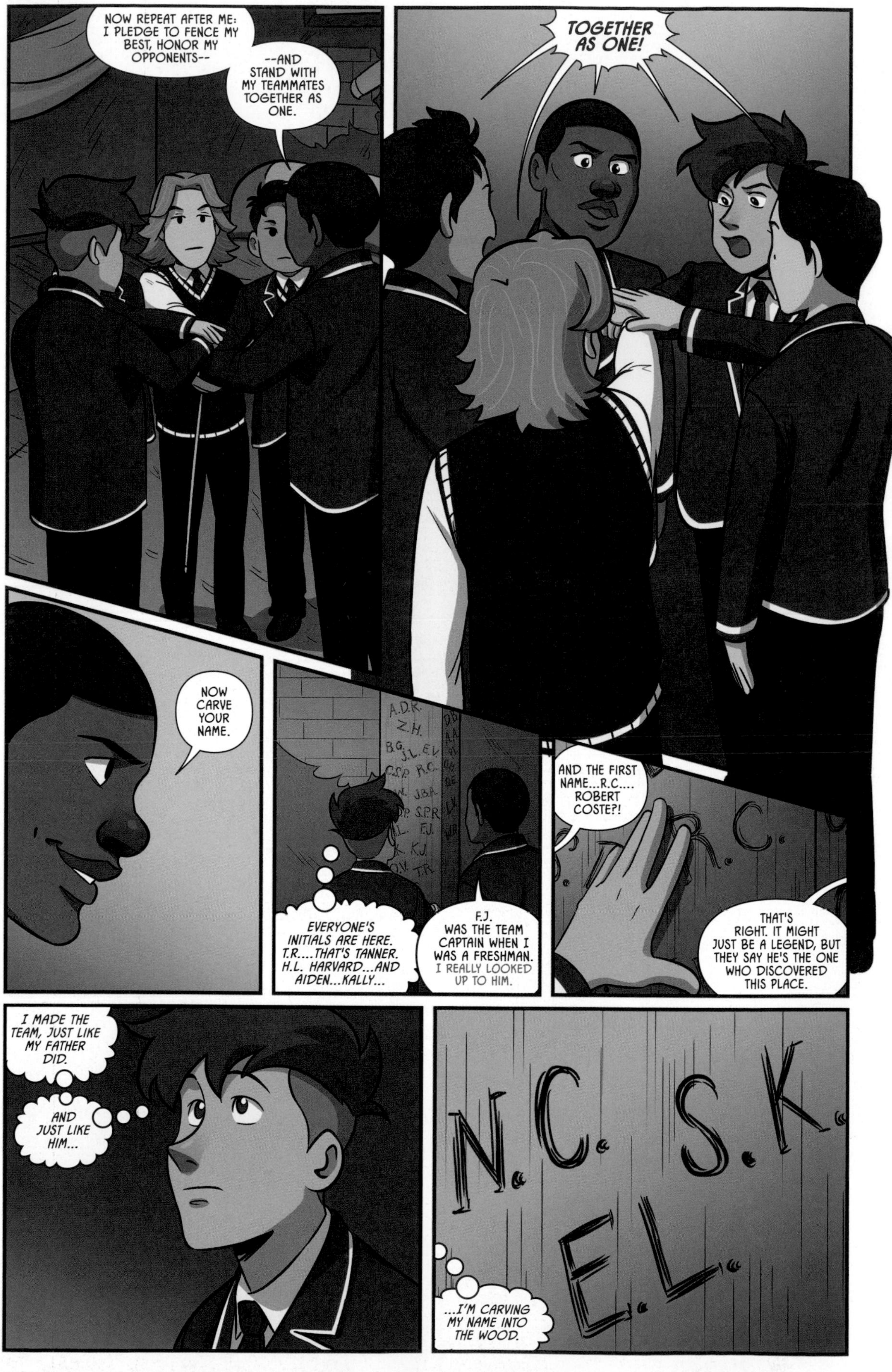
NOW REPEAT AFTER ME: I PLEDGE TO FENCE MY BEST, HONOR MY OPPONENTS--
--AND STAND WITH MY TEAMMATES TOGETHER AS ONE.
TOGETHER AS ONE!
NOW CARVE YOUR NAME.
EVERYONE'S INITIALS ARE HERE. T.R.... THAT'S TANNER. H.L. HARVARD... AND AIDEN... KALLY...
F.J. WAS THE TEAM CAPTAIN WHEN I WAS A FRESHMAN. I REALLY LOOKED UP TO HIM.
AND THE FIRST NAME... R.C.... ROBERT COSTE?!
THAT'S RIGHT. IT MIGHT JUST BE A LEGEND, BUT THEY SAY HE'S THE ONE WHO DISCOVERED THIS PLACE.
I MADE THE TEAM, JUST LIKE MY FATHER DID.
AND JUST LIKE HIM...
N.C. S.K.
E.L.
...I'M CARVING MY NAME INTO THE WOOD.

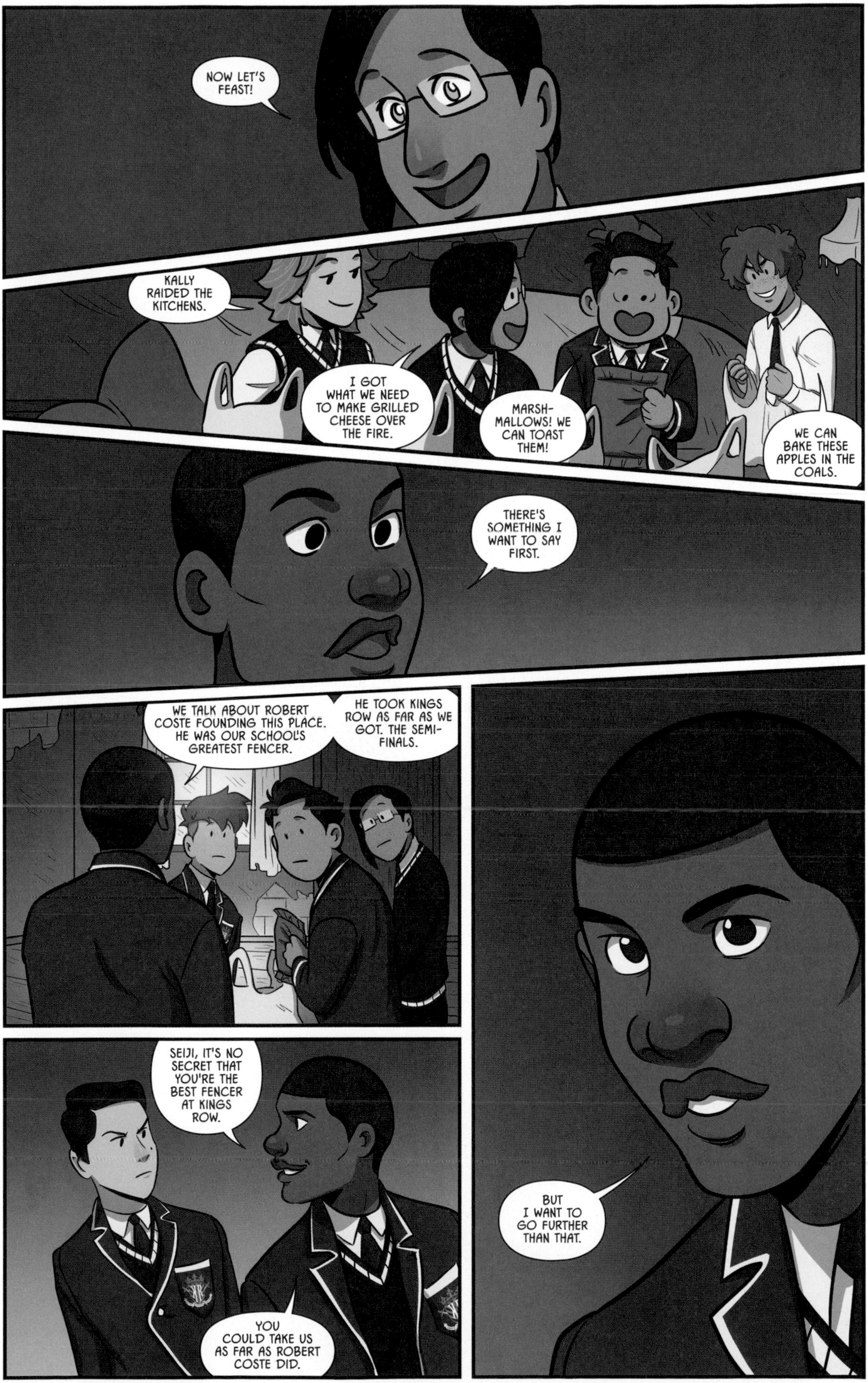
NOW LET'S FEAST!
KALLY RAIDED THE KITCHENS.
I GOT WHAT WE NEED TO MAKE GRILLED CHEESE OVER THE FIRE.
MARSH-MALLOWS! WE CAN TOAST THEM!
WE CAN BAKE THESE APPLES IN THE COALS.
THERE'S SOMETHING I WANT TO SAY FIRST.
WE TALK ABOUT ROBERT COSTE FOUNDING THIS PLACE. HE WAS OUR SCHOOL'S GREATEST FENCER.
HE TOOK KINGS ROW AS FAR AS WE GOT. THE SEMI-FINALS.
SEIJI, IT'S NO SECRET THAT YOU'RE THE BEST FENCER AT KINGS ROW.
YOU COULD TAKE US AS FAR AS ROBERT COSTE DID.
BUT I WANT TO GO FURTHER THAN THAT.

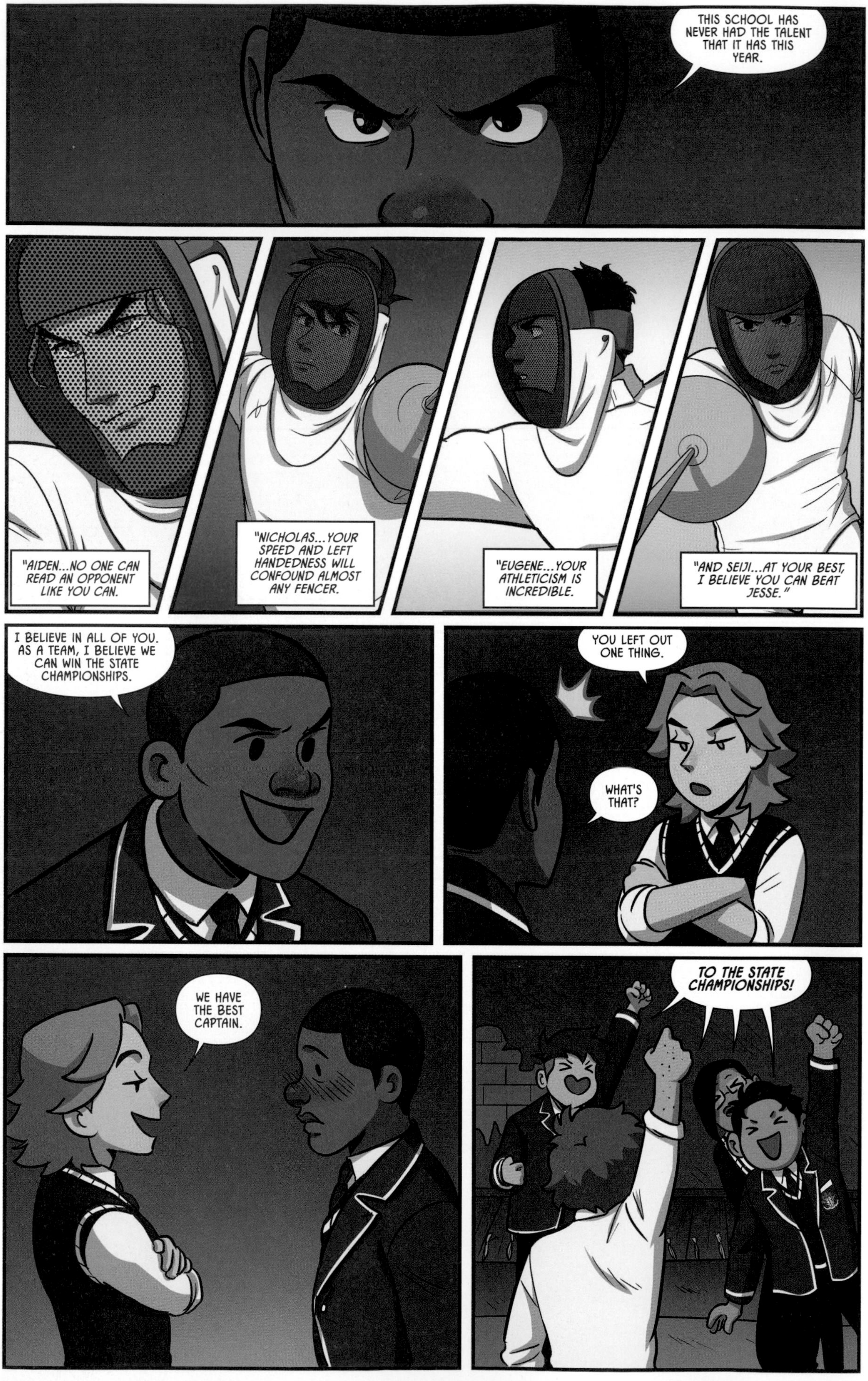
THIS SCHOOL HAS NEVER HAD THE TALENT THAT IT HAS THIS YEAR.
"AIDEN...NO ONE CAN READ AN OPPONENT LIKE YOU CAN.
"NICHOLAS...YOUR SPEED AND LEFT HANDEDNESS WILL CONFOUND ALMOST ANY FENCER.
"EUGENE...YOUR ATHLETICISM IS INCREDIBLE.
"AND SEIJI...AT YOUR BEST, I BELIEVE YOU CAN BEAT JESSE."
I BELIEVE IN ALL OF YOU. AS A TEAM, I BELIEVE WE CAN WIN THE STATE CHAMPIONSHIPS.
YOU LEFT OUT ONE THING.
WHAT'S THAT?
WE HAVE THE BEST CAPTAIN.
TO THE STATE CHAMPIONSHIPS!

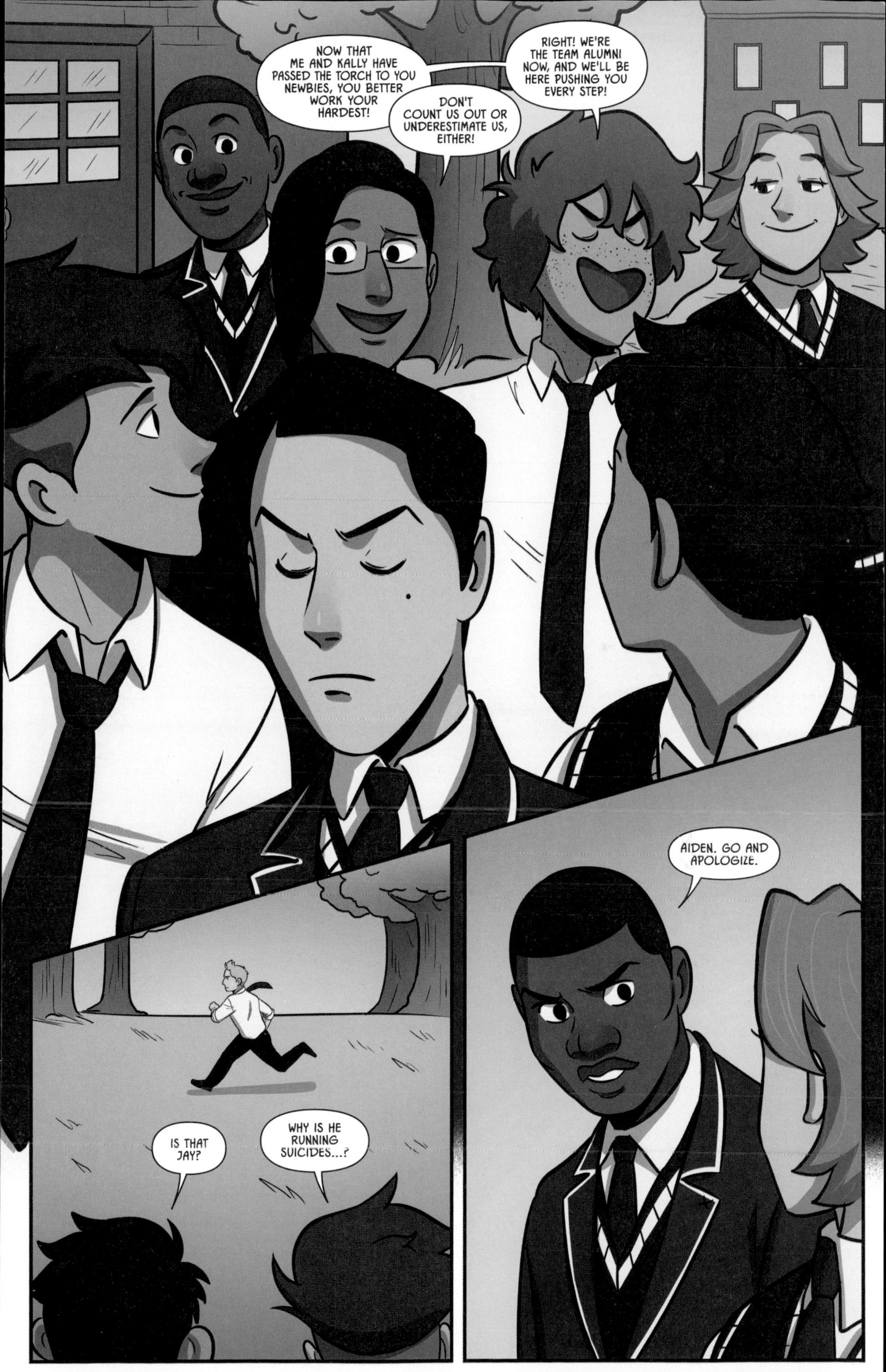
NOW THAT ME AND KALLY HAVE PASSED THE TORCH TO YOU NEWBIES, YOU BETTER WORK YOUR HARDEST!
DON'T COUNT US OUT OR UNDERESTIMATE US, EITHER!
RIGHT! WE'RE THE TEAM ALUMNI NOW, AND WE'LL BE HERE PUSHING YOU EVERY STEP!
IS THAT JAY?
WHY IS HE RUNNING SUICIDES...?
AIDEN. GO AND APOLOGIZE.

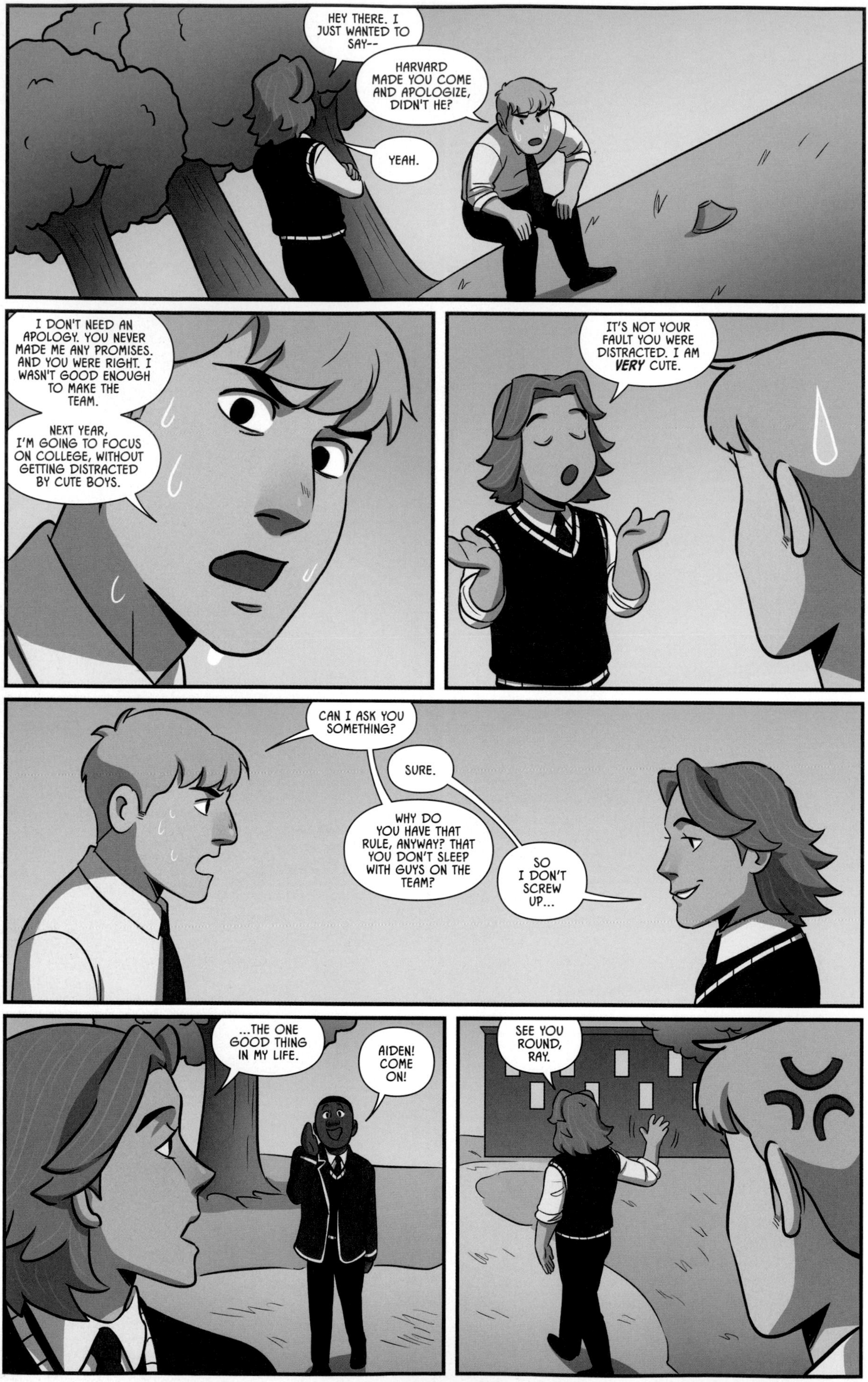
HEY THERE. I JUST WANTED TO SAY--
HARVARD MADE YOU COME AND APOLOGIZE, DIDN'T HE?
YEAH.
I DON'T NEED AN APOLOGY. YOU NEVER MADE ME ANY PROMISES. AND YOU WERE RIGHT. I WASN'T GOOD ENOUGH TO MAKE THE TEAM.
NEXT YEAR, I'M GOING TO FOCUS ON COLLEGE, WITHOUT GETTING DISTRACTED BY CUTE BOYS.
IT'S NOT YOUR FAULT YOU WERE DISTRACTED. I AM **VERY** CUTE.
CAN I ASK YOU SOMETHING?
SURE.
WHY DO YOU HAVE THAT RULE, ANYWAY? THAT YOU DON'T SLEEP WITH GUYS ON THE TEAM?
SO I DON'T SCREW UP...
...THE ONE GOOD THING IN MY LIFE.
AIDEN! COME ON!
SEE YOU ROUND, RAY.

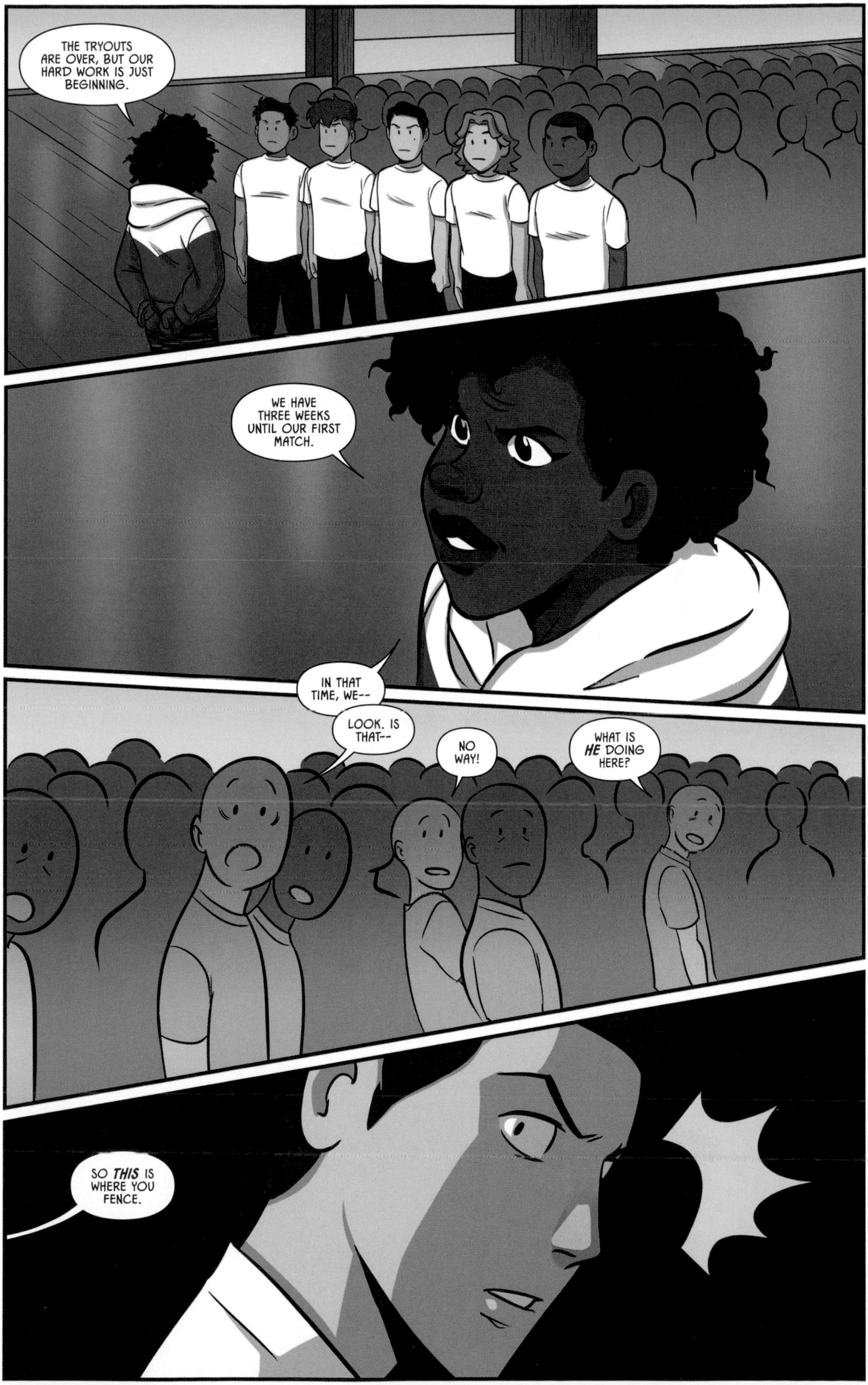

THE TRYOUTS ARE OVER, BUT OUR HARD WORK IS JUST BEGINNING.
WE HAVE THREE WEEKS UNTIL OUR FIRST MATCH.
IN THAT TIME, WE--
LOOK. IS THAT--
NO WAY!
WHAT IS *HE* DOING HERE?
SO *THIS* IS WHERE YOU FENCE.

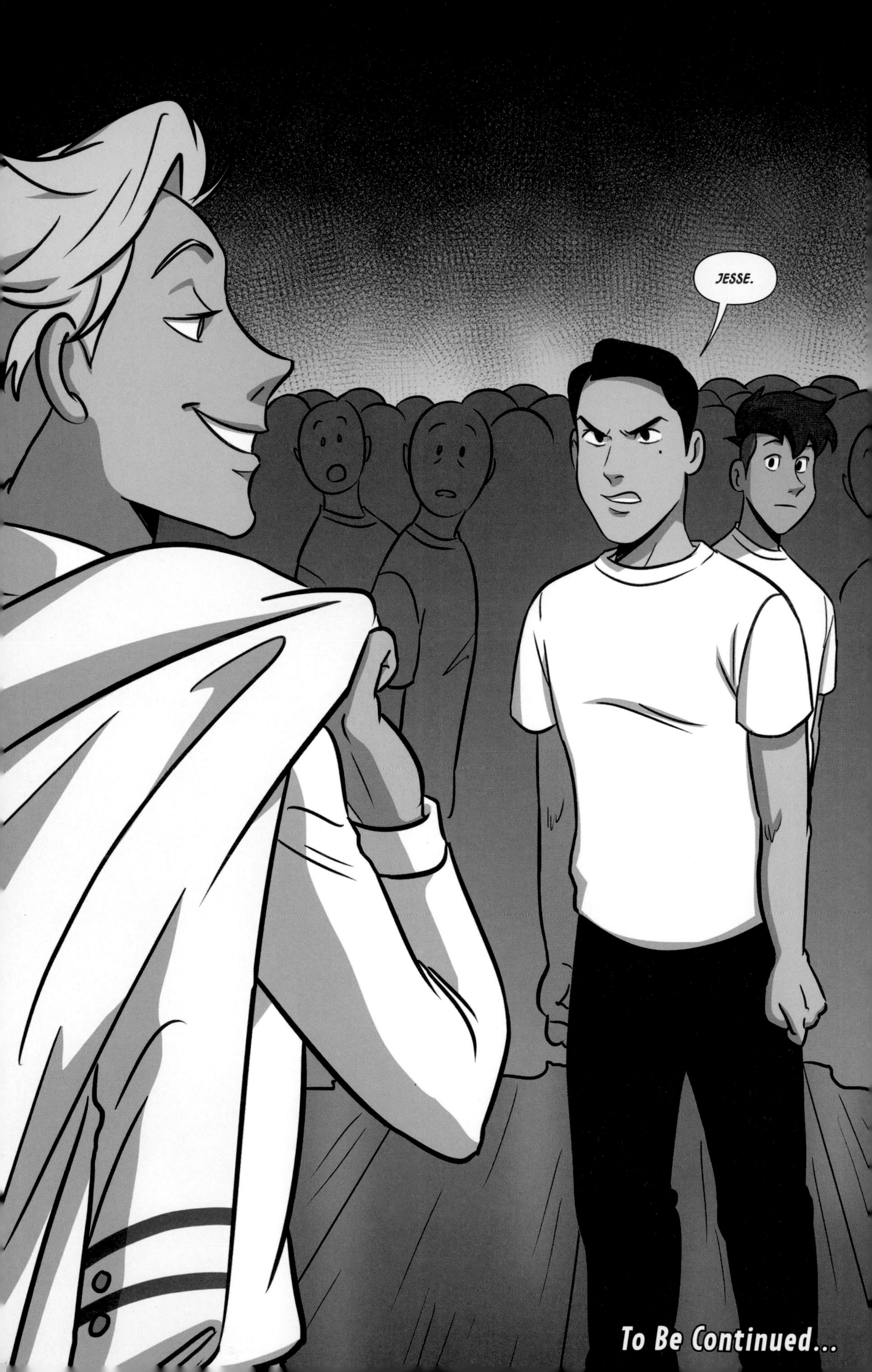
JESSE.
To Be Continued...

COVER
Gallery

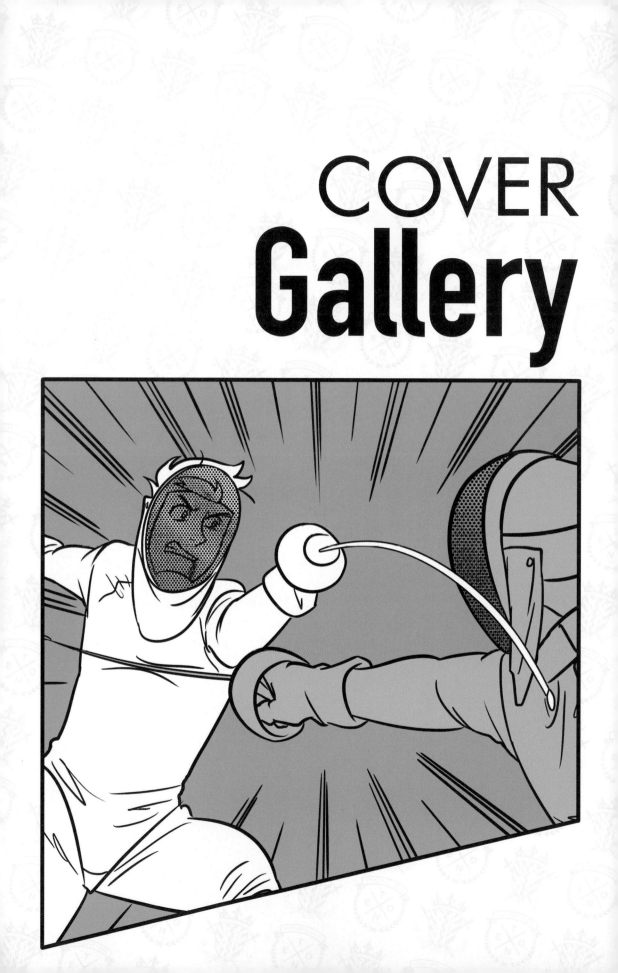

ISSUE 09 COVER BY
HamletMachine

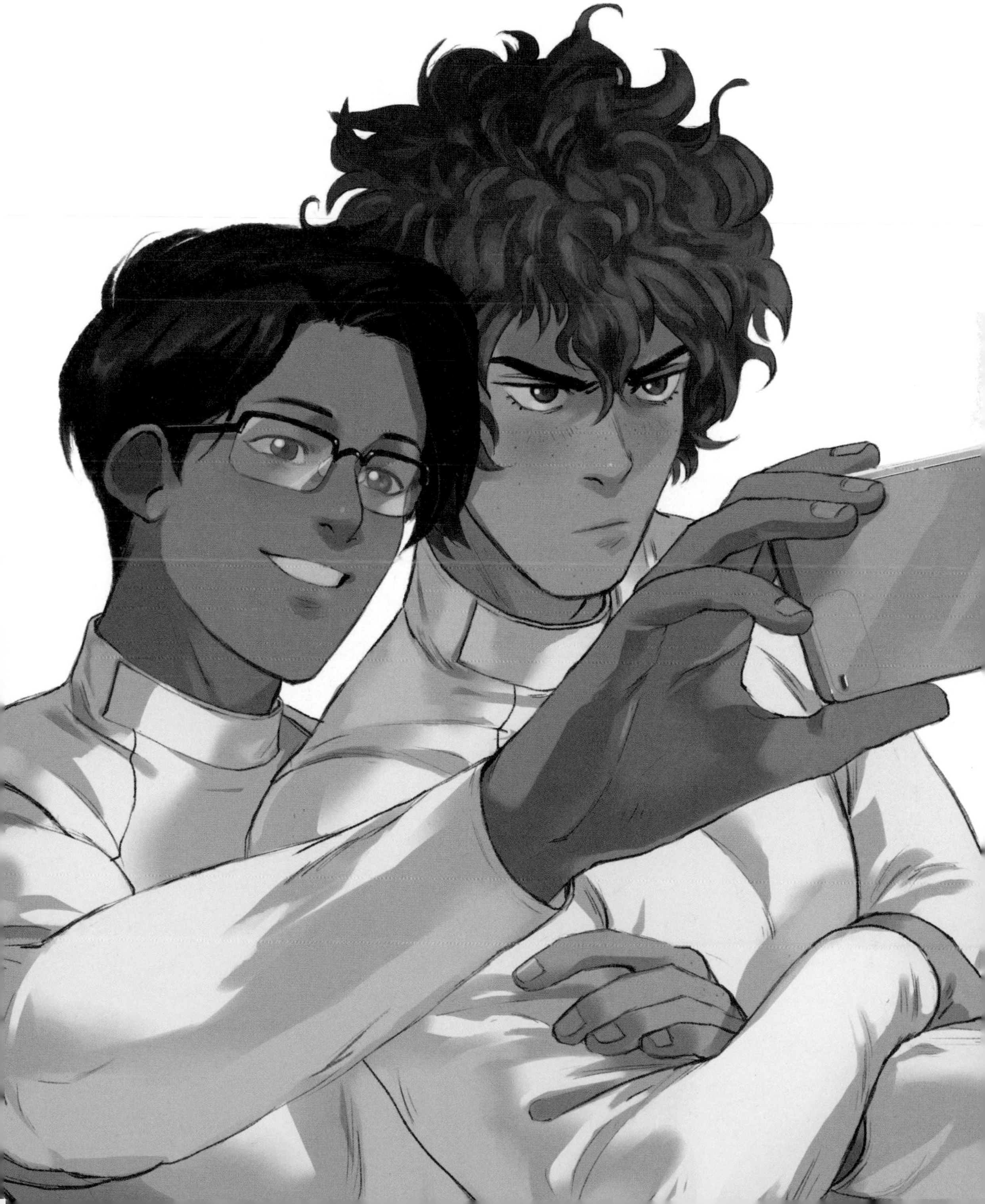

ISSUE 10 COVER BY

HamletMachine

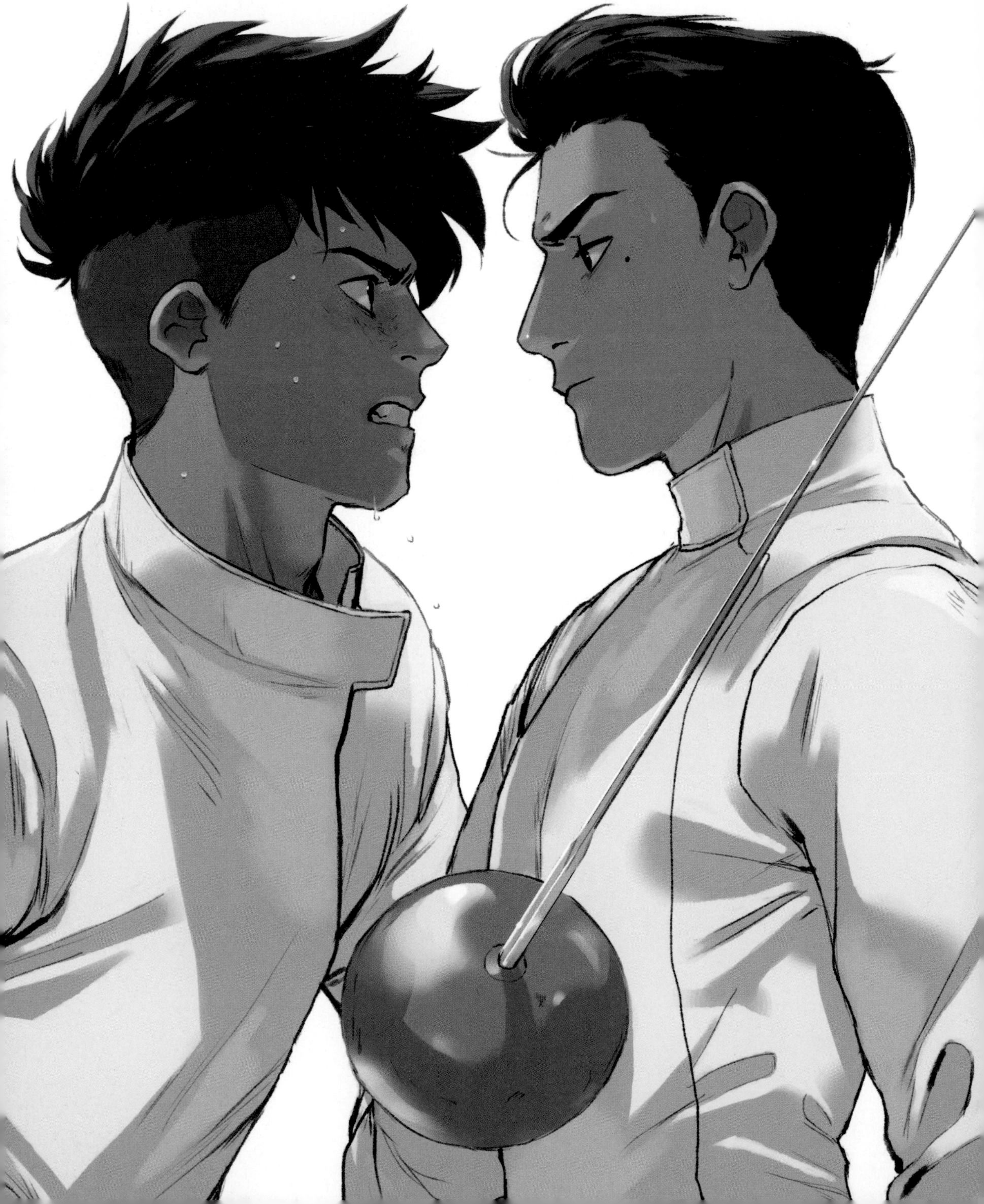

ISSUE 11 COVER BY
HamletMachine

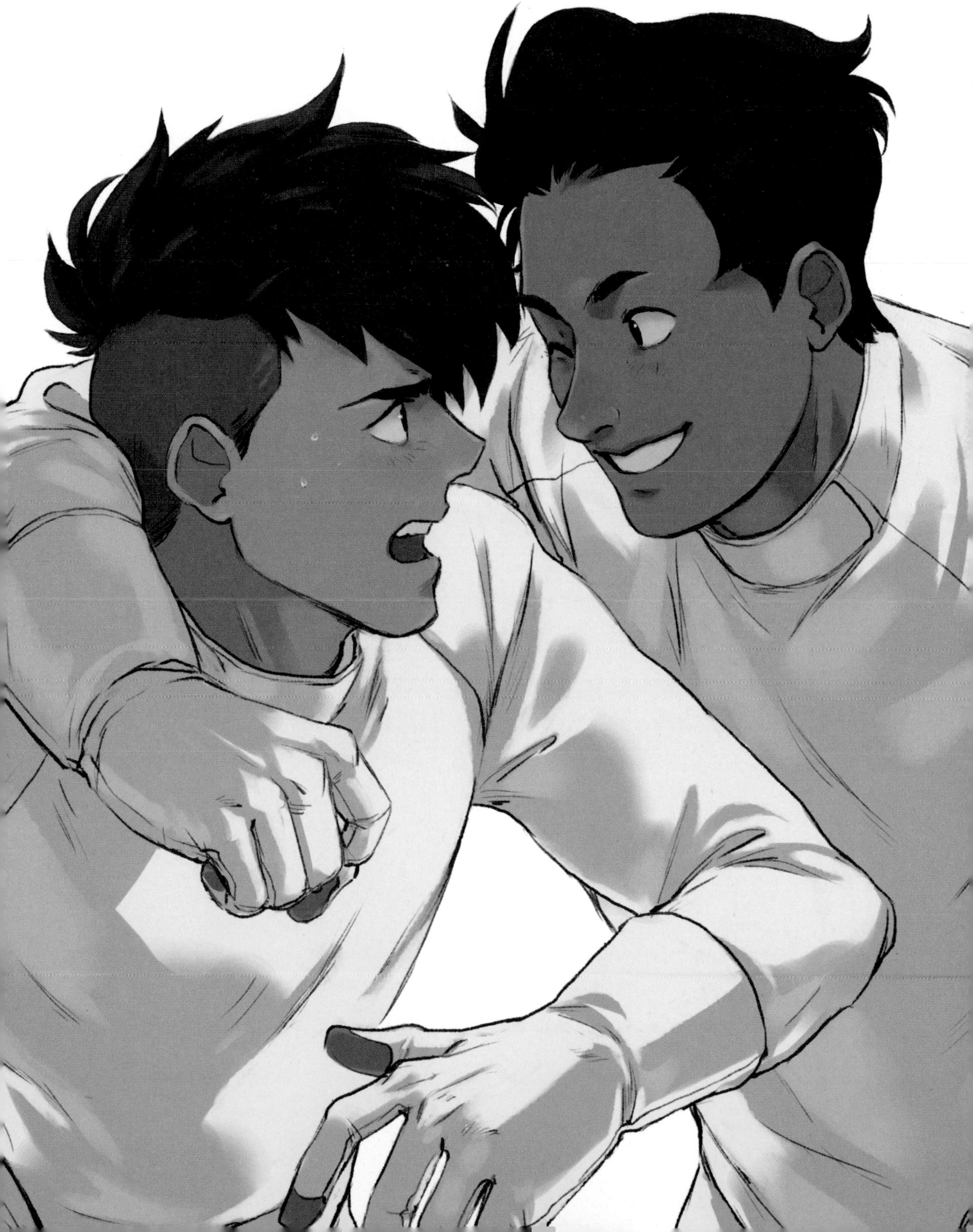

ISSUE 12 COVER BY

HamletMachine

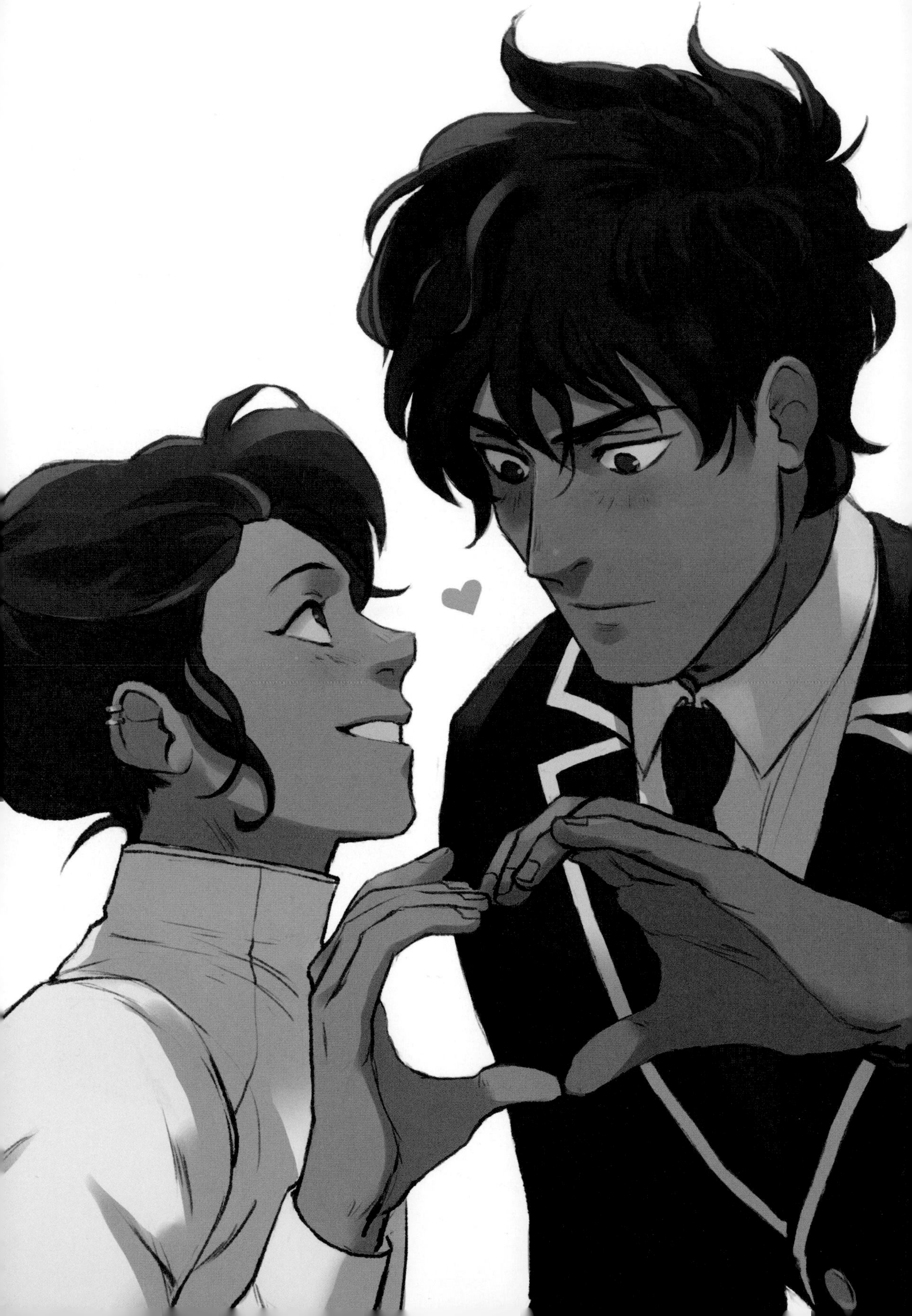

PENCIL PAGES
Gallery

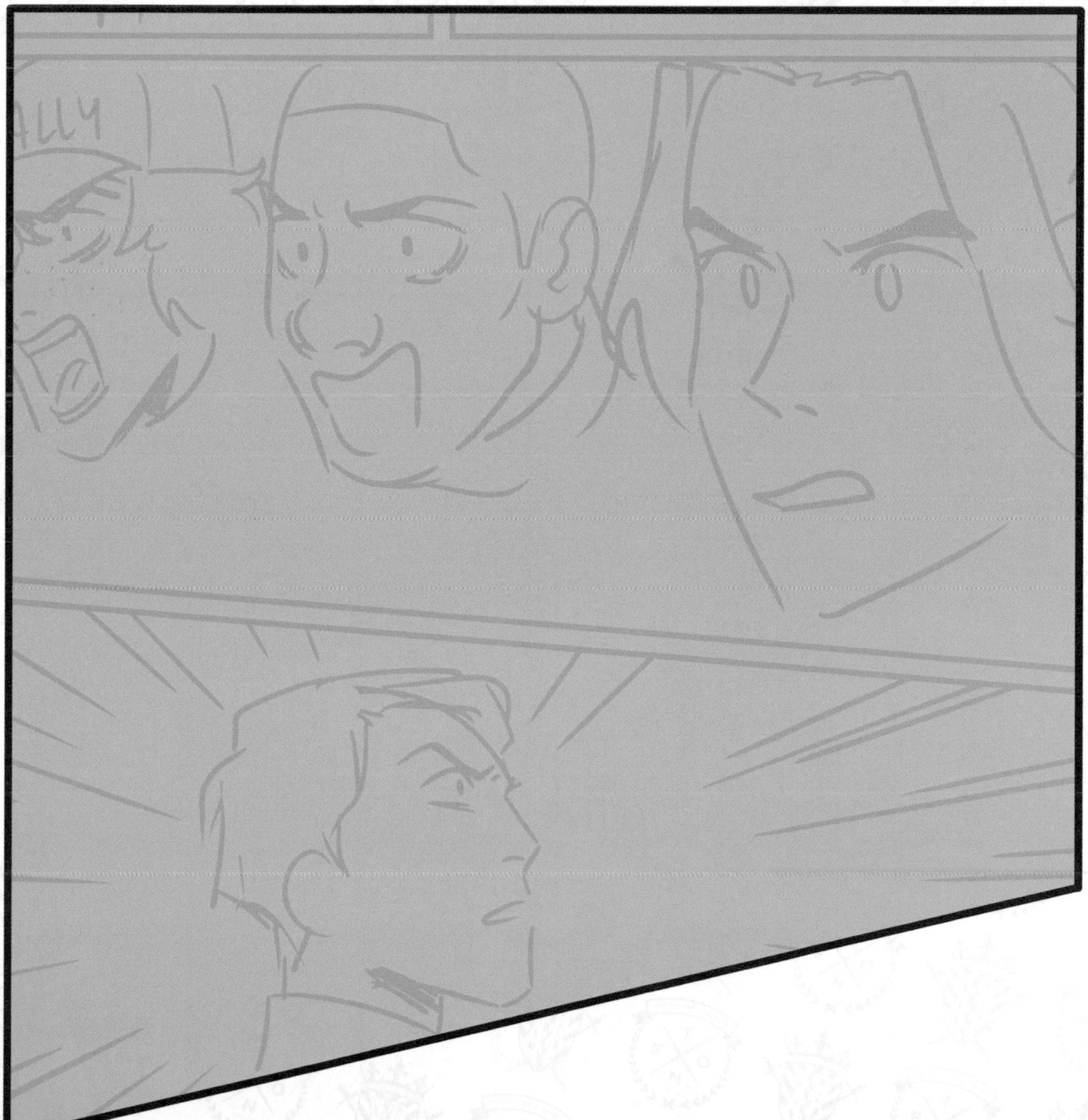

ISSUE 09, PAGE 04

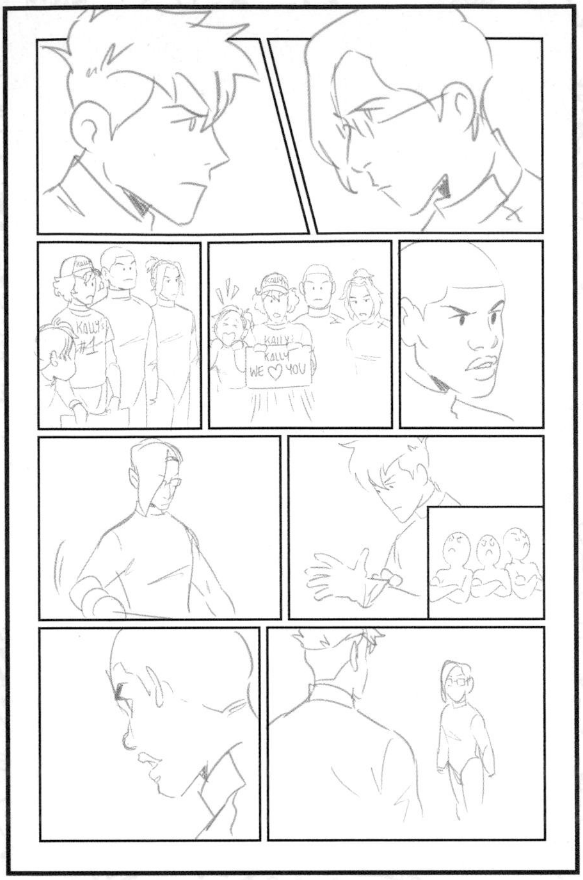
KALLY's #1
KALLY KALLY WE ♥ YOU

ISSUE 09, PAGE 05

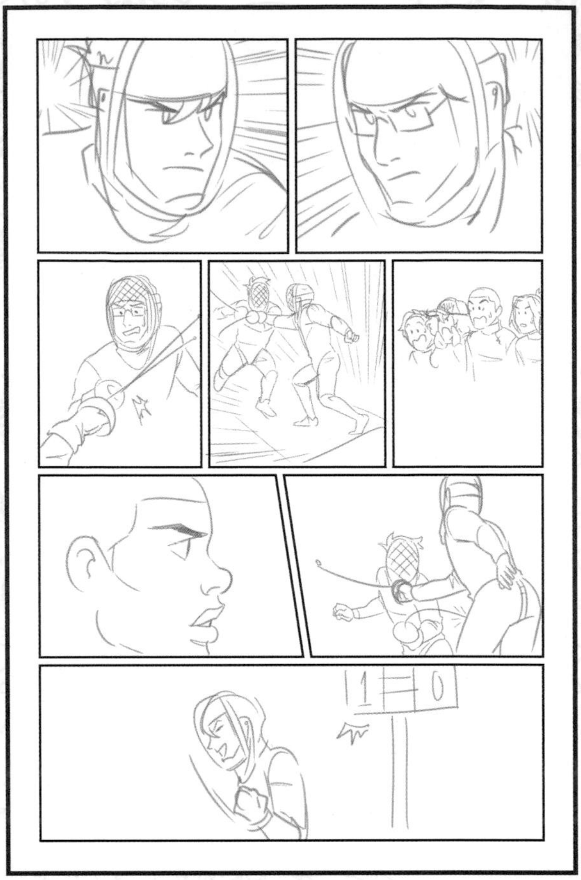
1 0

ISSUE 09, PAGE 06

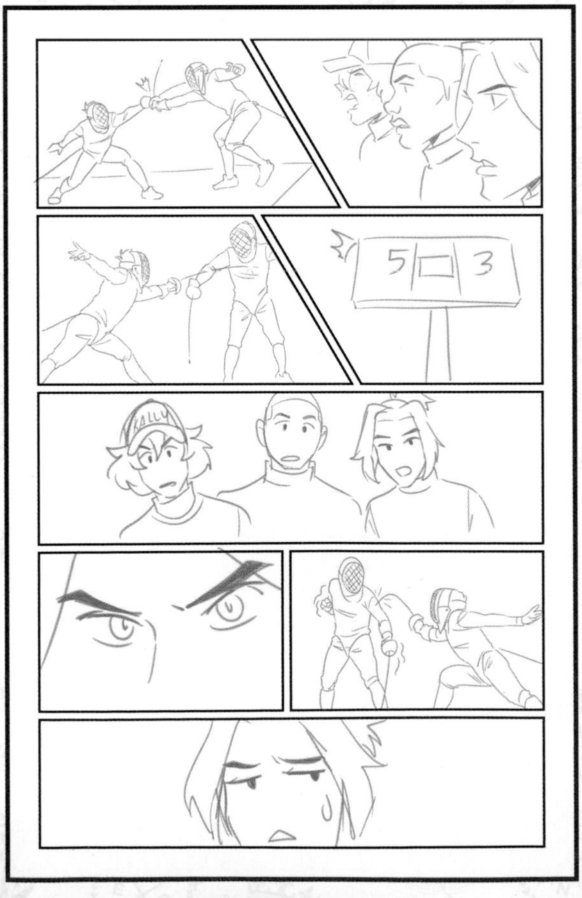
5 3

ISSUE 09, PAGE 07

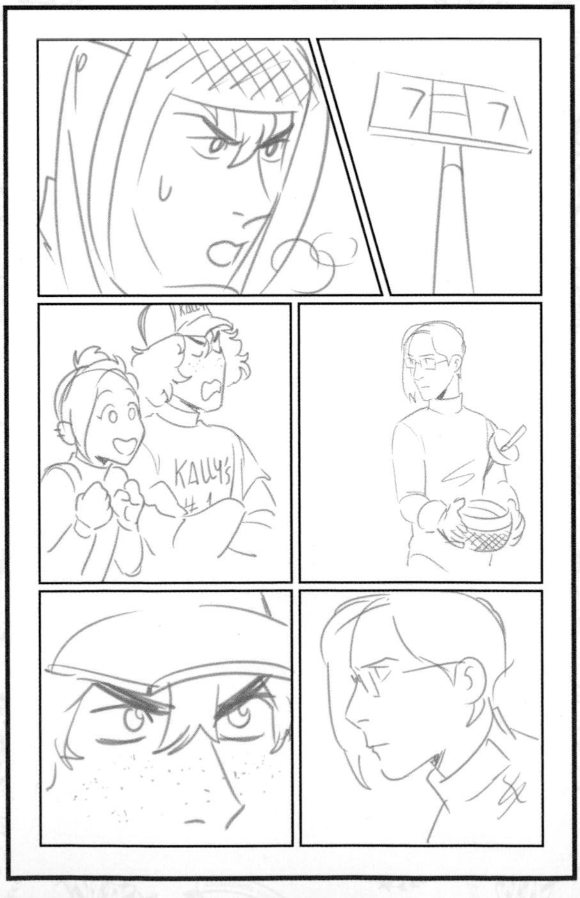
7 7
KALLY's #1

ISSUE 09, PAGE 11

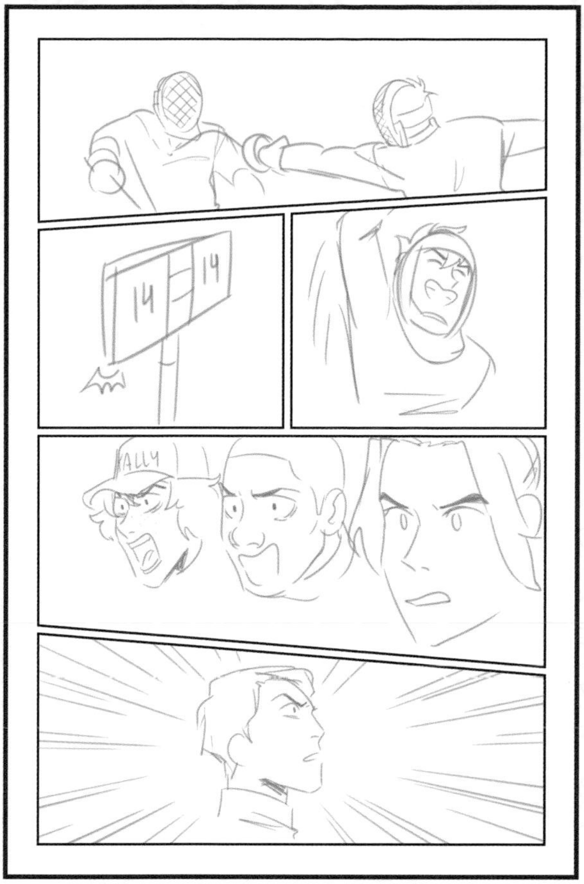
14
14

ISSUE 09, PAGE 12

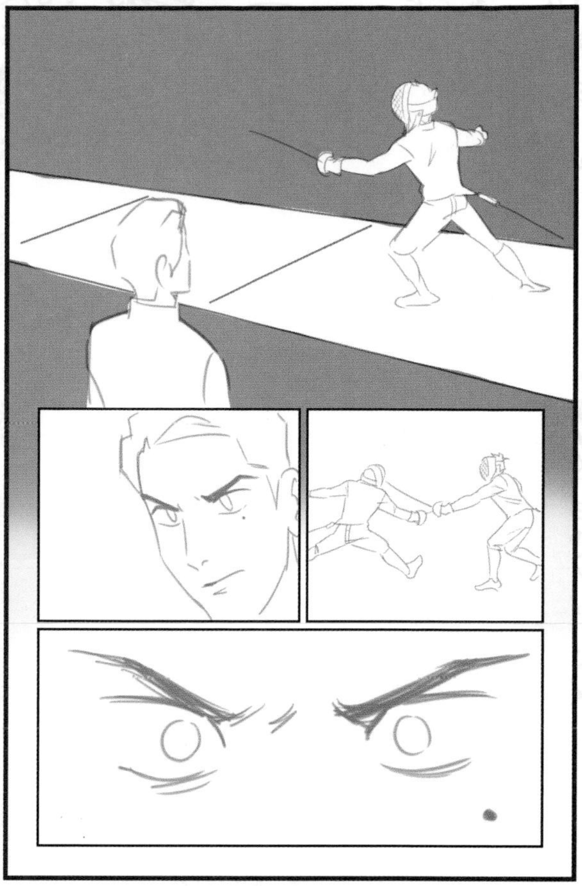

ISSUE 09, PAGE 13

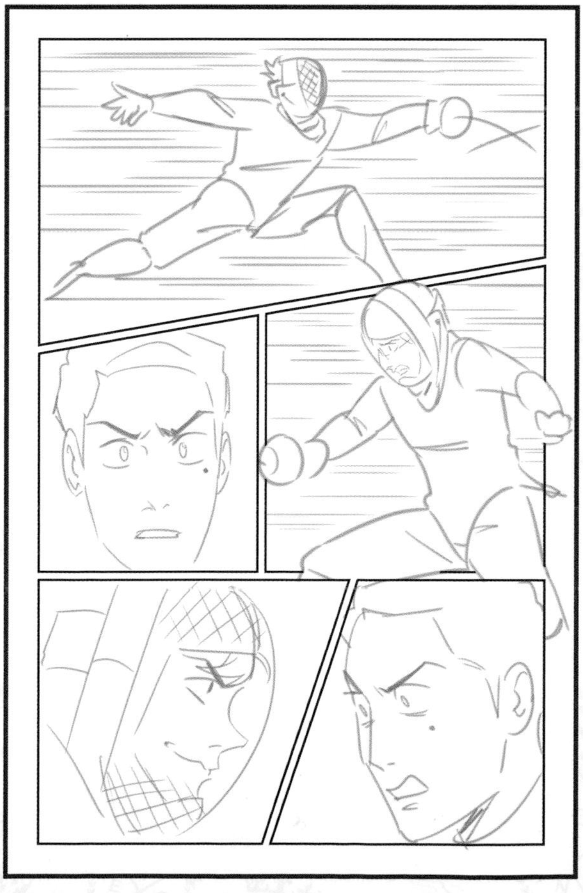

ISSUE 09, PAGE 14

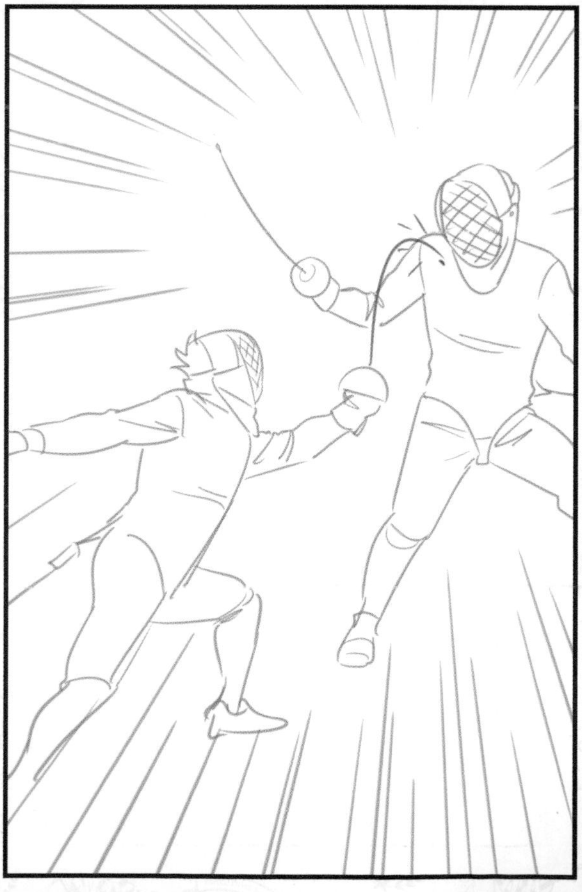

ISSUE 10, PAGE 13

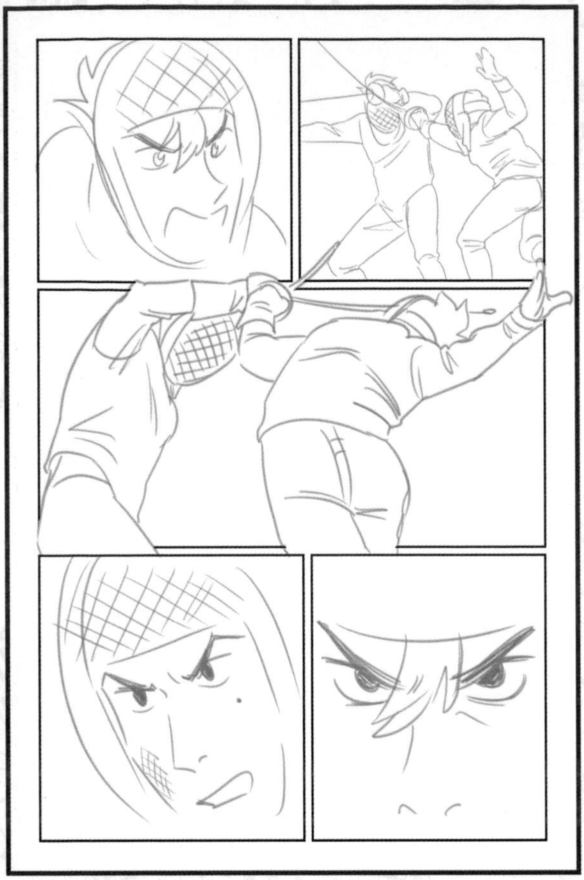

ISSUE 10, PAGE 14

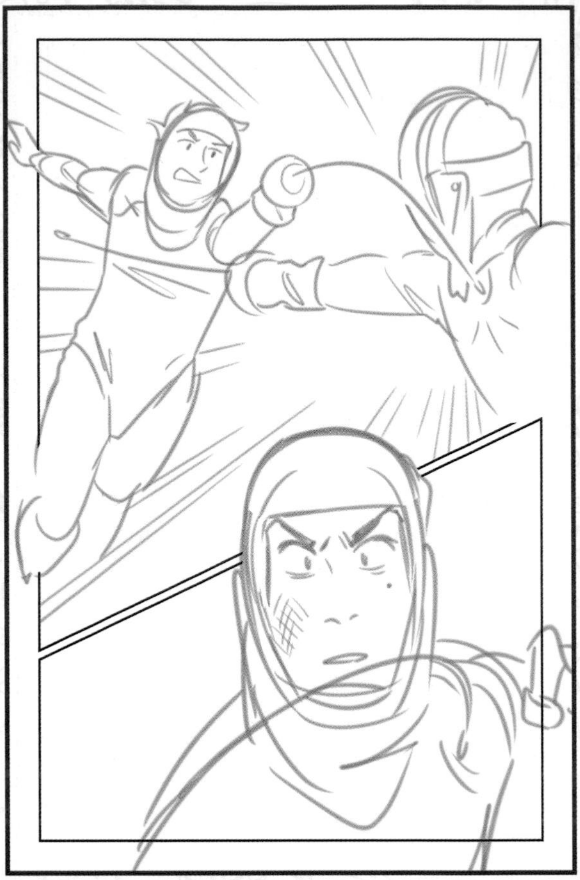

ISSUE 10, PAGE 15

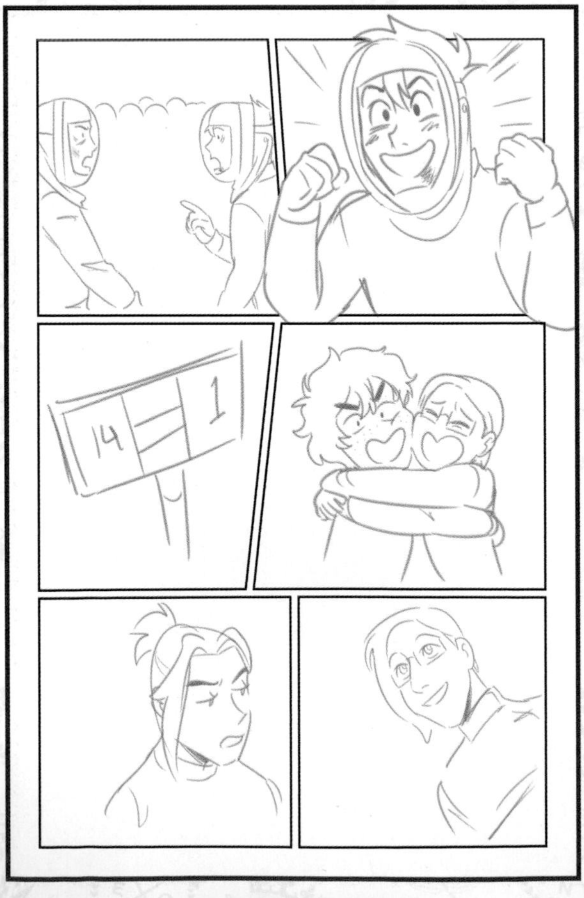
14
1

ISSUE 10, PAGE 16

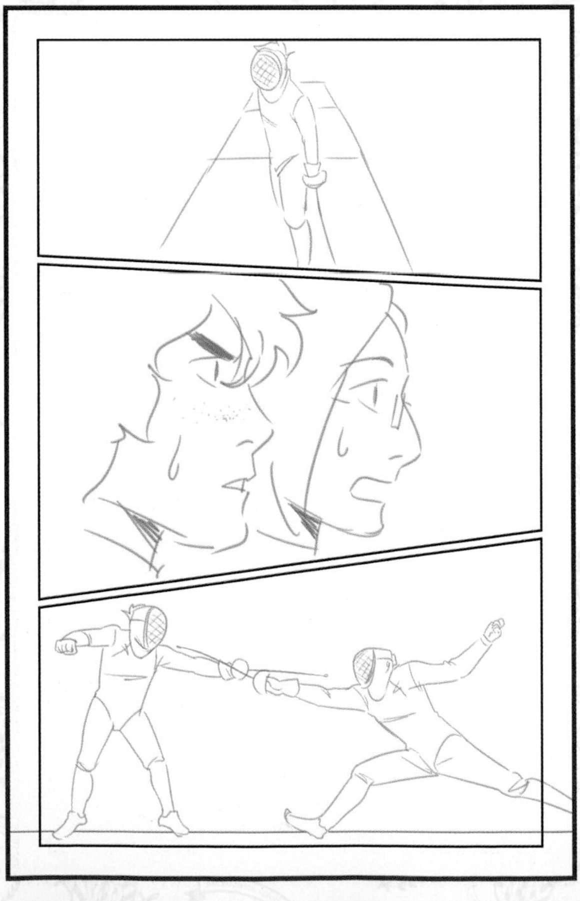

ISSUE 11, PAGE 12

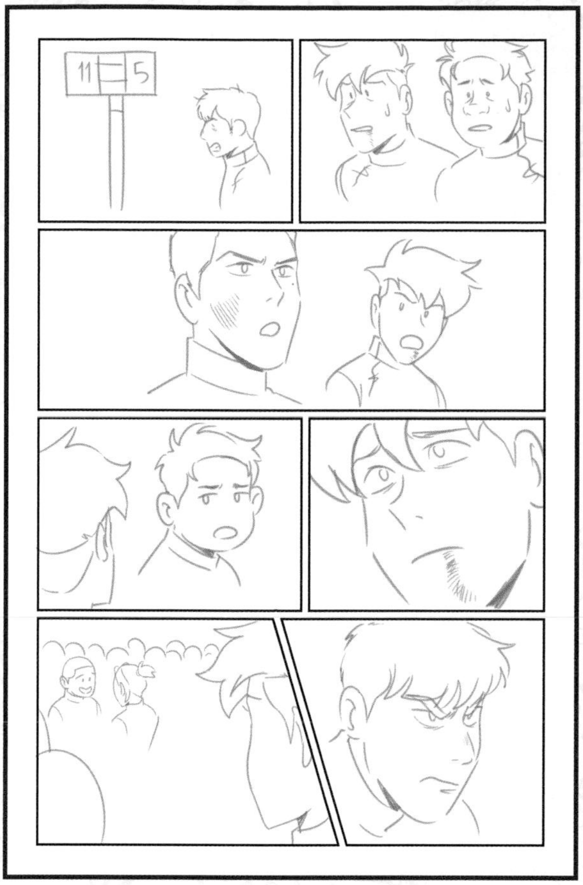
11
5

ISSUE 11, PAGE 13

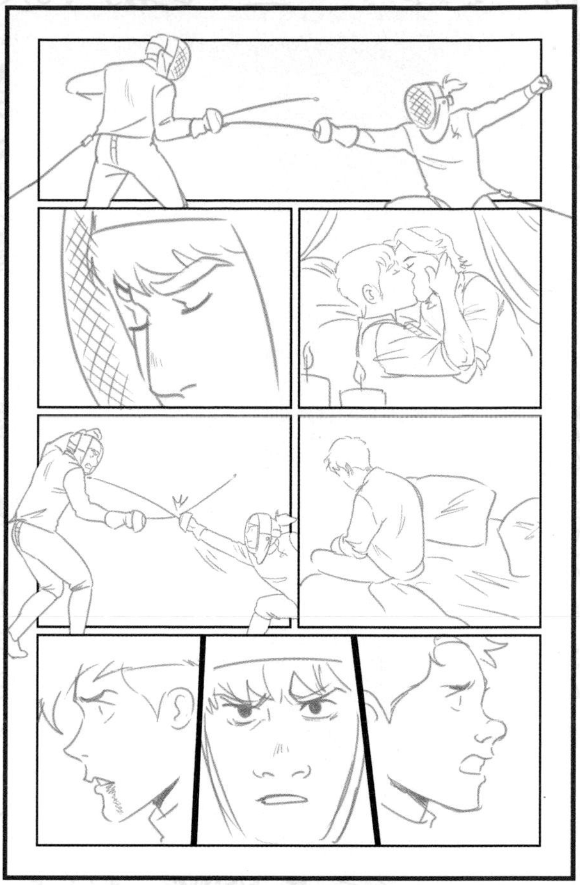

ISSUE 11, PAGE 14

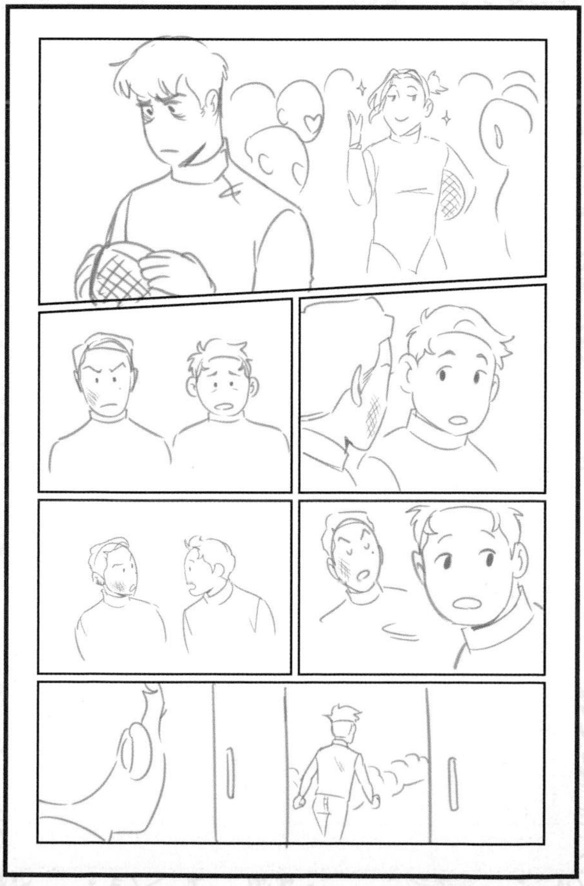

ISSUE 11, PAGE 15

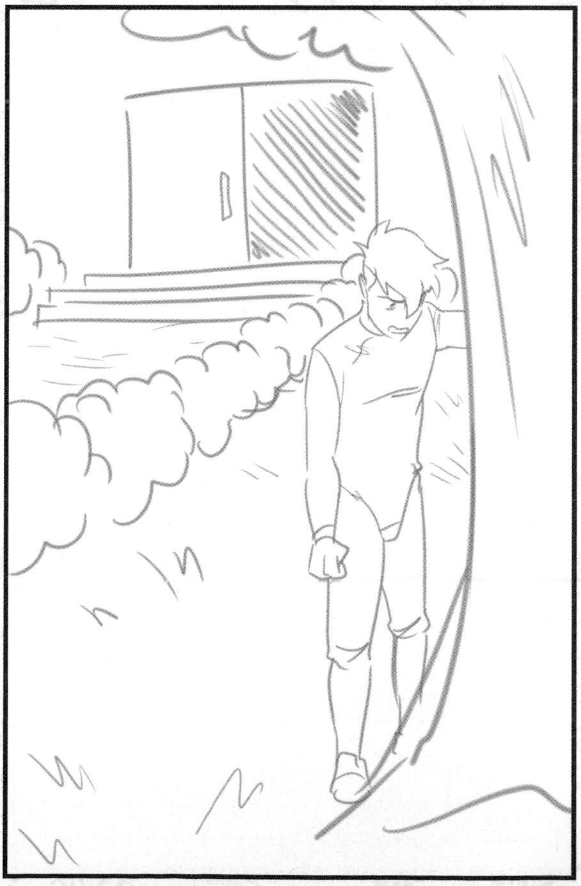

DISCOVER
ALL THE HITS

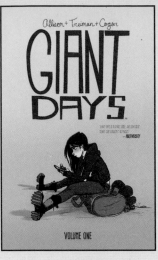

Lumberjanes
Noelle Stevenson, Shannon Watters, Grace Ellis, Brooklyn Allen, and Others
Volume 1: Beware the Kitten Holy
ISBN: 978-1-60886-687-8 | $14.99 US
Volume 2: Friendship to the Max
ISBN: 978-1-60886-737-0 | $14.99 US
Volume 3: A Terrible Plan
ISBN: 978-1-60886-803-2 | $14.99 US
Volume 4: Out of Time
ISBN: 978-1-60886-860-5 | $14.99 US
Volume 5: Band Together
ISBN: 978-1-60886-919-0 | $14.99 US

Giant Days
John Allison, Lissa Treiman, Max Sarin
Volume 1
ISBN: 978-1-60886-789-9 | $9.99 US
Volume 2
ISBN: 978-1-60886-804-9 | $14.99 US
Volume 3
ISBN: 978-1-60886-851-3 | $14.99 US

Jonesy
Sam Humphries, Caitlin Rose Boyle
Volume 1
ISBN: 978-1-60886-883-4 | $9.99 US
Volume 2
ISBN: 978-1-60886-999-2 | $14.99 US

Slam!
Pamela Ribon, Veronica Fish, Brittany Peer
Volume 1
ISBN: 978-1-68415-004-5 | $14.99 US

Goldie Vance
Hope Larson, Brittney Williams
Volume 1
ISBN: 978-1-60886-898-8 | $9.99 US
Volume 2
ISBN: 978-1-60886-974-9 | $14.99 US

The Backstagers
James Tynion IV, Rian Sygh
Volume 1
ISBN: 978-1-60886-993-0 | $14.99 US

Tyson Hesse's Diesel: Ignition
Tyson Hesse
ISBN: 978-1-60886-907-7 | $14.99 US

Coady & The Creepies
Liz Prince, Amanda Kirk, Hannah Fisher
ISBN: 978-1-68415-029-8 | $14.99 US